Marxism and the Proletariat

Marxism and the Proletariat

A Lukácsian Perspective

Stephen Perkins

Pluto Press
LONDON • BOULDER, COLORADO

First published 1993 by Pluto Press
345 Archway Road, London N6 5AA
and 5500 Central Avenue
Boulder, Colorado 80301, USA

British Library Cataloguing in Publication Data
A catalogue record for this book is available from the British Library
ISBN 0 7453 0492 3 hb
ISBN 0 7453 0499 0 pb

Library of Congress Cataloging in Publication Data
Perkins, Stephen
Marxism and the proletariat : a Lukácsian perspective / Stephen Perkins.
260p. 22 cm.
Includes bibliographical references and index.
ISBN 0-7453-0492-3. — ISBN 0-7453-0499-0 (pbk.)
1. Communism. 2. Proletariat. 3. Lukács, György, 1885–1971. 4. Capitalism. 5. Class consciousness. I. Title.
HX73.P485 1993
335.4'11–dc20 93-20550
CIP

Designed and produced for Pluto Press by
Chase Production Services, Chipping Norton
Typeset from author's disks by Stanford DTP Services, Milton Keynes
Printed in Great Britain by T.J. Press, Padstow

Contents

Abbreviations

Capital: Karl Marx, *Capital: A Critique of Political Economy*, 3 Vols (London: Lawrence & Wishart, 1954, 1974, 1974)

DR: Georg Lukács, *The Destruction of Reason* (London: Merlin Press, 1980)

Gemein: Ferdinand Tönnies, *Community and Association* (London: Routledge & Kegan Paul, 1955)

Grundrisse: Karl Marx, *Grundrisse: Foundations of the Critique of Political Economy* (rough draft) (Harmondsworth: Penguin, 1973)

HCC: Georg Lukács, *History and Class Consciousness: Studies in Marxist Dialectics* (London: Merlin Press, 1971)

MECW: Karl Marx and Frederick Engels, *Collected Works* (London: Lawrence & Wishart, 1976–)

MESC: Karl Marx and Frederick Engels, *Selected Correspondence* (Moscow: Progress Publishers, 1965)

MESW: Karl Marx and Frederick Engels, *Selected Works* in one volume (London: Lawrence & Wishart, 1968)

Money: Georg Simmel, *The Philosophy of Money* (London: Routledge & Kegan Paul, 1978

PW: Georg Lukács, *Tactics and Ethics: Political Writings, 1919–1929* (London: New Left Books, 1972)

Acknowledgements

This book is based upon a thesis of the same title completed at the University of Kent in 1989. I would like to express my thanks to David McLellan who supervised the thesis from first to (long) last. I acknowledge the financial assistance of the Social Science Research Council, which, in a relatively minor act of reactionary vandalism, was renamed the Economic and Social Research Council mid-way through its funding of my research. Thanks anyway are due, and in particular to the then Secretary of State for Education and Science, Keith Joseph.

'Grey are all theories, and green alone life's golden tree'; for assorted greenery I am indebted to (amongst others): Miles Davis, Art Pepper, Jimi Hendrix, Keith Jarrett, Buddy Rich, Thomas Mann, John Lennon, Raymond Chandler, Stanley Clarke, John Surman, John McLaughlin, Jimmy Page and Thelonius Monk.

Especial thanks and love to Helen and to Anna.

Introduction

In this book I examine the role of the proletariat in the evolution of marxist political philosophy. The book falls into three sections. In the first (chapters 1 and 2) I examine how Marx developed an understanding of the proletariat that was a response and proposed solution to the problems associated with the dissolution of hegelian philosophy, as well as being influenced by the political environment of mid-nineteenth century Paris, and which stressed the liberatory–emancipatory characteristics of the proletariat and the democratization of the hitherto elitist and speculative conception of philosophy, before going on to emphasize the social power role played by the proletariat in capitalist society. In the second section (chapter 3) I look at the creation of a marxist orthodoxy and how it altered the conception of the proletariat developed by Marx by stressing its epistemological dependence upon a political theory developed independently of it – most notably by a vulgar, Feuerbachian-inspired materialism, but also by a bureaucratic or vanguardist political party that would represent its interests. Finally, in chapters 4, 5 and 6 I look at the achievement of Georg Lukács in redrawing the theoretical parameters in which marxism locates the proletariat; at how he was able to reestablish the central importance of Marx's early writings and also, by virtue of the influence exerted upon his thought by the emergent school of German sociology, to extend these insights to the political conditions of the modern world, and in particular to account for the failure of the proletariat to conform to the revolutionary role ascribed to it by Marx.

The central problem to which the book is directed is the apparent failure of marxism at precisely the point at which many would argue it makes its most original and vital contribution to social theory, namely the relationship between theory and practice. This failure is evidenced by the absence of successful proletarian revolutions in the economically advanced conditions of western Europe and the United States, by the marginalization of marxist politics in those countries and by the particular nature of those 'socialist' revolutions that have occurred in the less advanced countries, especially the former Soviet Union.

The book is concerned to assess both the consequences of this failure for marxist political philosophy, and also the extent to which it may itself be said to have contributed to this failure.

My argument is that the conception of the proletariat originally developed by Marx in 1843 continued to be a central feature of his political thought, but that changes in political conditions after 1848 led Marx increasingly to stress the economic contradictions within capitalism which were revealed by his economic writings and which determined the nature and degree of class conflict. This had the (unintended) consequence of devaluing the emancipatory–liberatory characteristics of the proletariat. This tendency was taken a stage further by the development of an orthodoxy that stressed, on the one hand, the social weight of the proletariat – its numerical and strategic dominance in modern society – and, on the other, the economic contradictions that would bring about socialism as a consequence and which would make possible the prefigurement within capitalism of certain aspects of socialism. This devaluation of political agency – in the sense in which Marx originally conceived it – was buttressed by a version of materialism that regarded political and class struggles as the automatic response to economic stimuli.

Lukács' thought is important because it reestablishes the importance of Marx's early writings by demonstrating their relationship to his later writings, and because he does this by placing at the core of marxist political theory the liberatory function of the proletariat. This would at first sight appear to make the failure of marxism all the more complete. However, Lukács' methodology also provides a solution to this dilemma. On the one hand his essence/appearance dichotomy allows him to escape the preemptive judgement of any particular historical epoch; on the other, his theory of reification demonstrates how the revolutionary mission ascribed to the proletariat has been systematically – and systemically – thwarted or diverted by the ability of bourgeois society to shape and to distort the consciousness through which it is perceived.

I

The application of marxist political ideas to the modern world is faced with the major obstacle that whatever insights and understanding, scientific and otherwise, it might generate about the nature of the modern world, it nevertheless breaks down in relation to the symbiotic relationship it posits between theory and practice. Its theoretical analysis of the history and structure of capitalist society might reveal much about modern society, but marxism was never intended to be a positivist science;

its scientific credentials were regarded by its founder as being weapons in the struggle for economic and social liberation, weapons forged for the use of the proletariat, but weapons, however, that the proletariat has left to smoulder in the common rooms – both senior and junior – of the universities (whether traditional or recently renamed).

Thus, where we find marxist ideas today we do not usually find the proletariat; and where the proletariat is organized and active, for example in trade unions, we do not often find marxist ideas. And where political revolutions have broken out in recent (and not so recent) times, we do not find workers in their vanguard, but rather peasants, artisans and/or intellectuals; where workers have constituted an organized political majority they have more often rejected the marxist model of political and social revolution. Indeed, even the single major exception to this pessimistic scenario – the Great October Socialist Revolution – tends to confirm the rule. Socialist revolution was possible in Russia because a combination of favourable circumstances allowed the formation of a revolutionary alliance between industrial workers, peasants and intellectuals, with a combination of workers and intellectuals in the vanguard, organized under the aegis of the Bolshevik Party. However, the same circumstances that favoured revolution in Russia also ruled out both socialism and the preservation of proletarian political hegemony. The subsequent substitution of the rule of the Communist Party for proletarian self-rule itself fed into the alienation felt by workers elsewhere toward marxist politics; this point hardly requires labouring after the events of 1989 and 1990.

Having acknowledged all this, however, it is also necessary to look a little deeper into the matter. Political circumstances have never been particularly favourable to marxist ideas: exclusion, ostracism, isolation and repression have all played a part in the marginalization of marxist political ideas. Equally, the environment in which all political ideas operate tends systematically to undermine those which are opposed to and seek the destruction of that environment. It would thus be inappropriate to hold marxism responsible for the unfavourable conditions in which it must operate. Rosa Luxemburg's description of communism as the party of permanent opposition signifies not merely her condemnation of those who would seek to administer capitalism, but also a recognition that marxists are bound by their convictions to be social outcasts, 'dead men on leave' as Levine put it.

However, permanent opposition does not imply that marxism is a utopian doctrine with no realistic expectation of political success. For most of the last century or so marxist political influence, in the form of working-class politics, seemed to be very much on the ascendancy; what made marxism unique, its advocacy of proletarian politics, seemed to make it an irresistible power that would eventually sweep all before it to inaugurate a socialist commonwealth. It is this expectation that seems no longer reasonable. Working-class politics is nowadays in most advanced industrial, that is to say capitalist, countries profoundly a- or anti-marxist. (It is also, incidentally, increasingly a- or anti-political.) By whatever measure, the influence of marxism upon the workers' movement is probably as low as it has ever been.

Lukács' interpretation of marxism in his book *History and Class Consciousness* (1923) offers, I would argue, a solution to this so-called and long-standing 'crisis of marxism'; a crisis that has two elements to it. The first concerns that problem Perry Anderson has identified[1] as a key factor in the dissolution of marxism in post-war France, namely the difficulty in adequately reconciling the competing claims of structure and agency (or subject).[2] This is, of course, a long-standing problem not only within marxism but in all the social sciences and can be traced back, as I shall shortly show, to the writings of Marx himself (and further). The second element concerns the failure of marxism in terms of its liberatory promise. In the east, political victory – achieved under possibly unique conditions – did not lead to any great advertisement for socialism but on the contrary to a veritable festival of anti-communism, while in the west, political defeat and failure have long been recognized by the opponents of marxism – and also by some marxists – as important indicators of its shortcomings.

These two characteristics of the crisis of marxism carry with them two separate and distinct routes to correction. The first of these is the more straightforward since it is cast in terms of academic research; it concerns examining how Marx himself conceptualized the relationship between structure and agency, the extent to which his successors followed his example in this matter and the political consequences of their interpretations. This is, in other words, a matter of marxology, or marxist interpretation. But even were this task to be satisfactorily accomplished (to put aside for a moment the question of how we might judge such a project in terms of success or failure), it is my belief that rather than bringing the second aspect of the crisis nearer to a solution it in fact makes the central tenets of Marx's conception of politics ever more out of accord with actual political situations, at least in the sense of predicting their outcome.

II

There is within the marxist tradition a somewhat ambiguous relationship to the notion of agency that can be traced back to certain of Marx's writings, but whose origins are to be found in Hegel. This ambiguity has usually been seen in the context of Marx's intellectual development, in his progression away from a subjective activism towards a more rigid determinism. Thus, in *The Holy Family*, Marx and Engels write in a justly famous passage:

> History does nothing, it possesses no immense wealth, it wages no battles. It is man, real living man who does all that, who possesses and fights; history is not, as it were, a person apart, using man as a means to achieve its own aims; history is nothing but the activity of man pursuing his aims.[3]

This passage, whose political implications persisted in the drawing up of the statutes of the First International ('that the emancipation of the working classes must be conquered by the working classes themselves'[4]) makes a fairly clear categorical assertion that history is the product of human agency – and nothing more.

On the other hand – and this position became increasingly dominant in Marx's later writings – there is the notion that upon closer examination, human agency proves to play a far less significant role, being constrained (and indeed determined, if not caused) by a whole range of other factors. This perception is typified in another equally famous passage, this time from *The Eighteenth Brumaire of Louis Bonaparte*, that:

> Men make their own history, but they do not make it just as they please; they do not make it under circumstances chosen by themselves, but under circumstances directly encountered, given and transmitted from the past. The tradition of all the dead generations weighs like a nightmare on the brain of the living,[5]

and is made even more forcibly in Marx's preface to *Capital*, where he favourably cites a Russian reviewer who gives this interpretation of the book: 'Marx treats the social movement as a process of natural history, governed by laws not only independent of human will, consciousness and intelligence, but rather, on the contrary, determining that will, consciousness and intelligence.'[6] Here, then, is the prescriptive injunction that a theory of history cannot limit itself to the observation of history as the direct expression of the desired ends of people, but must be seen as the product of circumstances beyond their immediate control or comprehension.

This problem is partly one of definition, since the term agency carries with it two senses: an agent may be one who is an active initiator of a particular event, but may also be one who acts on behalf of another and so, with respect to the event in question, is merely a passive instrument.[7] But it would be a mistake to regard the matter as merely one of semantics, for much hinges on the distinction between the two senses of the term, particularly when we are concerned with political acts and ideas, the intention of which is to exert some influence over, or to initiate some kind of change in any given social environment. We are here talking of the capacity to *make* history: either for ourselves, or on behalf of others, or of impersonal forces or categories.

This debate has for long been a central issue in the socialist movement; it could even be said to be the central problem of socialist politics. But its origins are to be found in Marx's own writings and, in particular, in the nature of his relationship to Hegel's philosophy of history. The difference between Hegel and Marx has traditionally been said to be[8] that whereas Marx created a *theory* of history, a scientific means of explaining reality in terms of categories derived from it, Hegel's *philosophy* of history consisted of elaborate speculations quite independent of reality itself. However, if we pursue this matter a little further we can discover some interesting, and illuminating, parallels between the two approaches.

For Hegel, the march of history is the march of the spirit towards freedom.[9] But since freedom can only consist of a union of subjective and objective elements (as the subject cannot be said to be free so long as it remains dependent on an object outside itself), that freedom can only be realized on the basis of an absolute: by God. Thus Hegel's 'world spirit' controls and directs the course of world history, which takes the form of a succession of national spirits. The form of knowledge that corresponds to this development is characterized in terms of an epistemological ascent by consciousness, to the ultimate plateau of a subject–object union in reason. This is in fact the goal of consciousness: the realization of freedom through action and exploration.

Hegel's idealist creations could not retain any credibility if they remained at this theological level; they had to be brought into a relationship with reality itself, through which the realization of freedom could be seen to be a real and concrete possibility. Hegel achieves this by discovering in reality – or more precisely in the rationality of humankind – the means through which the objective world can be brought under the conscious mastery of world spirit. It is people's passions that generate and promote the capacity to develop reason, with the conscious intent of mastering their environment. As Hegel puts it:

'needs, passions and interests are the sole springs of action – the efficient agents in this scene of activity.'[10] Science and philosophy add to this process by making possible an 'advance to a closer insight into the inner harmony and uniformity of nature',[11] or a penetration of the veil of external contingency, through the discovery of those laws which express the inner necessity of this whole process. When this is done, people can base their decisions not on the contingent or accidental but on a thorough knowledge of their environment.

So far, then, people come to master nature through the acquisition of knowledge gleaned from their active participation and involvement in it. But nature and history still remain external to them. People gratify their passions, exercise their will and develop themselves in accordance with the laws that they discover; nevertheless, Hegel says: 'in history an additional result is commonly produced by human actions beyond that which they aim at and obtain – that which they immediately recognize and desire.'[12] This additional result is the product of Hegel's so-called cunning of reason, which operates in the background, setting people's passions to work for itself.

Now in Marx's shift of attention towards the laying out of the foundation of an anatomy of society, though certain elements of his earlier philosophical preoccupations were carried over, these were not given direct systematic expression. This tardiness has carried with it certain consequences, first in Marx's own later writings, but also, more crucially, in the interpretation of these later writings and their development by his followers. For example, in *Capital* Marx pays very little attention to agents in history as efficient causes; rather he sees them if not as passive, then as blind instruments of forces beyond their comprehension or control, forces which determine the social conditions under which they live, the social relations through which they correspond with one another and even the thoughts and ideas that they develop with regard to this social universe. Individuals are dealt with only as the personification of economic or social categories, as the embodiment of particular class interests and relations. History develops 'behind the backs' of human beings; in such a situation, the freedom enjoyed by such individuals is no more than, in Spinoza's phrase, the freedom a thrown stone would have if it had consciousness.

This derogation of human agency is not confined to the actions of individuals but is also reflected by the absence of any systematic exposition of the collective subject: of social classes. The third volume of *Capital* notoriously breaks off with an incomplete chapter on classes. Now it may quite rightly be countered that this other aspect of Marx's thought was taken for granted and remained as an heuristic device, or that it was developed elsewhere, or that it was actually displayed in the 'historical' chapters of *Capital*. Nonetheless, the ambiguity remained to perplex later generations of marxists.

But if *Capital* was ambiguous, the interpretation of it was not. Successive generations of marxists, beginning with Engels, who based their interpretation of Marx's theory primarily upon his economic writings, developed a tendency towards a positivism that signified a serious divergence from Marx's more subtle and fluid dialectical thought. For Kautsky and Plekhanov, as well as for the Lenin of *Materialism and Empirio-Criticism*, external reality yielded objective laws with which human beings could interfere only in the sense either of passing a moral judgement on the movement of history, that lay forever external to them, or perhaps by attempting to modify such laws by means of technical action based upon knowledge and utilization of them. In this way the dialectical notion of socialism came to be transformed into a 'scientistic' socialism that regarded science and history quite independent of any human evaluation or moral judgement. Intervention in history took the form either of a neo-Kantian critique, or a political complement to this objectivity.

In such a situation it is easy to comprehend how this model of social-historical technology could go hand in hand with a political movement increasingly – though at first unconsciously – integrated into the existing order. This indeed became the increasing preoccupation of German social democracy, the revisionist controversy representing a desire by Bernstein and others to reconcile the contradiction between revolutionary phraseology and reformist practice in favour of the latter. But even the orthodox reply to Bernstein failed to appreciate the dialectical element in Marx's socialism, relying instead upon a determinism and evolutionism derived from Darwin, and thus merely reproducing the dualisms of science and ethics, past and present, history and politics that were the very motifs of Bernstein and the neo-Kantians. Witness this quotation from Kautsky:

> Nor can the social democratic organization of the proletariat, in its class struggle, do without the moral ideal, without ethical indignation against exploitation and class oppression. But this ideal has nothing to do with scientific socialism, the scientific study of the laws of evolution of the social organism in order to know the trends and the necessary ends of the proletarian class struggle.
>
> It is true that in the case of a socialist, the thinker is also a militant, and no man can be artificially cut in two parts of which one has nothing to do with the other; so sometimes even in Marx's

> scientific research we perceive a moral ideal. But he always, correctly, tries to exclude it as far as possible. For in science, the moral ideal becomes a course of errors, if it attempts to prescribe the ends of science.[13]

Here, then, we find if not a Marx 'cut in two parts', a marxist science cut in two: scientific research and moral ideal – the one scientific in so far as it expels the other; the other morally superior in that it motivates human action.

Now there is a sense in which the tendency towards a mechanistic and reductionist theory was encouraged by some of Engels' later writings. But the letters Engels wrote in the 1890s in which he tried to counter the increasing economic reductionism of his (and Marx's) followers, may best be understood within the context of an intervention in an ideological debate centred not upon the relative importance of the 'economic', 'political', or 'ideological' categories, but as an attempt to counter the mechanized determinism and fatalism of these marxists.[14]

It is true, however, that Engels implicitly accepts an equation between the objective necessity of the economic side and the social element of the superstructure, in which the active element was of rather more importance. But in trying to bring these into a more dialectical relationship within the social totality, Engels is in fact attempting to address two problems at the same time. First, he is trying to counter the tendency to delimit the materialist conception of history to a study solely of the 'economic' side at the expense of the 'formal' side of history. And second, he is also attempting to counter the tendency to regard the prioritization of the economic side as a sequence of cause and effect.

However, Engels' attempt to reformulate the role and position of human actions in history, and to relate these actions to their actual outcome, are ultimately unsuccessful. Thus his remarks to Bloch, for example, take us little further forward:

> We make our history ourselves, but ... under very definite antecedents and conditions ... history proceeds in such a way that the final result always arises from conflicts between many individual wills, and every one of them is in turn made into what it is by a host of particular conditions of life. Thus, there are innumerable intersecting forces, an indefinite series of parallelograms of forces which give rise to one resultant, the historical event. This may in its turn again be regarded as the product of a power which operates as a whole unconsciously and without volition ... the wills of individuals ... do not achieve what they want but are merged into an aggregate means, a common resultant.[15]

Engels speaks here of individual wills and their relationship to historical development, and at that level this may be an accurate representation of the effectiveness of human actions. But if we substitute social classes for individual wills, the end result is that we find that the ultimately decisive material basis finally asserts itself over historical developments and that the will of individuals and the collective will of classes cancel each other out in the process. There thus still seems no way in which humankind can escape the iron cage of historical determinism.

III

It is my contention that the ambiguities carried into Marx's writings by their contact with Hegel's philosophy, and the particular interpretation of his later writings made by social democracy that led to the tendency to evolutionism and positivism, can be overcome only by reading these later works in the context of their predecessors. In particular, it is in the 1843 Introduction that the key elements of Marx's politics are established, elements that were later given a more substantive social and economic basis to be sure, but which remained fundamentally unaltered throughout Marx's lifetime. These concern such matters as the relation between theory and practice, the democratization of theory and, above all, the universal, liberating function of the proletariat: its revolutionary mission. These were not later inserted into the economic structures of capitalism that Marx depicted in *Capital* as the determinant and determining factors of social and political life, but quite the opposite: the determinism of the economic structure was the factor that constrained, limited, restricted the emancipatory characteristics of the proletariat; that set limits to its revolutionary capacity, but which could not do so indefinitely because the consequences of bowing to this economic determinism would be catastrophic to the essential humanity and humanizing mission of the proletariat. Marx's concern with the proletariat was not so much so that capitalism could be better understood, his concern with capitalism was so that the proletariat could change, or overthrow it.

The standpoint of the proletariat, then and the advocacy of its revolutionary mission I take to lie at the heart of marxism: the analysis of capitalism is but the means to help further this end. For all the scientific insights generated by this analysis, this is not an end in itself. Indeed, in so far as it comes to take on this appearance – and this is particularly so in non-revolutionary epochs like our own – then the danger is that the theory will succumb to scientistic passivity and acquiescence, will retreat into a withdrawal from the world that, though not entirely voluntary (in the sense that political engagement becomes increasingly difficult/problematic), has the consequences, first, that conditions for limited political engagement are dismissed or disregarded and second, that alternative mechanisms for effecting social change are elaborated which then make it difficult to recognize and to take advantage of a more favourable political environment (should one arise).

The act of revolution is the link between the old world and the new, between capitalism and socialism. But to assert this is not to delineate the mechanisms of that revolution adequately, the extent to which it is created in the preconditions of capitalism, or the extent to which it is the irruption of a new political force. Capitalism creates the preconditions for socialism, but in a non-revolutionary epoch, such as existed in the epoch of social democracy, this could then be taken to mean that the one system evolves into the other, the transition between the two being signified by the rise to power of the proletariat in the form of a parliamentary majority. Here the act of political change is nothing but the signifier of change brought about by the development of the productive forces.

If, however, one's standpoint on this issue is based upon the revolutionary class consciousness of the proletariat, then the concept of revolution necessarily entails a revolutionizing effect upon this class consciousness which then has the result of denying such an evolutionary model, not by rejecting those developments within capitalism that make revolution possible, but by regarding them as mere preconditions that will themselves be transformed in and through the process of revolution itself (state capitalism and nationalization are pertinent examples).

Thus, at this level of analysis, the proletariat can be seen to be the mediating category between structure and agency, the development of its class consciousness being the determining element in whether or not capitalism is overthrown. Such mechanisms as industrialization, centralization, urbanization, the tendency to economic crisis and so on are but preconditions – or opportunities – for the development of that revolutionary class consciousness, not substitutes for it.

It is obvious to most people, however, that the proletariat is not and for the most part only very rarely has been, a revolutionary class. Disputes over the available evidence are interminable, but it would seem to me clear that any claim on empirical grounds for the existence of a revolutionary class would be forced to disqualify the proletariat and plump instead for the peasantry (or possibly the bourgeosie). However, Marx's claim that the proletariat is the revolutionary class par excellence is not based on empirical grounds but relates to his understanding of what constitutes the essence of the proletariat.

'The working class is revolutionary or it is nothing', Marx wrote in a letter to Schweitzer in 1865,[16] and from this many have drawn the conclusion that it is indeed nothing.[17] What Marx meant by this, however, may be clarified by reference to his earlier remark that 'I have always defied the momentary opinions of the proletariat'[18] and his famous analysis of the proletariat given in *The Holy Family*, that:

> It is not a question of what this or that proletarian, or even the whole proletariat, at the moment *regards* as its aim. It is a question of *what the proletariat is* and what, in accordance with this *being* it will historically be compelled to do.[19]

The link between the non-revolutionary working class and the revolutionary proletariat – for such a link there must be if marxism is to avoid utopianism – is two-fold: first, what Marx referred to as the 'steeling school of labour',[20] that is, the class struggles which the dynamism of bourgeois society forces upon it and which causes it to escalate from individual sabotage and resistance, through collective economic resistance to political organization; and second, the theory of the falling rate of profit, which is first developed in the *Grundrisse* but is a refinement of the theory of crisis elaborated in *The Communist Manifesto*.

The most obvious question then is, or should be: if this advocacy of the proletariat's revolutionary mission is to some extent autonomous or perhaps independent of empirical evidence, why should we pay any attention to it at all? The temptation must be to be drawn to the other pole of attraction offered by the proletariat, namely its centrality as the major material force in capitalist society, which has only to be yoked to some guide external to it – intellectuals, philosophy, the party or whatever – to be in a position to bring about revolutionary change.

Since Marx's death and perhaps even before, this has indeed been the result: the working class has been regarded as the most important social class, not because of its revolutionary potential as such (which, to be fair, it has only very rarely exhibited), but because its centrality, its importance and its majority have made it an exciting and promising ally for the revolutionary (and not so revolutionary) intelligentsia.

The proletariat, then, has two characteristics in Marx's theory: it is the class that suffers most from the alienated conditions and social misery of capitalist society; and it is also the class which, by virtue of the potential it possesses to abolish those conditions in and through its own act of liberation, is destined to assume the political leadership of society hitherto exercised by the bourgeoisie. Thus, its objective social weight and political power, derived from its role as direct producer, makes it a potentially powerful political force; while its subjective role as both the representative of humankind's alienation and exploitation as well as of its universalizing negation of the same – achieved in and through class struggle – makes it a revolutionary power. Obviously, the first of these characteristics continues to exist even where the latter does not. The point is that the former, namely the proletariat's social weight, may be co-opted into non-revolutionary political directions in the absence of the latter and that to appreciate the importance of this latter element requires a non-empiricist assessment of what the proletariat is. Furthermore, as the case of Maurice Merleau-Ponty well illustrates, the adoption of the standpoint of the proletariat without this non-empiricist perspective can lead to its abandonment at the impossibility of reconciling truth with success.[21]

The following chapters return to the two tasks faced by marxist political thought which I raised earlier. On the one hand I provide an exegetical analysis of the role of the proletariat in Marx's thought together with a discussion of the consequences of such an approach; on the other, by also highlighting Marx's non-empircist background and methodology I can demonstrate how this perspective deserves (indeed is required) to be retained despite the evidence that apparently contradicts it. Furthermore, this opens the way to the interpretation developed by Lukács that shares this perspective and which also offers a solution to this challenge of the empirical.

1 Karl Marx and the Discovery of the Proletariat

It was with the appearance of the *Deutsche-Französischer Jahrbücher* at the end of February 1844 that Marx first appended his name to the cause of the proletariat. In the journal that he jointly edited with Arnold Ruge, Marx contributed two major articles, 'On the Jewish Question' and 'Contribution to Critique of Hegel's Philosophy of Law. Introduction', as well as three letters to Ruge which, along with other letters by Ruge, Bakunin and Feuerbach, made up a section 'From the Correspondence of 1843'. Engels also contributed two major articles: 'Outlines of a Critique of Political Economy' and 'The Condition of England. Past and Present by Thomas Carlyle'.[1] The political views of the journal were thus dominated by the views of Marx and Engels, and their contributions not only gave the journal the radical tinge that was to bring upon it and its contributors the wrath of the Prussian government,[2] but were also significant in their adoption for the first time of views that were to characterize the future marxist movement.[3]

This is not to say of course that Marx completed his world outlook with these essays: far from it. The essays do represent, however, a significant moment in the development of his thought; such future changes that did take place in his intellectual development did so on the basis of these views, and were dictated not by their denial, but by the need to widen and deepen the analysis contained therein – as well as to act upon the conclusions.

This view might appear to be contradicted by Marx's claim in the 1859 preface to 'Contribution to the Critique of Political Economy' that his and Engels' concern in *The German Ideology* was to 'settle accounts with our erstwhile philosophical conscience',[4] and that this settling of accounts amounted to the abandonment of his earlier views in favour of later ones. However, far from denouncing the 'idealism' that allegedly permeates these early writings, Marx notes on the contrary that they led to the result that legal relations as well as forms of state are to be grasped neither from themselves nor from the so-called general development of the human mind, but rather have their roots in the material conditions of life...that...the anatomy of civil society is to be sought in political economy.[5]

Further evidence on this point is provided in the third section of *The German Ideology* where Marx writes of the relationship between the left-hegelians and himself, and Feuerbach. For after the latter had demonstrated the earthly illusions upon which religion was based, the question that Feuerbach left unanswered, namely how people got those illusions into their heads in the first place, paved the way to the materialistic view of the world. Marx himself pursued this very question in his 1843 contributions to the *Deutsche-Französischer Jahrbücher*, but in such a manner that allowed the left-hegelians to pretend that nothing more was being given than 'a new turn to their worn-out theoretical garments'. Thus Marx does not reject these 1843 writings but merely regrets that their 'philosophical phraseology, the traditionally occurring philosophical expressions' leaves them open to misinterpretation and misrepresentation. It is true that this same passage contains the notorious statement that 'philosophy and the study of the actual world have the same relation to one another as onanism and sexual love' as well as the declaration that 'one has to leave philosophy aside...one has to leap out of it and devote oneself like an ordinary man to the study of actuality',[6] but this turn by Marx, away from (speculative) philosophy to study of the actual world is unchallenged. What is at question is whether in effecting this change Marx at the same time abandoned or broke from the philosophical position he had developed in opposition to both Hegel and the other left-hegelians.

I would suggest two possible responses to this question. The first, exegetical, would conclude from the comments made by Marx (cited above) that what Marx actually abandoned was the philosophical form in which his earlier writings were cast, and that he preserved the conclusions and much of the content in his (so-called) scientific writings. The second response would be to argue that the sorts of questions to which Marx sought solutions in his anatomy of civil society are indeed philosophical questions in the widest sense: questions which deal with the meaning and destiny of existence, but seek answers in social and historical terms rather than in ontology or metaphysics.

Marx's own testament is therefore ambiguous. On the one hand he talks of 'settling accounts' with his philosophical conscience; on the other he does this not by criticizing his own philosophical writings but by writing with Engels two lengthy philosophical critiques of post-hegelian philosophy (*The Holy Family* and *The German Ideology*). Any self-critique is thus at best implicit, evidenced by Marx's abandoning of his manuscripts to 'the gnawing criticism of the mice',[7] by his turn to economic studies and his concern with the form in which these earlier writings were composed.

Moreover, such changes as there undoubtedly were are best understood in terms of the consequences of the philosophical positions worked out in these early writings, rather than their simple abandonment. If we look in some detail at the conception of revolution worked out by Marx in this period we shall see that it is this which accounts for his subsequent interest in economic matters and political activism, as well as his apparent abandonment of philosophical preoccupations. It is this too that serves as the major foundation stone of Marx's social thought. Marx sought not to ignore the philosophical questions that dominated the German intellectual scene at the time, but to realize them in a social critique. In the 1843 introduction Marx expressed this view in contradistinction to those liberal reformers who had to his mind derided the contribution of philosophy by concentrating solely on constitutional reform. What these people forgot, Marx claimed, was that 'the real living germ of the German nation has grown so far only inside its *cranium*. In a word – *you cannot supersede philosophy without making it a reality*.'[8]

Marx and Revolution

What, then, is Marx's conception of revolution? And in what sense can this be said to constitute a social critique?

When Engels declared at the funeral of Marx in 1883 that his friend was 'before all else a revolutionist'[9], he invested in this term a quite specific meaning whose origins go back to Marx's 1843 Introduction and which requires some elaboration to clear away the myths and caricatures that surround it now, as they did then. A revolutionist in the sense in which Engels spoke is not someone who merely desires a revolution, but someone who subscribes to (at least) three further sets of beliefs. The first is an understanding of that which is to be overthrown which penetrates to the essence and origin of the ills and evils for which a revolution is required as a remedy. Second is a recognition that that change cannot be brought about through piecemeal reforms and alterations, but requires a radical, thoroughgoing break with existing social and political relations. The third is an account of the social, class relations that maintain and reproduce existing conditions, and those that can overthrow them. These sets of beliefs are problems to be solved; the history of marxism might be said to be a history of attempts to solve them.

There were – and are – of course, non-marxist revolutionists: people who believe that they understand the true causes of the wretchedness of existing conditions and who desire and recognize the necessity for a revolutionary upheaval to overturn them. But what was and remains unique to the marxist view of revolution concerns two things: the claim to put that understanding of existing conditions on to a scientific basis; and thus the claim to have discovered within those conditions the force that is not only capable but is compelled to bring about that revolutionary change, namely the proletariat.[10]

There are many alternatives to this approach: the substitution of the moral example of the revolutionary, for example; the armed seizure of power by the small group; the location of revolutionary agency in other social groups or classes (the bourgeoisie, the peasantry or the lumpen-proletariat); or frontal attacks upon the power of the state in an attempt to ignite the 'volatility of the people'. All of these strategies have been utilized at one time or another by groups of self-proclaimed revolutionaries, with varying degrees of failure. It was Marx and Engels, however, who were to 'discover' and make the basis of their political strategy the force within existing conditions that could bridge the gap between the enlightened desires of the revolutionary and the stubborn inertia of existing reality, between philosophy and the world, between the 'is' and the 'ought'. Marx expressed the basis of his strategy in the 1864 provisional rules to the International Working Men's Association when he said that 'the emancipation of the working classes must be conquered by the working classes themselves'.[11]

This view, which appears nowadays innocuous and straightforward, is in fact quite the opposite. For upon this principle rests a conception of revolutionary change that is as unique and central to the modern marxist movement as it was to Marx and his companions in the last century. This point may be established by examining the different ways in which the principle has been interpreted since Marx's death, by orthodox social democracy and by communism as well as by the currents of socialism in opposition to which Marx developed his own views.

Before doing this, however, it is necessary to draw the theoretical parameters within which Marx was involved in this earlier period, to examine both how it was that he came to the views he did and also, thereby, to appreciate their true novelty, importance and relevance. For it was remarkable that a German doctor of philosophy came to regard a social class with which he had only the remotest of contact as the force capable of redeeming the world of its sins and of remedying the social ills that had taxed, or so it was said, the best brains of what Marx described as 'the most philosophical country in Europe'. It was equally remarkable that this task (or achievement) was left to the citizen of a Germany that was then, economically, socially and politically, one of the most backward in Europe – with the consequence that it barely possessed a proletariat at all. This apparent paradox is stimulating not only for its own sake, but because in seeking to account for it we can learn much about Marx's understanding of the modern proletariat; what precise role it plays in his thought at this time; whether this view was dependent upon certain historically contingent factors; and also how Marx came to the views he did in the first place.

The Evolution of Marx's Thought

Hegel and the Left-Hegelians

Marx took from post-hegelian German philosophy two strands of thought that he bound together, giving each a radical twist. The first was that criticism of religion was transformed into a social critique of civil society; instead of concentrating criticism upon the heavenly abstractions of theology, it was now directed at the social conditions that gave rise to the demand for – and creation of – religious or spiritual feeling. The existence of religion was not a philosophical error but an alienated form of protest by humanity against the inhumanity of the world in which it found itself. Post-hegelian philosophy, and especially the writings of Feuerbach, had signified the raising to consciousness of this fact, but it had been unable to proceed any further, first, because it was unable to perceive how consciousness of this fact could proceed to change the fact itself (or, more accurately perhaps, because it regarded the raising to consciousness as a change in the fact itself) and second, because its critique of Hegel's dialectic had led it to reject all mediation as at best irrelevant, and at worst anathema to its position of 'absolute negation',[12] of total opposition to all that exists. This misconception of Hegel's dialectic was made possible by the combination of an apocalyptic persuasion and an idealistic faith in the power of (critical) ideas, a combination which led to a belief that inevitable change was about to occur; in Heine's phrase, thought preceded action as lightning did thunder.[13] This investment of hope in radical change found its embodiment in the accession of Frederick William IV to the Prussian throne in 1840 and the relaxation of censorship shortly afterwards, but was revealed to be wildly optimistic by the government's reactionary return to censorship in 1842–3.

Marx's view was that the criticism of religion could be completed only when full recognition of the social determinants of religious feeling was complemented by a revolutionary, practical critique of its social basis:

> To abolish religion as the illusory happiness of the people is to demand their *real* happiness. The demand to give up illusions about the existing state of affairs is the *demand to give up a state of affairs which needs illusions*. The criticism of religion is therefore *in embryo the criticism of the vale of tears*, the *halo* of which is religion.[14]

Once humanity is made aware of its own religious creations it must then go on to rectify the social conditions that led it to religion in the first place. This amounted to a democratization of theory, in that criticism of religion was no longer the abstract province of the philosopher, but part of a social critique. This leads to the second feature of Marx's position, namely the basis of his social critique in a radically democratic relationship between thought and reality, between theory and practice, a relationship founded in political activity.

While Marx took over from left-hegelianism, and in particular from Feuerbach, its radical criticism of religion and philosophy, his emphasis on radical-democratic politics was largely absent in Feuerbach, whose political attitude consisted of an unrealistic counterposition of aspiration with existence. This absence of a realistic political strategy was in no small part due to the failure to grasp the importance of Hegel's dialectic and the role of mediation in it. Marx's break with left-hegelianism, which was in one respect a result of the political clarification forced upon the Young Hegelians by government repression,[15] was in another respect shaped by the retention in Marx's thought of a more positive attitude to Hegel's dialectic, and in particular the importance of mediation. The absence of the latter among the Young Hegelians had left them to the mercy of political events over which they had no control, while for Marx, his discovery of the proletariat had made possible – or so he thought – the means through which philosophy could realize its (radical-critical) mission at the same time that it undermined its own authoritative autonomy.

In his discussion of the dialectic in the *Economic and Philosophic Manuscripts of 1844,* Marx discusses its positive aspects within the realm of estrangement, and notes that despite the weaknesses exposed by

Feuerbach (which had been largely ignored by the other Young Hegelians)[16] Hegel's dialectic nevertheless expresses the premise that mediation, even of estranged forms, is necessary for the supersession of those forms through a process of self-discovery. Hegel grasps, Marx notes,

> the *positive* meaning of self-referred negation (although again in estranged fashion). Hegel grasps man's self-estrangement, the alienation of man's essence, man's loss of objectivity and his loss of realness as self-discovery, manifestation of his nature, objectification and realisation. In short, within the sphere of abstraction, Hegel conceives labour as man's act of *self-genesis* – conceives man's relation to himself as an alien being and the manifestation of himself as an alien being to be the emergence of *species-consciousness* and *species-life*.[17]

While Marx utilizes Feuerbach's transformative method to criticize the formal and abstract character of Hegel's dialectic and its idealistic subject-bearer, as well as to advocate a humanistic starting point for philosophy, he does not reject the dialectic (and the necessity of mediation) as such, merely the particular character of them found in Hegel. Once the real essence of humans – their labour – has been discovered, this can then be examined under the light of the dialectic.

Marx's future writings could thus be said to be a series of engagements with these positions: investigations into the conditions of life in civil society and the critique of the social underpinnings of such phenomena as religion and (abstract) philosophy were complemented by a democratization of theory and realization of criticism in political activity. This latter required both practical activity at the formal, organizational level, and also analyses of positions that hinder this process. We thus find that Marx's concrete investigations of social analysis are formulated in terms of a critique – both theoretical and political – and that they are directed at social transformation rather than passive contemplation. Marx is no watcher of Minerva's owl.

There is therefore a considerable degree of overlap between these two positions: in particular, the conditions of life and role of the proletariat is that central category that unites these two strands of Marx's thought. The proletariat suffers the dehumanized exploitation and indignities of civil society, and the forms of resistance which it offers to its condition involve both a consciousness of the world and its situation in it, and a determination to alter that world. This confluence of theory and practice involves a democratization of theory – something that Marx saw as a significant advance beyond the contemplative, speculative thought of Hegel and the Young Hegelians.

Marx and Feuerbach

If we now go on to look in detail at how Marx effected these two radical criticisms of left-hegelianism, we can see both how he came to adopt the cause of the proletariat and, more importantly, what meaning this had for his thought. While Marx shares the general approach of left-hegelianism that proposed a union between German philosophy and the French spirit, and was in this respect particularly influenced by Feuerbach, he moves away from philosophical debates amongst intellectuals to advocate the adoption of revolutionary politics in union with the proletariat. In 1843 Feuerbach had finally turned Hegel's method against its system, portraying the hegelian system as the last refuge of religion, to be overthrown by the dialectical inversion that would start with the finite rather than the absolute, with humanism rather than idealism. The invocation of the French spirit marked for Feuerbach, and for those like Marx inspired by his article, the belief that 'being is the subject, thought the predicate. Thought arises from being – being does not arise from thought',[18] and that the dissolution of this abstract philosophy would be achieved by a critical philosophy of 'Gallo-Germanic blood' that took the senses as its starting point.

Marx enthusiastically embraced Feuerbach's humanistic criticisms of Hegel's idealism, but preferred politics rather than nature and the senses as a basis for its criticism and dissolution. In this sense, Lukács is correct in his claim that Marx was never a Feuerbachian; that he retained Hegel's dialectic – albeit in an inverted form[19] but allied it to politics rather than to nature.[20] In politics there was a possibility of mediating philosophy and the world. Feuerbach's (unmediated) invocations of the primacy of the senses, of nature, of anthropology and of love could usefully subvert Hegel's philosophy (and in this respect were not criticised by Marx), but they could not be realized in political activity and thus remained, for all their usefulness and radicalism, contemplative and static.

We can take as a further example of the difference between Feuerbach and Marx the famous quote from *The Holy Family* where Marx and Engels distinguish their position – under the influence of Max Stirner – from the other left-hegelians:

> History does nothing; it does not possess immense riches, it does not fight battles. It is men, real, living men, who do all this, who possess things and fight battles. It is not 'history' which uses men as a means of achieving – as if it were an individual person – its own ends. History is nothing but the activity of men in the pursuit of their ends.[21]

At first reading this would appear to support those who argue that Marx was under the influence of Feuerbach at the time, and indeed the letter Marx wrote to Feuerbach in the same year in which he states that Feuerbach has provided a 'philosophical basis for socialism'[22] adds to this impression. However, partly under the influence of Engels, Marx was increasingly to distinguish his views from Feuerbach. Only three months later, in November 1844, Engels writes to Marx of his impressions upon reading Stirner, saying that they must base themselves on Stirner's (albeit one-sided) egoism against Feuerbach's theological 'man': 'we must take our departure from the Ego, the empirical, flesh-and-blood individual ... we must take our departure from empiricism and materialism if our concepts and notably our "man" are to be something real.'[23]

While Feuerbach was useful in terms of his critique of Hegel's idealism, his proposed solution was inadequate since it remained essentially philosophical. The shared terminology of Feuerbach's 'man' or 'species' and Marx's 'men' disguises the more fundamental divergence between the two, and the different uses to which these similar concepts are put. While Marx shares Feuerbach's criticisms of Hegel in terms of his transformative critique,[24] Marx was clear from an early stage that to be effective this critique must be realized – and this required a conception of 'man' based upon active, historical agency, rather than Feuerbach's divination of species and worship of nature. The skeletal conception of 'man' Marx took from, or shared with Feuerbach requires fleshing out with more than Feuerbach's own concern with the stomach, in terms of 'empiricism and materialism', and the social and historical circumstances in which the interrelation of humans and nature takes place.

Further evidence with respect to Marx's relationship to Feuerbach is provided by Marx's letter to Feuerbach written in the summer of 1844, in which he tries to encourage the reluctant Feuerbach to engage his philosophical preoccupations with their political implications, which Marx now thought lay with the movement of the French proletariat rather than with the intellectual circles of conservative Germany. Marx has thus shifted both from philosophy to politics, and from intellectuals to the proletariat. This is how Marx interprets his new understanding of revolutionary politics to Feuerbach:

> in contrast to the eighteenth century, religiosity has now passed to the middle and upper classes while on the other hand, irreligiosity – but an irreligiosity of men regarding themselves as men – has descended to the French proletariat. You would have to attend one of the

> meetings of the French workers to appreciate the pure freshness, the nobility which burst forth from these toil-worn men.

And he concludes that 'it is among these "barbarians" of our civilized society that history is preparing the practical element for the emancipation of mankind.'[25]

In this letter Marx is clearly calling upon Feuerbach to follow the example set by himself, to follow the same path he has taken: from abstract to real philosophy, from philosophy to politics. By emphasizing that the solution to the problem that Feuerbach concerned himself with to the virtual exclusion of all others, namely the religious question, could not be found within philosophy but must be located within the social (and hence political) conditions that both men saw as lying at the root of religion, Marx hoped that Feuerbach could be encouraged to take a radical step towards political engagement. In this he was to be disappointed. Indeed, Feuerbach's refusal to make such a move signifies the real division between the two: that while Feuerbach shared with Marx the desire to humanize religion, he regarded the accomplishment of this task as the duty of philosophy, of thought,[26] whereas Marx saw philosophy itself, or at least the abstract version of it, as being incapable of bringing about its own realization. For this a dialectical mediation was necessary.

While Feuerbach saw humankind as the true anthropological basis of religion, his philosophical critique of religion – the demonstration of this truth – was insufficient and required a material embodiment that Marx now discovered among the proletarian circles he encountered in Paris. Religion, (abstract) philosophy and even critical philosophy shared a common origin in the wretchedness of social conditions; one could not simply be replaced by another. The solution to the religious question as posed by Feuerbach and the other left-hegelians lay not in its replacement by philosophy, or even by anthropology, nor in its suppression, but in its realization in the concrete existence of which it was an expression, through the proletariat.

Marx and the Proletariat

So far then, it would seem that Marx's change in orientation is clear and straightforward. Whereas hitherto he had been a conventional left-hegelian, on his expulsion from Germany and his exile to Paris he encountered a social force, the proletariat, that solved philosophical questions by its promise of revolutionary change. Thus, on this interpretation,

Marx abandoned philosophy in favour of politics (and later economics) as he abandoned intellectuals for the proletariat.

There is, however, more to this question than would at first appear to be the case from such a reading of Marx's change of orientation. It would be mistaken to suppose that Marx simply abandoned philosophy upon discovering in Paris an active, politically conscious proletariat. To begin with, there is some truth to Tucker's accusation[27] that Marx did not know any real proletarians, and that those workers Marx met in Paris were most often German émigrés and/or artisans.[28] There were relatively few factory workers in Paris at that time,[29] and those that there were were not likely to be counted among the revolutionaries of Marx's acquaintance. I will consider further below this criticism of accuracy.

More importantly however, Marx's views did not arrive ready-formed: they developed (albeit rapidly) during a period in which he assimilated the radical socialist ideas of his new environment.[30] As I have already indicated, the call for a union between German philosophy and French politics was a theme common to the hegelian left disappointed both by the failure of the promised reforms of Friedrich Wilhelm IV and by their own political impotence. In most cases, however, this theme signified nothing more radical than a call for alternative sources of support. Marx was himself influenced by this approach, his earlier writings arguing in typical left-hegelian vein for a union in which philosophy plays the active, enlightening role, while the proletariat plays the merely secondary role of having its consciousness reformed by exposure to this philosophy. Thus, even if it were true to say that Marx abandoned philosophy for the proletariat – and it is not – what is crucial is the meaning the proletariat has for Marx's thought at the time.

Marx's understanding of the proletariat was, to begin with, shaped by his left-hegelian background, which viewed the proletariat as Feuerbach, for example, viewed the senses: as the instrument through which critical philosophy could overthrow abstract philosophy and religion. At first, as we shall soon see, Marx's conception of the proletariat shared some of the characteristics of this theoretico-elitist model.

The difference between Marx and the other left-hegelians was that he ended this period of development by incorporating both elements – philosophy and the proletariat in a social critique in which each draws upon the strengths and support of the other to resolve the weaknesses or partiality of its own predicament in favour of a radical-democratic emphasis upon social transformation. While Marx shared Feuerbach's view of religion and philosophy as expressions – in abstracto – of a real social problem, namely the problem of society, the hegelian heritage persisted in his laying equal emphasis upon the social critique, upon the ability of the proletariat to utilize its understanding of reality – its philosophy – to overthrow that reality. In other words, Marx does not speak of philosophy in the abstract manner of the hegelian tradition, and nor does he regard the proletariat as merely the social counterpart of this (abstract) philosophy. Rather, philosophy is moderated by its association with the proletariat and the proletariat moderated by its association with philosophy. Philosophy is no longer abstract, because it now enjoys this material embodiment, and the proletariat is no longer merely empirical because of its association with philosophy. The proletariat signifies the mediating concept between philosophy and the world, making possible true criticism, i.e. practical-critical activity, because its situation in the world is both actual and critical.

Marx develops the concept of the proletariat to solve the dilemma of political impotence which left-hegelianism could not transcend. The call to humanize religion, to recognize people in God, was a necessary step in the critique of theism. However, Marx came to recognize that religion and its critique were both founded upon an earthly existence which must itself be subjected to a radical criticism if the basis of religion was to be effectively challenged. This could not be done without challenging the ideas and conceptions that people had developed to support their religious beliefs, and also finding within the social basis of religion the mediator that can both formulate and operationalize that critique.

Changes in Marx's Thought

The changing character of Marx's views may be demonstrated by comparing his contributions to 'From the Correspondence of 1843' with the two works written soon after, either shortly before or during his residence in Paris:[31] 'On the Jewish Question' and the 1843 Introduction. The letters Marx wrote to Ruge illustrate Marx's increasing radicalism as he travels the continent from Holland to Kreuznach via Cologne. His intention is, even now, to ground philsophy in reality, but the left-hegelian influence is not yet cast aside and this frustrates his intention at a key point, when he calls for a 'reform of consciousness' to accomplish this task.

The two focal points of German philosophical debate, namely religion and politics, are to be confronted not by a ready-made system but by active intervention and opposition; philosophy is no longer to be abstract or dogmatic, no longer the province of withdrawn academics, but the 'ruthless criticism of all that exists',[32] afraid neither of the results arrived at nor of conflict with the powers that be. In a manifesto intended for the new journal and written shortly before his move to Paris, Marx sums up his new political perspective thus:

> Hence, nothing prevents us from making criticism of politics, participation in politics, and therefore real struggles, the starting point of our criticism, and from identifying our criticism with them. In that case we do not confront the world in a doctrinaire way with a new principle: Here is the truth, kneel down before it! We develop new principles for the world out of the world's own principles. We do not say to the world: Cease your struggles, they are foolish; we will give you the true slogan of struggle. We merely show the world what it is really fighting for, and consciousness is something that it *has* to acquire even if it does not want to. The reform of consciousness consists *only* in making the world aware of its own consciousness, in awakening it out of its dream about itself, in *explaining* to it the meaning of its own actions.[33]

The tension in this work between the practical, material tasks of philosophy and the idealist premises on which it is based is resolved in favour of the latter in the last two paragraphs, where Marx declares 'our motto must be: reform of consciousness not through dogmas, but by analysing the mystical consciousness that is unintelligible to itself'[34] and he sums up the trend of the journal as

> self-clarification (critical philosophy) to be gained by the present time of its struggles and desires. This is a work for the world and for us. It can only be the work of united forces. It is a matter of confession, and nothing more. In order to secure remission of its sins, mankind has only to declare them for what they actually are.[35]

Marx was soon to realize, however, that necessary as this declaration was, more than this is required to 'secure remission' from them. But it would be churlish not to appreciate equally that the tendency of this document is precisely a move away from philosophical idealism, 'the reform of consciousness', to a concern with the actual mechanisms through which this is to be achieved, mechanisms whose implications are anything but idealist, precisely because they must be declared for what they actually are rather than as they appear to us.

First, the passage implies the uniting of theory and practice, but at the level of practice. Theory does not have the task of introducing truth into the world on the rationalist model, but distils truth out of the world itself. Only to the extent that new principles – for example, socialist consciousness – exist in the actions of the world, albeit implicitly and unrecognized, can theory develop into consciousness. As Marx somewhat immodestly puts it in the passage cited above: 'we merely show the world what it is really fighting for.'

Second, this political task is not voluntaristic in the sense that one reason, or set of ideas, is substituted or confronted by another. Marx's version of the 'reform of consciousness' is more radical than the rationalist model adopted by Feuerbach and the other left-hegelians, since it does not take place through the simple replacement of a faulty (or false) consciousness by a superior model, but rather it is a replacement forced upon dreaming consciousness by its own location in the world. That is to say, the mechanism for change lies not at the level of thought, but at practice guided by thought.

Third, this passage implies the alienation model of people that accounts for the struggles and actions which are the basis and support for this 'reform of consciousness'. It is not merely shame, nor material interests alone that force people to resist, but rather the brutal, animal-like, dehumanized world in opposition to which religion has created a perfect world in abstraction, and Hegel's political philosophy a falsely realized reflection.

Marx has at this stage irrevocably broken with abstract philosophy. He has shifted the locus of his criticism from the level of theory to the social reality that produces the theory to which he is opposed. He has thus located not only the cause but also the solution to bad philosophy in reality itself. Yet he is still (as he was to put it later) at the end point of religious criticism, not yet at the starting point of his own mode of criticism. This was to come later, beginning with the other major articles published in the *Deutsche-Französischer Jahrbücher.* 'On the Jewish Question' providing an account of the necessary link between religious and political criticism while at the same time further elaborating on what precisely is at fault in reality; the 1843 Introduction providing a recapitulation in manifesto form of the conclusions drawn to date, and, crucially, specifying what it is in reality that has the potential of rectifying what is wrong in it. In his contributions to the *Deutsche-Französischer Jahrbücher* Marx does two things. He offers an account of what he sees as wrong in reality, its effects and causes, together with his vision of its self-annulment. He then goes on to apply this approach both to the universal conditions of bourgeois society, as well as to the more specific conditions of Germany.

His essay 'On the Jewish Question', while dealing with a problem real and specific to Germany, namely religious persecution, does so in terms of the relationship of this political problem with the social conditions that lie at its origin. Marx berates his former colleague Bruno Bauer for his inability adequately to differentiate between political and human emancipation, and his consequent failure to appreciate the limits and extent of political emancipation. In Marx's view the religious problem is not a problem of the form of state organization, irrespective of whether the Christian state practices discrimination against Jews, since even where the state has freed itself from religious sectarianism – for example in the United States – religion not only continues to exist 'but displays a fresh and vigorous vitality'.[36] The political emancipation of people and of the state from religious persecution is 'a big step forward', indeed it is 'the final form of human emancipation within the hitherto existing world order',[37] but it is not yet human emancipation, which can be achieved only by striking at the origin and source of religion – which is also the origin and source of the state.

Marx thus draws an analogy between religion and the state, each of which he sees as merely the idealized expression of the essential powers of people that are denied them in their everyday lives: 'the state is the intermediary to whom man transfers all his non-divinity and all his human unconstraint',[38] that is to say, those things which make people truly human, in particular their freedom, are transferred to the state. Marx draws this analogy to show that neither the state nor religion can be reformed or transformed on its own basis, since each rests upon a social basis that must itself be challenged. What lies at the heart of this problem is 'the dualism between individual life and species-life, between the life of civil society and political life'[39] which creates in people the need for both religious and state worship, a situation in which:

> man – not only in thought, in consciousness, but in *reality*, in *life* – leads a twofold life, a heavenly and an earthly life: life in the *political community*, in which he considers himself a *communal being*, and life in *civil society*, in which he acts as a *private individual*, regards other men as a means, degrades himself into a means, and becomes the plaything of alien powers.[40]

By this measure even the most perfect form of political democracy is extremely limited, since it is based upon the notion of the individual as sovereign:

> man in his uncivilized, unsocial form, man in his fortuitous existence, man just as he is, man as he has been corrupted by the whole organization of our society, who has lost himself, been alienated, and handed over to the rule of inhuman conditions and elements – in short, man who is not yet a *real* species-being.[41]

We can thus see how Marx has taken a specific German circumstance and used it to highlight the universal significance of which it is an amplified expression. The religious problem of the Jews has become for Marx the problem of religion, political emancipation has become human emancipation, and the source and origin of problem and solution have been located in the material conditions of life which generate the demand for both religion and politics, but which also prevent either sphere from bringing about people's universal emancipation. Political emancipation, including emancipation from religious persecution, while welcome, is only a step forward within the existing order and also carries with it disadvantages: 'throwing off the bonds which restrained the egoistic spirit of civil society'[42] leaves as the sole source of social cohesion the unrestrained greed of egoistic human beings. No social ties between people remain save 'natural necessity, need and private interest, the preservation of their property and their egoistic selves'.[43]

In the second part of the essay, similarly, Marx relates the causes of anti-semitism and the possibilities of reducing it to its social element. For him, the problem of jewry is not a religious question but a matter of the secular basis and 'worldly religion' of jewry and the Jew, which Marx describes as 'Practical need, self-interest...Huckstering...[and] Money'.[44] Marx has thus transferred the Jewish problem to its empirical essence – 'huckstering and its preconditions'[45] are the source, as he sees it, of the world's ills.

Marx has thus created a model of alienated humanity in which the inability of people to live authentically, according to their true attributes, needs and desires, leads to the transubstantiation of those attributes, needs and desires elsewhere, to their alienated expression in religion and politics. Both these spheres, however, while they stand in ethical superiority to their material opposite in reality, are in fact subordinate to and dominated by that earthly existence. And people suffer in both spheres: in their lives as 'real individuals' they suffer the consequences of the absence of all moral and social restraint; in their political and spiritual lives they likewise suffer the exclusion of their real, material lives: '[man] is the imaginary member of an illusory sovereignty, is deprived of his real individual life and endowed with an unreal universality.'[46]

But the next stage of the argument is crucial. For after noting the limitations of political emancipation, Marx goes on to offer his own alternative vision of human, social emancipation. This vision is not, however, a dogmatic imposition upon existing political life, but can be shown to grow out of it. Marx notes the specific characteristics of society that concern him: the separation of civil society and political life; the dominance of the former over the latter; and the consequences this has on the warped social relationships created on this basis – 'man who is not yet a *real* species-being'.[47] A further specification of this 'man' reveals his separation from and opposition to others, his egoism and his worship of private property.

The struggle for purely political liberation signifies the 'completion of the materialism of civil society' with its consequent withdrawal of all restraints on the 'egoistic spirit of civil society',[48] and this in turn creates the demand, as it prepares the ground for the next stage: true human emancipation. By destroying all semblance of a universal content in political life, political liberation makes manifest the corruption, inequality and inhumanity of civil society, and creates a demand for liberation from it, for its overthrow. The conditions for this final form of human liberation are the reabsorption of real individuals into their lives as abstract citizens on the ancient Greek model, and the organization and recognition of people's powers as truly social.

What remains to be demonstrated is the means through which this full human emancipation will be achieved. We know most of the conditions upon which it is to be defined: that it is located in the material world of civil society; that it cannot nor will it be satisfied by political emancipation alone; and that it suffers the social persecution paralleled by the political persecution of the Jew. It is in the 1843 introduction that Marx announces its discovery.

Marx's 'Discovery' of the Proletariat

Robert Tucker argues that Marx came to communism through the influence of the 'communist rabbi' Moses Hess, the French anarchist Joseph Proudhon and the 'conservative hegelian and one-time Prussian police agent'[49] Lorenz von Stein. Marx's image of the proletariat was not of empirical origin, Tucker argues: 'He did not come by it, for example, by observation of contemporary factory conditions, by direct contact with industrial workers and work, or even by the study of political economy.'[50] On the contrary, 'the only proletarians he knew were the ones he read about in books, in particular von Stein's *Der Socialismus und Communismus des heutigens Frankreichs.*'[51] Shlomo Avineri has accepted the influence of von Stein's book on Marx but questions Tucker's overestimation of its influence, arguing that it merely expressed a general view which, for example, had been expressed even earlier – by Adam Muller in 1815 and Franz von Baader in 1835. This concern with the proletariat was part of the 'mood and...general malaise prevalent at that time in intellectual circles in Germany among radicals and conservative romantics alike',[52] and he concludes that 'Marx's intellectual tour de force must be approached by confronting his description of the proletariat with the universal postulates of Hegel's political philosophy.'[53] Both Avineri and Tucker, then, argue that Marx's discovery of the proletariat was primarily an intellectual discovery, that it was theoretically a priori rather than empirical in origin.

David McLellan's view is that Marx came to adopt the cause of the proletariat as a consequence of his shift of attention from German to French matters, specifically as a result of his study of the French Revolution and his move to Paris in October 1843, which for the first time took him outside the comfortable, intellectual atmosphere of the newspaper office or study and placed him in a radical socialist atmosphere in which 'first hand contacts with socialist intellectuals'[54] could not but exert a radical influence on the radical Marx. Thus Marx's immersion in the politics of French society led him into contact with workers who made a favourable contrast with the verbose but politically impotent intellectuals who had hitherto constituted his contact group.

It is certainly true that the Paris Marx moved to was a world away from the Germany that he had grown up in; the city had had an electrifying effect upon many of the German émigrés, who breathed there the free air of political debate for the first time. Ruge, Marx's co-editor on the *Deutsche-Französischer Jahrbücher,* expressed the views common to the hegelian left:

> We are going to France, the threshold of a new world. May it live up to our dreams! At the end of our journey we will find the vast valley of Paris, the cradle of the new Europe, the great laboratory where world history is formed and has its ever fresh source. Even our philosophy, the field where we are in advance of our time, will only be able to triumph when proclaimed in Paris and impregnated with the French spirit.[55]

We might add to this the description of the ideological maelstrom of post-1830 France offered by Franz Mehring in his biography of Marx, a country, says Mehring, where 'a ceaseless battle of intellects raged – rolling now here, now there – such as could be found nowhere else in Europe and certainly not in Germany, which lay motionless in the silence of intellectual death.'[56] On the one hand then, we have the intellectual influence of Marx's reading; on the other, the political effects of Marx's move to Paris. The truth lies somewhere between the two.

It is almost certainly the case that Marx's first acquaintance with workers came through reading books, but it was also his direct and first-hand contact with workers – and socialists – in Paris that gave a reality to these theoretical reflections. His theoretical leanings were thus influenced by experience, though, equally, his experience was also itself affected by theoretical considerations. It was this political experience that enabled Marx, as we shall shortly see, to advance beyond the elitist and one-sided relationship between theory and the masses posited by his former left-hegelian fellow thinkers. On the other hand, is is also true to say that what Marx discovered in Paris in 1843 was not the result of observation alone; he added to this an intellectual faculty that influenced his assessment of what he saw about him. His understanding of the proletariat is not reducible to what the proletariat actually constituted in Paris at that time, nor even to what the socialists Marx mixed with thought that it constituted.

This is a matter of more than historical importance, since what we are concerned to explicate is not so much how Marx came to 'discover' the proletariat, but the meaning of that discovery for Marx himself and for the movement that bears his name. The essential point to scientific discovery, or indeed to any other, is precisely the search itself: to search for something invariably means that one knows broadly – in abstract as it were – what one is looking for. The quest to split the atom yielded new insights once accomplished, but the essential groundwork for this and other scientific discoveries had been laid at an earlier stage. Similarly with Marx, it was the philosophical environment of post-hegelian philosophy that led him to the search for what only the discovery in Paris of the proletariat could fulfil.

It is a matter also of political import. For some commentators the revelation that Marx's 'discovery' of the proletariat was based upon a faulty empirical understanding of French conditions has led to (or is perhaps derived from) two conclusions. The first is that Marx's understanding of the proletariat was at this point non-empirical, and that this therefore puts Marx in the Judaeo–Christian tradition in which the proletariat plays the role of messianic salvation,[57] and that his own views express moral indignation at the condition of the proletariat. The second is that the marxist movement is discredited, or at best compromised, by the refusal of the proletariat to play the role written for it and its consistent failure to measure up to the historical mission of universal salvation this tradition would have it perform.[58]

The charge, then, is that Marx makes two errors: an error of accuracy and an error of prophecy. Swept along on a tide of radicalism, he mistakes the artisan and intellectual milieu of Paris for a revolutionary proletariat,[59] and second, because he mistakenly takes the conditions of life of these radical artisans to be typical of those of the proletariat, he places the burden of his theory of revolution upon a social class – the proletariat – that never warranted such expectations.

It is not sufficient to rebut this criticism by citing evidence that shows the deep impression made upon Marx by the workers he encountered in Paris. This is because first, the evidence does not overwhelmingly disprove the hypothesis; on the contrary, it consistently suggests that Marx viewed the French proletariat through spectacles that focused on something other than the immediate appearance of the workers he encountered. This was true also in the case of Marx's understanding of the revolt of the Silesian weavers (discussed below). Second, because while the hypothesis that Marx's understanding of the proletariat was at this stage purely philosophical or even religious may, as David McLellan points out, be mistaken as a total explanation,[60] it does contain an element of partial truth. It is a different matter, of course, to specify what that truth consists of. Is it the location of Marx in this Judaeo–Christian tradition? Is it the assessment of Marx's thought as the expression of moral indignation against the condition of the proletariat? Is it the ascription to the proletariat of a messianic mission? Or is it the understanding that the proletariat constitutes something that will be expressed historically and is not immediately apparent? In the remainder of this chapter I will go on to answer these questions by examining in some detail the development of Marx's theory of the proletariat, and will assess the extent to which the criticism of accuracy made against Marx is justified. I will discuss the criticism of prophecy in the next chapter.

Marx's Specification of the Proletariat

Marx's discussion of the proletariat in his 1843 Introduction continues his critique of the 'wretchedness of existing conditions', but also draws upon his study of the French (bourgeois) Revolution and his understanding of the way in which the French bourgeoisie made itself the ruling class of society to show certain parallels with the future role of the proletariat. The proletariat thus takes on two aspects: it is the class that suffers most from the alienated conditions and social misery of existing conditions; and it is also the class which is, by virtue of the potential it possesses to abolish those conditions in and through its own act of self-liberation, destined to assume the political leadership of society previously exercised by the bourgeoisie.

Two problems are immediately evident in this account. The first concerns whether Marx regards the proletariat as a revolutionary class because it is the most miserable class: whether it is the more or less passive recipient of a revolutionary character determined by the wretchedness of its existence – the so-called immiserization problem. The second arises from the consequences for its consciousness of those conditions of its existence: whether it has the ability to surmount the mystifications that arise in consciousness from the alienated and alienating reality in which it finds itself.[61]

The first of these problems is additionally complicated by the very backwardness of the Germany Marx knew and upon which he based the revolutionary conclusions of this work – until, that is, Engels introduced him to the new world of industrial England. For it is at first difficult to see how under such backward conditions a revolutionary social force based upon modern, bourgeois conditions could be said by any but the most utopian to be a realistic possibility. Marx argues, however, that Germany's backwardness has yielded advantages as well as disadvantages. For while it is indeed true that Germany to a large extent lacked the material basis for the political revolution that had completed the development of the modern state in the more advanced countries, and in so doing had freed the dynamic capacities of civil society of their feudal fetters, and while it suffered from both the shortcomings of the modern world as well as the 'barbaric deficiencies of the ancien regime',[62] these had also given it the opportunity to develop in consciousness, in thought, the criticisms of those social conditions that were at the time more apparent than real.

Thus, German philosophy had developed radically as a form of compensation for Germany's economic and social backwardness, and though this had the consequence of encouraging 'the abstraction and conceit of its thought',[63] this state of affairs could be remedied by reuniting the radical philosophical critique of existing conditions with a social force both capable of and willing to alter those conditions, in other words of bringing about the reunification of thought and reality, of theory and practice. Indeed, this reunification is itself encouraged by German conditions. On the one hand the advanced stage of development of its philosophical critique of the modern world brings about a dissatisfaction with any proposed solution which offers merely a partial political revolution. And on the other, its social backwardness makes this latter a utopian dream, for only the radical social revolution with general human emancipation as its aim is a truly realistic solution to Germany's problems.

This appeal to German conditions offers us two possible roads of interpretation. We might argue that Marx's radicalism, which has already caused him to mistake Parisian artisans for proletarians, has now led him to exaggerate vastly the revolutionary potential of German conditions – precisely because this potential is deduced philosophically rather than derived empirically. Just because there is a gulf between actual conditions and human aspirations does not mean that the mediator posed between these will be able to realize its project, particularly if its own actual existence is weak and tendential. On the other hand, however, we might argue that Marx was content at this point merely to postulate the model of revolutionary change and was not (yet) in a position to detail the actual, empirical working out of it. In other words, Marx was not seeking to describe an actual state of affairs but was providing an essential account of what he believed would ultimately be brought about.

I think this latter approach is the most accurate account of what Marx was developing: an analysis of the social developments that must eventually lead – even in Germany – to general human emancipation. This ambitious task requires a material force, but Marx does not call on one defined in opposition to thought or to philosophy; he notes on the contrary that the two must go together, that 'theory also becomes a material force as soon as it has gripped the masses'.[64] It is at this point that Marx, having rejected the German bourgeoisie or middle class as the class capable of remodelling German society, introduces the proletariat. It is this class which is alone capable of playing the mediating role between philosophy and society and of remodelling the 'barbaric deficiencies' of modern Germany.

To begin with Marx is concerned with the capacity of the class to formulate itself as the ruling class of the nation; any class may claim to suffer wrong and may seek to mitigate its own sufferings, yet only under certain conditions can a class not merely aspire to but rightly claim leadership of a nation. These conditions coalesce around whether the generalized defects of society are concentrated upon that class such that its own liberation has the necessary consequence of liberating society as a whole. In this way 'liberation from that sphere appears as general self-liberation'.[65]

It is important to note here that Marx does not claim that the proletariat is immediately that class, merely that it alone has the potential to assume the leadership of the nation against the evils that beset it. He notes that no particular class enjoys the consistency, courage or consciousness to declare itself both as the wronged and also as the liberator of the social world, that no existing class yet possesses 'that revolutionary audacity which flings at the adversary the defiant words: *I am nothing and I should be everything*.'[66] Such a class can and will evolve out of the conditions of society because these will impose upon that class the need and capacity for general emancipation as a material necessity.[67] Marx concludes in a well-known passage that the possibility for German emancipation lies

> In the formation of a class with *radical chains*, a class of civil society which is not a class of civil society, an estate which is the dissolution of all estates, a sphere which has a universal character by its universal suffering and claims no *particular* right because no *particular wrong* but *wrong generally* is perpetrated against it...a sphere, finally, which cannot emancipate itself without emancipating itself from all other spheres of society and thereby emancipating all other spheres of society, which, in a word, is the *complete* loss of man and hence can win itself only through the complete *rewinning of man*. This dissolution of society as a particular estate is the proletariat.[68]

The proletariat possesses a revolutionary character by virtue of its position in the social world of bourgeois society – it exists at the centre of this world and it suffers not as other classes or groups have suffered in the past, because of natural disasters or shortages, but is 'artificially impoverished' by the structural organization of society.

There is a two-fold character to that impoverishment. On the one hand the proletariat is denied the material benefits of modern production; on the other it suffers the spiritual degradation of humanity as a whole. Because the 'notorious crime of the whole of society'[69] is concentrated upon it, the proletariat suffers not only the material want that is the fate common to all subordinate classes but also the denial of human self-fulfilment upon which modern society is based.[70] More important even than this, however, the proletariat is *made to become aware of this*. Workers suffer exploitation not in the economic sense alone, in the confiscation by their employers – or, more accurately perhaps, by the employing class – of the products of their labour, but also in the sense that what is essentially human – their human essence – is also denied to them. These two aspects are characteristics of a single process, and it would be equally incorrect to separate and emphasize any one over the other.

For example, by stressing the economic exploitation and material impoverishment of the working class there has arisen the tendency to interpret the struggles and demands of the class as purely economic, and thus to regard the true expression of its character as lying in trade unionism. Under such an account its revolutionary character is made determinant upon absolute impoverishment, that is the working class is expected to resort to revolutionary methods only when all other means of satisfying its material wants have failed. This sort of explanation is based upon a one-sided interpretation of Marx's thought, one which fails to appreciate the power and revolutionary logic expressed in these early writings of Marx, which is not solely based upon the immiserization of the working class but which supplements this with the dehumanization and degradation of the working class and its resistance to this.

Similarly, however, the notion that the sufferings of the proletariat are the result of the social relations – and in particular the inhuman production methods – through which it is located in the world also has the tendency to shift emphasis toward the personal element involved in those relationships, and thus downplays their class element.[71] Such an approach can also draw on strong support in the modern world, serving as the basis for state intervention in the capitalist economy as a means of mitigating the arbitrary and oppressive element in the workings of private industry. Both sides of this equation, then, are one-sided and thus incomplete interpretations of Marx's own approach; they lead logically and historically to non-revolutionary conclusions. Both tendencies fail to recognize the central essence of the modern world, the 'secret of its own existence'[72] which is based upon the economic, social and human exploitation of the proletariat and which at the same time generates within the proletariat resistance to this exploitation, both in its own name and in the name of humanity.

It is true that Marx has at this stage little to say about what form resistance by the proletariat to its conditions of existence would take. But it is not and cannot simply be a matter of responding to the miserableness of those conditions; it must encompass both creative and defensive elements: *defensive* in that it reacts against the particular economic and social conditions in which it finds itself, *creative* in that because those conditions express the dehumanization of the world, resistance to them must take the form of making human once again this alien and oppressive world. It is in this sense that the proletariat is the legitimate heir of hitherto bourgeois humanism and plays a similar role to that performed by the bourgeoisie in the revolutions of 1688, 1789, 1830 and 1848. It resists with the explicit and conscious aim of righting the particular wrongs from which it suffers, but does so in the name of humanity, whose sufferings have passed onto its shoulders along with its striving for freedom. All of this is the outcome of Marx's prefatory characterization of the structure of civil society.

We can see how Marx makes the link between this conception of the revolutionary role of the proletariat with his understanding of the structure of bourgeois society, and in particular the relationship between political and social revolutions, by looking at his next published essay, his polemic against Arnold Ruge: the 'Critical Marginal Notes on the Article "The King of Prussia and Social Reform", by a Prussian', published in August 1844. In this article Marx takes up once again the question of the relationship of state to civil society and criticizes those who think that Germany's problem of pauperism can be rectified by the adoption of a modern form of state government. He points to the abysmal failure of the most modern state in Europe – the English – to deal with its problem of pauperism and says 'The *state* and the *system of society* are not *two* different things...the state is the system of society',[73] by which he means that the one, the state, cannot reasonably be expected to rectify the faults of the other that was, and is, responsible for its own existence. He goes on: 'the state is based on the contradiction between *public* and *private life*, on the contradiction between *general interests* and *private interests*', and hence the 'slavery of civil society is the natural foundation on which the *modern* state rests'[74] and which it cannot therefore be expected to challenge.

This (semi-anarchistic) denigration of the progressive potential of the state is complemented by Marx's view of the revolts of the Silesian weavers, whom he praises for their revolutionary consciousness: itself a product, as he sees it, of their 'social instinct'[75] which leads them not, as it does the German bourgeois, to waste their time with calls for a purely political revolution, but to the call for *social* revolution.

It is here that the specific revolutionary character of the proletariat is revealed. It does not share the political illusions of the bourgeois, because its social existence is characterized not by political impotence but by social slavery. The worker is isolated from a community more universal in character than the purely formal character of politics and government, hence rejection of the world goes beyond rejection of the form of government or state. The worker is isolated from

> *life* itself, physical and mental life, human morality, human activity, human enjoyment, human nature. *Human nature* is the *true community* of men. The disastrous isolation from this essential nature is incomparably more universal, more intolerable, more dreadful, and more contradictory, than isolation from the political community. Hence, too, the *abolition* of this isolation...is just as much more infinite as *man* is more infinite than the *citizen*, and *human life* more infinite than political life.[76]

Marx concludes from this that 'however *partial* the uprising of the industrial workers may be, it contains within itself a universal soul.'[77]

Marx was soon to raise this issue of the universal content of the proletariat's revolutionary role again, this time in the context of an article on List's book on political economy, where Marx ridicules the notion that the capitalists may take credit for the liberating potential of that which they have conjured up as a by-product of their 'huckstering interest'.[78] The forces of nature and the social forces of industry, such as the proletariat itself, are all seen by capitalists as mere objects of their manipulative lust for profit, and yet these forces also represent in embryo something different, something that will at some point (Marx says tomorrow)

> break their chains and reveal themselves as the bearers of human development which will blow him sky-high together with his industry, which assumes the dirty outer shell – which he regards as its essence – only until the human kernel has gained sufficient strength to burst his shell and appear in its own shape.[79]

There is some doubt as to whether the revolt of the Silesian weavers truly represented this universal soul, and certainly whether Marx's estimation of their revolutionary character is sufficiently judicious. Even Mehring remarks that Marx's historical estimation

> seems extraordinary to us today. He reads tendencies into it which were certainly not present, and Ruge seems to have estimated the revolt more correctly when he declared it to be no more than a hunger revolt without any deeper significance.[80]

But just as someone once remarked that it was 'better to be wrong with Sartre than right with Aron', so too here perhaps Marx's faults are more worthy than Ruge's correctness. For Marx undoubtedly perceived something in the revolt of the Silesian weavers that escaped Ruge. That point is surely that the revolts of those engaged in production – no matter how partial the terms on which they are fought, nor how disappointing the outcome – enjoys a potential far greater than could reasonably be attributed to the possibility of reforming the reactionary and backward character of German political life. Indeed, it took a major defeat in war and the outbreak of social revolution to finally achieve this task. In this respect Mehring's comment that 'to be formally in the right against genius is the whole error of the Philistine'[81] is particularly apt.

It is thus clear that Marx's understanding of the proletariat was at this stage not an empirical understanding, but rather was based upon Marx's philosophic – though soon to become socio-economic – analysis of the modern world. When Marx referred to the proletariat he did not simply mean the (relatively) few factory workers that lived in Paris at the time, nor did he mean the distressed and soon to revolt artisans and émigrés of that and other cities. The proletariat represented for Marx an embryonic social force which he came to discover through a favourable combination of various factors: his attempt to ground philosophy, and in particular Hegel's philosophy of estrangement, in the world; the influence of Feuerbach's humanism; his contact with the politically articulate artisans and émigrés of Paris; and Engels' introduction to the English proletariat as the class of the future. Put all these together and the conception of the proletariat thus constituted is philosophically derived, the locus of political mediation between philosophy and the world, present and future, and the embodiment of a radically democratized theory. It is, in short, a potential rather than an actual revolutionary force.

This point is illustrated by Marx's factional dispute with his former colleagues which continued to exercise his mind, and pen, in *The Holy Family*, where he subjects his former left-hegelian comrades to an uncompromisingly vitriolic polemic, not merely because they failed to recognize the democratic and progressive character of 'the masses', but because they created an unbridgeable gap between their idealized form of 'critical criticism' and the 'materialism and vulgarity' of these despised masses. Marx takes his stand with the masses against this elitist idealism. But he does not do so by embracing everything the masses, or rather the proletariat, stand for.

By this time Marx knows a little more about the actual conditions of life of the proletariat – introduced and spurred by Engels' knowledge and writings on this subject Marx has begun his study of political economy – and the consequence these conditions have upon its consciousness. Marx thus makes a distinction between the *actual* consciousness of the class and the *reality* of its existence, whose contradictory nature *forces* it to take part in a process – the 'steeling school of labour'[82] – that reveals to it its degraded position and obliges it to rebel against this:

> It is not a question of what this or that proletarian, or even the whole proletariat, at the moment *regards* as its aim. It is a question of *what the proletariat is*, and what, in accordance with this *being* it will historically be compelled to do.[83]

Conclusion

It is important to stress the importance of this early phase of Marx's intellectual development because by so doing we can achieve a better understanding not only of that earlier period of Marx's political life, but of later developments as well. These earlier writings provide us with an invaluable insight into the sorts of problems that preoccupied Marx before, during and after his period of residence in Paris. They show that the influence of Paris, though necessary to Marx's future development, was not entirely self-sufficient, since it found in Marx a recipient (almost) uniquely open to its spell. The move to Paris signified not a new start but a culmination of a process of political clarification and development that had its origins in Germany and in German conditions and whose intention lay precisely in its application to Germany, where the elements necessary for the creation of a unity of theory and practice were strangled by that country's oppressive political atmosphere and economic and social backwardness.

Criticism had indeed reached a cross-roads in Germany: it could progress no further without breathing the liberating air that Marx, and others, found in Paris. But this criticism, this *religious* criticism, was itself the necessary premise for, the indirect fight against, what was now recognized by Marx as an open political struggle but which seemed to his former colleagues as a diversion from the philosophical pursuit of truth: 'Marx has plunged into German communism here – socially, I mean, for he can hardly consider the dismal affair of any political importance', wrote Ruge to a friend back in Germany in July 1844. He went on: 'Germany can stand the minor damage the artisans (particularly the baker's dozen converts here) are likely to do without much doctoring.'[84]

The move to Paris had one other important consequence: it took Marx to the heart of the developing Europe-wide revolution that was to break out less than five years later. It carried him to an environment in which his rapidly developing philosophical and political ideas could be applied to a revolutionary situation – put to the test – and confirmed, modified, or rejected accordingly. Marx's political thinking was rescued from the particularities of German conditions and the limitations attendant upon these to achieve an internationalist and activist perspective which was denied, for example, to Feuerbach. His thinking was thus in a position to advance to the stage of practical application and hence further theoretical modification in the light of the most advanced and progressive, as against the most backward, political situation in Europe.

Paris was the crucial mediator between the advanced philosophical ideas Marx brought with him from Germany, the advanced economic and social conditions of its neighbour, Britain, about which Engels had written with such insightful force, as well, of course, as the radical political ideas handed down to the worker and artisan circles by the revolutionary history of that great city. It was here that the 'three sources and component parts' of marxism came together for the first time to formulate what we now think of as marxist political practice; it was here that Marx first adopted the 'proletarian standpoint'; it was here that he first published his discovery of the 'class with radical chains', and where he first made direct contact with workers' organizations.

As we have seen Marx indicate, however, this philosophical enterprise could not remain philosophical. Hegel's philosophy had broken down precisely in the interface between it and reality; to move beyond it required a more critical appreciation of the reality of which it was an expression, in the sense of a social force that could transform that reality. The historical dialectic thus put on to the agenda the quest for a social force that could exist only under certain, and not other, social and economic circumstances, but whose task it was to change, to overthrow and to transform those conditions of which it was a part.

The question of Marx's hegelian heritage is important in any general account of his theoretical development, but also specifically with regard to his discovery of the agent of social change, the role and assessment of which can be seen to have characteristics that differ according to whether it is seen within the paradigm Marx took with him to Paris, or was discovered alongside a paradigm shift. For example, many writers have seen Marx's discovery of the proletariat as an indication of a new approach to politics which, shorn of its hegelian-speculative problematic, sees the working class as the advocate of modernization and industrial development, either as an ally or a substitute for the weak bourgeoisie of absolutist Europe. Other writers, however, have held Marx's hegelian heritage to blame for his failure to recognize the true nature of the proletariat and thus to attribute to it characteristics it does not have. Hence it is said that 'Marx did not discover the revolutionary proletariat: he invented it';[85] that 'if the proletariat has failed to carry out the mission Marx assigned to it, the fault lies not with the proletariat but with the mission itself.'[86] This view leads to the conclusion that 'we shall get nowhere by looking to the industrial working class or by going in search of a "new" proletariat that will take its place.'[87]

I shall argue, however, that both these views are wrong, that Marx was quite serious in his advocacy of this revolutionary mission, that his discovery was primarily theoretical, based only tendentially upon empirical support, but that this had the paradoxical benefit of allowing a better understanding of reality compared with those who stake all upon the empirical evidence immediately available. Empirical evidence alone could not have convinced anyone that the proletariat, at the time Marx became a revolutionary, was the revolutionary class par excellence. Marx's theoretical background made that discovery possible, just as more recently it should cause us to question those who deny this essential ingredient of Marx's political theory simply because the proletariat has failed to display any revolutionary consciousness. This is not a question that can be settled by the facts themselves; it is a question that is above all concerned with explaining and contextualizing these facts.

Only such a perspective enables us to explain Marx's political activities during the revolutions of 1848, in which he came slowly, and at times reluctantly, to the conclusion that the proletariat could not enjoy the support of the bourgeoisie as its revolutionary ally. It explains the revolutionary intransigence of his two political manifestos, *The Manifesto of the Communist Party* and the *1850 Address to the Communist League*; it explains his willingness to trade political activism for a seat at the British Museum library; and it explains his critical relationship to existing working-class organizations, and indeed to individual workers.

For Marx, the revolutionary mission of the proletariat was given by his theoretical understanding of what he came to call capitalism. The ebb and flow of class struggles, whether revolutionary or not, could not undermine but only reinforce this understanding. Of course, this revolutionary mission could not exist solely at the level of theory, but neither did – or could – it exist perfectly in reality either; reality gave only an imperfect reflection of its presence. If social developments proceeded as Marx thought they must, then sooner or later this mission must be realized – but no arbitrary time limit could be imposed upon the broad sweep of history. Success or failure was determined by the contradictions that were present within society and which resulted in class struggles of one kind or another, and by the ability of the contending classes to draw the correct conclusions from their experiences in these struggles.

Marx's articles written in this period do two things: they give a theoretical account and justification for the adoption of the proletarian cause, and they apply this method, at least initially, to the specific conditions of Germany. Though Marx was later to reassess his revolutionary estimate of Germany's immediate political future, his advocacy on behalf of the revolutionary proletariat was to remain a constant, vital element throughout his life. It may have been the revolutionary optimism engendered by his move to Paris, and by his contact with the 'barbarians' of the Parisian workers' clubs, that at the time led him to recognize the revolutionary potential of the proletariat, but its revolutionary character was determined by neither the immediate political situation at any moment nor by the actual revolutionary character of any particular group of workers. As Engels was to comment in a letter to Marx written at the end of 1846: 'we can only appeal to a communist proletariat which has yet to take shape in Germany',[88] though he could equally validly have applied this state of affairs to the whole of Europe.

This brings us back to the second major problem that Marx's analysis must answer (the first was the 'error of accuracy'). A bridge must be constructed to link the empirically existent and postulated future, to connect the existing consciousness of the proletariat with its revolutionary mission. However, if the structure of society is such that it gives rise to a mystified consciousness, such as religion, then presumably the proletariat too will be subject to that same process of mystification. If this is so, how then can it be expected to break free of this pernicious influence? And how is marxism, the theoretical expression of the proletariat's revolutionary mission, able to declare itself untouched by that process without at the same time recreating that unbridgeable gulf between theory and the masses that Marx castigated in *The Holy Family*? Finally, given Marx's concern to unite theory and practice he is obliged to provide an explanation for any blocks to this process and, in particular, the practical barriers to the completion of a revolutionary consciousness among the proletariat.

It is to these questions that we must now turn.

2 Marx and the Proletariat: 1848 and After

This, then, is the advance Marx has made beyond post-hegelian philosophy: having become aware of the inadequacy of a purely philosophical critique of religion, he has gone on to elaborate a political critique of both religion and philosophy,[1] a task that has entailed subjecting the elitist tradition in philosophy to a radically democratic critique, with the aim of achieving a unification of theory and practice. Furthermore, because Marx was dissatisfied with the abstract absolutes of speculative philosophy, he was led to locate the mediations necessary to rescue philosophy from the contemplative polarities of classical German philosophy. Marx's version of philosophy – the self-emancipation of the proletariat – does not await the falling of the dusk to demonstrate its truth, but relies instead upon a critique, both philosophic and practical, of the 'wretchedness of existing conditions'. It is in this that the true significance of the proletariat to Marx's thought may be understood. On the one hand, the proletariat represents a logical link mediating between philosophy and the world (representing, at least potentially, the world made philosophic and philosophy made worldly), and thus at the same time mediating between the present and the future, between society and history, as well as possessing the universality that may reunify a divided and particularist social world through the creation of a classless society. On the other hand it is not merely a logical construct, but is formed in fact by a process of evolution of those social conditions which generate in the proletariat the capacity and energy to realize its historical mission: universal human emancipation. By appreciating this dualistic character of Marx's conception of the proletariat it is possible to avoid the error of reducing the role of the proletariat to either its empirical appearance or abstract ideal. The proletariat is not for Marx merely the agent for philosophy, and neither is it merely the discrete entity of everyday reality: it is rather both of these, the mediator between them. In his *Economic and Philosophic Manuscripts of 1844* Marx defines his position as a naturalism or humanism that 'is distinct from both idealism and materialism, and constitutes at the same time the unifying truth of both'.[2] This naturalism or humanism was materialist in so far as it was opposed to the idealist abstractions of Hegel, but it also injected into its materialism an otherwise absent social and historical, that is to say self-producing, conception of people, a conception that has particular consequences for Marx's (and our) understanding of the proletariat.

Marx's political thought is thus neither idealist nor positivist. The demonstration of its truth does not depend upon an act of faith (belief in the historical inevitability of its triumph and the eventual creation of a classless society), and neither does it run aground whenever reality fails to recognize its truth; it is neither an ideology nor a sociological description of empirical reality. It is a social critique, and must for this reason accurately – even scientifically – analyse the social conditions in which it seeks to intervene, but it finds merely evidence, not proof in the data it collects. Similarly, the proletariat Marx refers to as the bearer of a revolutionary mission is not a static thing to be studied in the same way that a scientist studies a particular object of enquiry, but is part of a dynamic social process, exhibiting both acceptance of and resistance to the role forced upon it by social conditions. Accordingly, it cannot be understood solely by reference to its empirical existence and behaviour.

There is, however, a major problem with this account. For if the proletariat is to act as the mediator between existing social conditions and the revolutionary future, while at the same time constituting the object and the subject of those social conditions, then a further mediation is also necessary, between the proletariat as constituted by bourgeois society, and the revolutionary role ascribed to it by Marx on the basis of his historical and social critique of that society. As we shall see in the next chapter, the necessity for this further mediation is not recognized by all who would call themselves followers of Marx. In this chapter I shall examine whether Marx's own position took sufficient care to acknowledge the importance of mediation in this respect. This will then make possible later an assessment of the extent to which the orthodox interpreters of Marx distorted, or perhaps merely exaggerated his views. For as we shall see, it is indeed the case that Marx's own development came increasingly to emphasize the revolutionizing character of bourgeois society itself, which forces the proletariat to act in a revolutionary way. The danger with this position is that the socio-economic tendencies which provide the necessary preconditions for revolutionary change could come to be regarded as sufficient on their own, and the crucial mediating role of class struggle and consciousness could be either forgotten or relegated to merely secondary importance. But this account would be incomplete if it failed to reflect Marx's equal stress on the self-emancipatory character of the revolutionary role of the proletariat. The problem is nonetheless a real one: how does the proletariat make the transition from capitalism to socialism? What form does its act of self-emancipation take? How can it be the essential product of bourgeois society and also its practical negation?

Two broadly based answers to this problem have been forthcoming in the history of marxism.[3] What might be termed the objectivist approach has regarded the proletariat as a largely passive recipient of external stimuli that propel it in either a revolutionary or non-revolutionary direction; the extent of its immiserization and misery, the decay or even the collapse of capitalist society, the concentration and urbanization of society's productive capacity – all these factors have been or are held responsible for the creation (or blunting) of the proletariat's revolutionary capacity. By contrast, the subjectivist approach has placed more emphasis on the creative, autonomous, organizing capacity of the proletariat itself, expressed through the organizations which have been its response to its life conditions – trade unions, workers' councils, political parties and so on – or the ideas it has generated or adopted, or the leaders it has followed. The questions to be raised in this chapter concern where Marx is to be placed in this schema.

As I noted earlier, there is evidence in Marx's writings to justify those who would argue that some change in outlook took place in the early or mid 1840s, that after this date Marx concerned himself exclusively, or at least predominantly, with empirical analyses of actual social conditions, abandoning his previously philosophical speculations with regard to the proletariat. The conditions for revolution came to be located exclusively among the objective conditions of capitalist development which propel the proletariat as historical agent in much the same way that Hegel's 'cunning of reason' propels his historical agents. Again, though, this evidence is not self-explanatory; that is to say it does not provide an explanation simply by explication. I have already argued against the view that Marx simply abandoned philosophy in 1843. Here I repeat the claim that any such change in emphasis has nothing to do with a theoretical rupture in Marx's thought, but is better explained by his attempt to draw the lessons of the 1848 revolutions and their aftermath, and to bring his theory into alignment with these developments. Such developments encouraged a far less sanguine political outlook by Marx, and shifted his concern to more long-term social developments, but they constitute a postponement, not an abandonment of the idea of proletarian self-emancipation.

It would in any case be false to suppose that a shift took place from a subjective to an objective understanding of the proletariat, that is from an understanding unrestrained by conditioning factors to one wholly determined by them. The attempt to draw an opposition between Marx's early voluntarism and mature determinism can be disproved from either direction: by showing the existence of 'voluntarist' remarks within the economic writings – for example, the chapters on 'Machinery and Modern Industry' and 'The So-Called Primitive Accumulation' in the first volume of *Capital*,[4] the references to the 'true realm of freedom' in the third volume of *Capital*,[5] or the interpretation of the Paris Commune as the form appropriate for the emancipation of labour[6] – or of determinist sentiments in the earlier writings (see below).[7] The point is that it is in the interface between these, in their dialectical relationship, that the central problem arose for Marx and his followers: how could the proletariat, a real, concrete product of social and historical conditioning, be both determined by these conditions and yet also represent their (and its) negation? How could the proletariat break out of its inglorious social role in bourgeois society to reconstitute society anew? From such a standpoint the changes that occurred in Marx's intellectual development are changes in perspective that allow for a greater understanding of the social determinants of class struggle, and not a rupture that marks a fresh start and an abandonment of his earlier views.

Marx's pre-1848 Conception of the Proletariat

In *The Holy Family*[8] Marx gives a short account of his understanding of the proletariat that highlights its dual character as both a logical category, derived in some way from the concerns of German philosophy, and as a real, objective social force. The proletariat, says Marx, is the logical antithesis of wealth in the world of private property, it is the 'negative side of the antithesis, its restlessness within its very self, dissolved and self-dissolving private property'[9] and because of this, that is because its existence is determined by private property, it is compelled to abolish itself and its opposite, private property. In contrast to the propertied class which feels quite at home in the world of human self-estrangement and abasement, the proletariat:

> feels annihilated in estrangement; it sees in it its own powerlessness and the reality of an inhuman existence. It is, to use an expression of Hegel, in its abasement the *indignation* of that abasement, and indignation to which it is necessarily driven by the contradictions between

its human *nature* and its condition of life, which is the outright, resolute and comprehensive negation of that nature.[10]

This idea of indignation against abasement bears some similarity to Marx's references in 'From the Correspondence of 1843' to the 'shame' of German patriotism and its attendant philistinism; however, here the indignation felt by the proletariat is not an attitude determined by exposure to enlightened ideas, but is something 'necessarily driven' by the contradiction between its human nature and the inhumanity of its condition of life. In a remarkable passage Marx goes on to emphasize those social conditions that compel both indignation and resistance:

> Private property drives itself in its economic movement toward its own dissolution...a development...which is unconscious and which takes place against the will of private property...it produces the proletariat *as* proletariat, poverty which is conscious of its spiritual and physical poverty, dehumanization which is conscious of its dehumanization, and therefore self-abolishing. The proletariat executes the sentence that private property pronounces on itself by producing the proletariat, just as it executes the sentence that wage-labour pronounces on itself by producing wealth for others and poverty for itself...Since in the fully formed proletariat the abstraction of all humanity, even of the semblance of humanity is practically complete; since the conditions of life of the proletariat sum up all the conditions of life of society today in their most inhuman form; since man has lost himself in the proletariat, yet at the same time has not only gained theoretical consciousness of that loss, but through urgent, no longer removable, no longer disguisable, absolutely imperative *need* – the practical expression of *necessity* – is driven directly to revolt against this inhumanity, it follows that the proletariat can and must emancipate itself. But it cannot emancipate itself without abolishing the conditions of its own life. It cannot abolish the conditions of its own life without abolishing *all* the inhuman conditions of life of society today which are summed up in its own situation...Not in vain does it go through the stern but steeling school of labour.[11]

While, therefore, the universalist mission of the proletariat is given by the concentration upon it of the particular evils of bourgeois society and which cast it in the role of humanity's collective saviour, that universal mission is performed as a reaction to what it feels as its *particular* suffering, resistance to which compels it towards a universalist revolutionary solution. The struggle for emancipation by the proletariat is not the result of a perceived contradiction between its life situation and inner desires, but arises because its actual life situation is based upon 'property, capital, money, wage-labour and the like...practical, very objective products of their self-estrangement...that therefore...must be abolished in a practical objective way.'[12] Thus the act of emancipation must be concrete and not abstract, based in everyday reality, not in consciousness. The proletariat has not only an 'idea' in revolution but a very real interest in it, a need for it; a need, moreover, that is spurred by its conditions of life and is 'the practical expression of necessity'.[13] We can see in this passage how the revolutionary role of the proletariat is a function of two things: first, consciousness of the inhuman conditions of life and society; and second, the need to revolt against these conditions and achieve emancipation. As in 1843, it is the conditions of life of the proletariat which sum up the depravity of bourgeois society and which propel resistance to it, but here there is a further element: Marx's reference to the 'steeling school of labour'. It is this experience that drives the proletariat to revolt against and to abolish the 'conditions of its own life', which are also the 'inhuman conditions of life of society'.

This is an important point for two reasons. To begin with it explains why Marx places such emphasis upon the proletariat rather than upon, say, the peasantry or lumpenproletariat, whose social misery is at least as great as the proletariat (though this was perhaps less true in Marx's time). Marx's whole understanding of modern society was predicated upon the absolute centrality of capitalism and upon its ability to subvert forms of life incompatible with it. Individuals who do not form part of the proletariat, and whose misery may appear to be caused by non-social, natural factors – poor soil, or climate, or ill-health for example – do in fact have their misery very largely determined by the development of capitalism: peasants have to compete with capitalist agriculture; natural economy loses out to the development of the market; artisans are undermined by competition from factories and by the growth of mass production; the unemployed and unemployable, the sick and disabled are disadvantaged by the dominance of a monied culture in which access to social resources is rationed by effective demand, that is by the possession of money or the means to acquire it. Second, the centrality of the proletariat is further heightened by the way in which the particular conditions of its existence bring about a particular form of resistance to them.

Marx elaborates on what he means by this in the final chapter of his *Poverty of Philosophy*,[14] where he discusses 'Strikes and Combinations of Workers'. Here he notes that workers continue to form combinations and trade unions to protect themselves against their employers and to engage in political struggles and industrial disputes despite the advice offered to them by economists and (some) socialists that such struggles are a waste of time.[15] Their felt need to engage in such activities overrides the 'well-meaning' advice offered to them by those who do not directly share their life conditions, and whose standpoint is thus quite different to their own. The point, though, is that workers reject such advice not merely because it is not based upon a shared experience of common conditions, but because their life situation forces them to perceive events from a perspective sometimes at odds with short-term immediate benefits and, moreover, to do so in collective rather than individual terms. As successive generations of economists have proved to their own satisfaction, the immediate day-to-day interests of individual workers are more usually served by obsequience and boot-licking than through collective struggle.[16] However, workers continue to embark on such seemingly self-destructive actions not just because they reject advice that is derived from experience beyond their own, but because their actual situation – whether they are aware of it or not – is such that satisfaction of the most moderate grievances or desire for social improvement requires collective organization for long-term change.[17] It is in this sense that Marx ridicules Max Stirner's advocation of public bakeries, arguing that

> for proletarians – owing to the frequent opposition of interests among them arising out of the division of labour – no other 'agreement' is possible than a political one directed against the whole present system. Where the development of competition enables the proletarians to 'come to an understanding', they reach an understanding not about public bakeries but about quite different matters.[18]

Marx goes on (in *The Poverty of Philosophy*) to give a systematic account of the historical development of those class struggles related to the development and growth of modern industry. To begin with, large-scale industry draws together large numbers of workers, unknown to each other and divided amongst themselves by competition. But this estrangement soon passes as workers combine together to defend an interest they do have in common: the maintenance of wages. And as the capitalists in their turn also unite 'for the purpose of repression', so these combinations become permanent and are invested with a (political) purpose over and above their tangible economic benefits; at this point 'association takes on a political character'. Marx thus shows how out of economic resistance a political struggle is created in a dialectic of class struggle that compels workers towards revolutionary politics. Through strikes, combinations and trade unions 'proletarians carry out before our eyes their organization as a class' and constitute themselves as a class, not only as a class in opposition to capital with a common situation and common interests but also, as the interests it defends become class interests and as class struggle is unavoidably a political struggle, so too it 'constitutes itself as a class for itself'.[19]

In *The Communist Manifesto*[20] we find an increased emphasis on the revolutionary conditioning of capitalism, a factor that was to be significant (in a negative sense) in accounting for the failures later in 1848 and 1849. In this work Marx and Engels sketch out the social-historical laws and tendencies operating in bourgeois society, and on the basis of these assert the necessity of the dictatorship of the proletariat. Modern bourgeois society is like the sorceror who is no longer able to control the powers he has summoned: 'commercial crises that by their periodic return put on its trial, each time more threateningly, the existence of the entire bourgeois society' are complemented by those who will judge and pass sentence, for 'not only has the bourgeoisie forged the weapons that bring death to itself; it has also called into existence the men who are to wield those weapons – the proletariat.'[21] Marx explains the necessity of the dictatorship of the proletariat on the basis of the social and economic conditions obtaining in bourgeois society: the proletariat is propelled to power by capital itself, in order to remove the fetters that bourgeois relations of production impose upon society as a whole. This propulsion takes two forms. First, the development of capitalism yields tremendous advances for humankind in the abstract, yet the real and actual distribution of these advances is extremely uneven, producing extremes of wealth and poverty; moreover, that development throws up periodic convulsions that aggravate the social misery inherent to it. Second, the development of bourgeois society itself develops and strengthens the social force that will abolish those conditions as well as itself, and educates it in the means to do so.

The development of capitalism also leads to a general recruitment into the proletariat from all classes of the population and a development of the proletariat itself. As capital develops industry, so too does it socialize all productive forces, the proletariat included, and this concentrates the latter in greater numbers and with increasing strength. Marx draws upon the chapter from *The Poverty of Philosophy* (cited above) to demonstrate how class struggle between proletariat and bourgeoisie changes and develops, how the creation of combinations becomes permanent in trade unions and then leads to the formation of political parties. 'The bourgeoisie finds itself involved in a constant battle':[22] to defeat the feudal classes it recruits the proletariat as its political ally, but in so doing it supplies the proletariat with its own political and general education which it will soon learn to use against the bourgeoisie itself. And even as the bourgeoisie faces battle with the proletariat, when 'the class struggle nears the decisive hour', a small section of the ruling class – the bourgeois intelligentsia – joins the revolutionary class, 'the class that holds the future in its hands'.[23] Marx and Engels conclude:

> The advance of industry, whose involuntary promoter is the bourgeoisie, replaces the isolation of the labourers due to competition, by their revolutionary combination, due to association. The development of Modern Industry, therefore cuts from under its feet the very foundation on which the bourgeoisie produces and appropriates products. What the bourgeoisie therefore produces above all, is its own gravediggers. Its fall and the victory of the proletariat are equally inevitable.[24]

The tendency toward socialism thus arises as an inevitable consequence of the progressive conquest of nature achieved by the advance of industry. Marx's conception of human agency and the revolutionary capacity of the proletariat is constituted within an overall law-governed process: the circumstances through which human beings encounter their environment constrain and determine both the choices and the actions available to them. The 'voluntarism' of the proletariat's revolutionary capacity is not counterposed to the actual conditions of historical development; rather, these two processes are complementary. But whereas before 1848 Marx tended to stress the former, he came later to emphasize the latter. This shift in emphasis, which, it should be noted, preceded the failure and disappointment of the 1848 revolutions, was given added weight by those events, which revealed the limitations of those – subjective or voluntarist – factors when taken on their own. Marx thus became engrossed in the analysis of the constraining factors in historical development, but this does not at all commit him to a rigid determinism that elevates the elements of constraint into a position of dominance. It could be argued that this is indeed what was required – that the constraining factors of historical and social development preclude the revolutionary commitment and class partisanship championed by Marx; and that as a result marxism unintentionally replicated the economic determinism of bourgeois economics that made eternal the social relations of bourgeois society, despite the wishes, intentions and origins of its founder. This was possible because the eschatological vision of the latter was displaced by an impassionate, scientifically rigorous account of the actual development of capitalism. Such an interpretation is put forward because in contrast to Marx's earlier philosophical preoccupations, Marx and Engels became involved after 1845–8 in a theoretical investigation of the empirical bases and conditions of modern life, in an analysis of the economic side of the social totality, since it was this that was thought by them to be the primary constituent of social life and which created the conditions upon which the rest of this social totality rested.[25] History – the process of class struggle – could not properly be understood until this aspect of the social world was secured on a properly scientific basis. As Marx was to explain in his introduction to the *Grundrisse*:

> It seems to be correct to begin with the real and the concrete, with the real precondition, thus to begin, in economics, with, for example, the population, which is the foundation and the subject of the entire social act of production. However, on closer examination this proves false. The population is an abstraction if I leave out, for example, the classes of which it is composed. These classes in turn are an empty phrase if I am not familiar with the elements on which they rest. Eg. wage labour, capital etc...Thus, if I were to begin with the population this would be a chaotic conception of the whole.[26]

Thus, no matter how fundamental classes and class struggle are to history, they nevertheless rest upon further conditions, the understanding of which alone makes history, and those class struggles, both possible and intelligible.

Marx was therefore drawn increasingly to stress one side of the dialectical understanding of history (historical determinism) against the other (revolutionary humanism). But note that I have used the term historical determinism. This is for the good reason that Marx never made the transition to economic determinism with which his detractors perennially charge him. Marx was not an economist in the modern sense. The persistence of hegelian themes in the *Grundrisse* and, indeed, in *Capital* itself; the repeated expressions of indignation and horror at the suffering, poverty and degradation of human life brought about by the development of bourgeois society; the contempt issued to the intellectual apologists for this state of affairs:[27] all these bear witness to Marx's concern to persevere in the decidedly non-positivist view of science as social critique, and this disproves Rosa Luxemburg's criticism that the abstractions in *Capital* result 'in a bloodless theoretical fiction which declares the struggle and the relations to be non-existent'.[28] Marx did not abandon his belief in the revolutionary mission of the proletariat, he merely gave to this a socio-economic foundation, one which would determine whether its mission was, at any particular moment, realizeable or merely something for the future.

The essential difficulty concerns whether the revolutionary character of the proletariat can be said to be truly revolutionary if it is merely the consequential response to externally generated stimuli and whether the development of capitalism and its possible breakdown become substituted for the revolutionary consciousness of the proletariat. This was indeed the tendency amongst orthodoxy and will be discussed in the next chapter. Here we must note the possibility within Marx of a conflict or contradiction between the two positions. The development of socio-economic conditions, Marx believed, would lead to socialism. However, this process had to be mediated through the revolutionary consciousness of the proletariat: it was not an automatic sequence. It is this latter view which is absent in so much of orthodoxy, or else is posed in such a way that consciousness is itself regarded as something generated external to the class. In the remainder of this chapter I will demonstrate that this process of mediation is indeed present in Marx's mature writings, first by looking at the reasons why Marx gave increased attention to the factors that constrained human social and political activity, and then by going on to show how Marx's mature theory of crisis also contains within it the requirement of political mediation.

Historical Inevitability

Having analysed the historical development of the capitalist mode of production, Marx is in the position of discovering the laws of development of that mode of production, the determinate conditions for its existence and negation. Thus, once constituted, the capitalist mode of production develops a number of contradictions which makes its passing as inevitable as its formation. *Pace* the bourgeois economists, history does not come to a close with the birth of capital, for

> as soon as the capitalist mode of production stands on its own feet, then the further socialization of labour and further transformation of the land and other means of production into socially exploited and, therefore, common means of production, as well as the further expropriation of private proprietors, takes a new form.[29]

This new form is actualized by the permanent laws of motion of capitalist production. The centralization of capital leads to further misery, oppression, slavery, degradation and exploitation. With this grows the revolt of those subject to this state of affairs, the working class – a class, moreover, that is armed, disciplined, educated and organized by the very process of capitalist production. Hence the very conditions of capitalist production lead to a situation in which its own existence is continually threatened by its development:

> The monopoly of capital becomes a fetter upon the mode of production, which has sprung up and flourished with, and under it. Centralization of the means of production and socialization of labour at last reach a point where they become incompatible with their capitalist integument. This integument is burst asunder. The knell of capitalist private property sounds. The expropriator is expropriated.[30]

The logical flow of this prose assumes an inevitability that dares (or perhaps invites) criticism. But while the purpose of *Capital* lies in explaining the existing order in terms of both how it is possible for it to exist, and at the same time belies its appearance as permanent, yet there is something missing. Since its breakdown, or rather, since the historical processes that lead to its breakdown operate despite (and indeed determine) the will, consciousness and intelligence of individuals and classes, these latter *appear* to be irrelevant: we may surrender ourselves to a fate decreed by these forces which are external to us.

But this is not Marx's conception. For him that 'will, consciousness and intelligence' is a crucial part of the total historical process – to be sure, not sufficient on its own to effect long-standing radical social change (the key lesson of 1848), but when exercised in conjunction with the laws and tendencies of historical development, absolutely vital. Actually, this belief did not require the production of *Capital* for its proof, and in fact it preceded the year 1848. For in October 1847 Marx could write:

> if...the proletariat overthrows the political rule of the bourgeoisie its victory will only be temporary, only an element in the service of the bourgeois revolution itself, as in the year 1794, as long as in the course of history, in its 'movement', the material conditions have not yet been created which make necessary the abolition of the bourgeois mode of production and therefore also the definitive overthrow of the political rule of the bourgeoisie.[31]

Marx again drew the parallel with 1794 in *The Eighteenth Brumaire of Louis Bonaparte*, and the necessity for the development of material conditions before any proletarian seizure of power could be anything but short-lived is clearly what lay behind the statement attributed to him after 1848 that 'the bourgeoisie must first come to the helm',[32] and also behind his initially far from sanguine attitude to the Paris Commune.[33] Indeed, after Marx resumed the economic work that had been interrupted by the events of 1848, his change in perspective not only signified a greater awareness of the constraining factors in historical development, but also brought about a split and eventual dissolution of the Communist League. Thus, in their *Review* of November 1850, Marx and Engels write of the dependence of the 1848 revolutions on the previous year's trade crisis and remark that in the changed situation of

> general prosperity, in which the productive forces of bourgeois society develop as luxuriantly as is at all possible with bourgeois relationships, there can be no talk of a real revolution. Such a revolution is only possible in the periods when *both these factors*, the *modern* productive *forces* and the *bourgeois forms of production*, come in *collision* with each other...A new revolution is possible only in consequence of a new crisis. It is, however, just as certain as this crisis.[34]

This general point assumed a particular importance to the German exiles who took insufficient account of the absence in their homeland of any large-scale modern productive forces based upon bourgeois forms of production, which, because of the manifest weakness of the bourgeoisie, would continue to be lacking for some considerable length of time. Consequently, those radicalized by the events of 1848 resented these limitations and were loath to take the sober advice offered by Marx and Engels. (This itself probably accounts for Marx's equally determined advocacy of such limitations.) In the meeting of the Central Authority of the Communist League on 15 September 1850, at which Marx proposed the removal of the Central Authority to Cologne and the splitting of the London groups, he characterized the errors of his opponents thus:

> The materialist standpoint of the Manifesto has given way to *idealism*. The revolution is seen not as the product of realities of the situation but as the result of an effort of will. Whereas we say to the workers: You have 15, 20, 50 years of civil war to go through in order to alter the situation and to train yourselves for the exercise of power, it is said: We must take power *at once*, or else we may as well take to our beds.[35]

That Marx was criticizing this tendency towards Blanquism, and not his own previous view,[36] is evidenced by his further criticism that Schapper and Willich, for all their talk of proletarian revolution, in the absence of real conditions for such a perspective 'in practice represent the petty bourgeois and not the proletarians'.[37] This raises the question of just how far the revolutionary impulses of the proletariat (in so far as they exist) could be stymied by the development of capitalism.

For Marx adds one important point of clarification concerning the preconditions for the emancipation of this and indeed for all oppressed classes, namely that 'the productive powers already acquired and the existing social relations should no longer be capable of existing side by side'. But since 'of all the instruments of production the greatest productive power is the revolutionary class itself' this is hardly a hurdle to revolutionary activity, as Marx recognizes when he concludes that 'the organization of revolutionary elements as a class supposes the existence of all the productive forces which could be engendered in the bosom of the old society'.[38] Marx thinks, then, that the proletariat does not have to await the development of all the productive forces possible under bourgeois relations of production before it is ready to achieve a social revolution, but that the very act of constituting itself as a revolutionary force serves notice that those productive forces are already sufficiently developed for revolution to be feasible. We may note at this point the contrast with Marx's opinion expressed twelve years later (in the 1859 preface), that:

> no social order ever perishes before all the productive forces for which there is room in it have developed; and new, higher relations of production never appear before the material conditions for their existence have matured in the womb of the old society itself. Therefore mankind always sets itself only such tasks as it can solve.[39]

It is a matter of deep controversy among marxist scholars, and probably even more so among marxists, how these two views are to be interpreted. The quotation from the 1859 preface obviously allows a more evolutionist interpretation, stressing the development within capitalism ('the womb of the old society') of those forces which will ripen into socialism. To this extent it implies a political quietism by placing less emphasis upon the idea of revolutionizing the social structure, giving to the old mode of production a veto over the new and taking on only those tasks for which a solution is possible.

There are political dangers, however, in elevating what is after all a broad, panaromic view of world history into a political strategy. First, there is no clear arbiter to decide which tasks are solvable and which are not. Under conditions of normal capitalist development, when there is no overt challenge to capitalist rule among the subordinate classes, the temptation must be to withdraw either into splendid isolation[40] or into those forms of working class activity which under such conditions are acceptable and normal (namely trade unionism and political reformism) and which remain not only oblivious but hostile to the attractions of revolutionary politics. Another related problem concerns the nature of that process whereby the new relations of production mature 'in the womb of the old'. While this dramatic analogy – upon which Marx repeatedly draws – is apt in highlighting the development from capitalism to socialism as a process, and thus in differentiating his view of history and of political change from the utopian drawing up of blueprints, it does have the drawback of under-emphasizing the revolutionary rupture between the two systems and the force required by the one to destroy the other. The analogy thus makes possible the conclusion that socialism is that system which will further improve the economic productivity of society without regard to the social relations under which that improvement is made possible – the problem of 'state socialism'[41] – or else that the course of maturation, the pregnancy, is an automatic process over which the mother has no power of acceleration or delay. In fact, capitalism has not developed an offspring over which it wields no parental authority; indeed, precisely because it has exercised authority over its prodigy, that prodigy has failed to conclude its adolescent rebellion successfully. As we shall see, Marx came to regard the ability of the parent body to yield authority as constrained by the convulsions brought on by economic crises and, later, by the tendency for the rate of profit to fall. But historical experience since Marx's day has shown that socialism does not develop out of capitalism as if through a process of gestation: capitalism provides at best only the preconditions of the future society; it provides the placenta but no uterus.

It is necessary to note, however, that the implication of these 1859 comments is to restrict the circumstances in which revolutionary activity is a realistic possibility. Marx registers this reservation because he wished on the one hand to provide an account of the failure of the 1848 revolutions to live up to his expectations of the time (and immediately afterwards), and on the other to distance himself from those who persevered with a strategy based upon social and political conditions that no longer existed. This change in political outlook was to no small degree encouraged by Marx's deepening interest in the study of political economy, and in particular his interest in the role economic crisis has to play in the determination of political possibilities.

Marx's Theory of Crisis

As we have already seen, as early as 1847 Marx had noted the dependence of the political victory of the proletariat upon the requisite development of material conditions, and following the debacle of 1848–9 he had extended this dependence to encompass the very possibility of revolution itself. The revolutions of those years had been made possible, indeed had been brought about, on the one hand by the general development of the capitalist system and on the other by the specific circumstance of the economic crisis of 1847. Marx also came to recognize at this time that a different form of political activity was called for in a period of general prosperity, and that a general crisis was a necessary precondition for revolutionary politics. This recognition led him to further study of both the 'normal' mechanisms of capitalist accumulation, and the threat posed to that process by the periodic outbreaks of economic crisis. In this section I propose to examine the degree of correspondence between Marx's understanding of crisis and his general theory of capitalism, and in particular to examine whether or not his theory of crisis may be said to constitute a theory of economic breakdown.

In attempting to set out an account of Marx's theory of crisis, one is faced with two major problems. First, there is no theory of crisis that may be isolated from the main body of Marx's writings on the functioning of the capitalist system; second, his reflections upon crisis change over time and are framed at different levels of abstraction. These problems do not arise from any failure by Marx to deal with the problem of crisis, but rather from the manner in which he does deal with the problem: they are intrinsic not extrinsic problems.

In *The Communist Manifesto* for example, his theory of crisis depends upon such mechanisms as the six-year trade cycle and the absolute impoverishment of the proletariat but, as Ernest Mandel points out,[42] this theory conflates those monetary crises that reflect crises of overproduction with autonomous monetary crises, and also grasps the duration of the business cycle in an empirical way, unconnected to the period of reproduction of fixed capital. These inadequacies, according to Mandel, led Marx incorrectly to forecast crises in 1852, 1853 and again in 1855.[43]

It was with the actual outbreak of crisis in 1857[44] that a significant development in the theory of crisis emerged. Marx collected material on the development of the crisis and utilized this when he came to write up his economic theories in the *Grundrisse.*[45] Even here though, Marx developed no theory of crisis as such, but rather incorporated his understanding of crisis into his general theory of capitalist production and accumulation.[46] It is true enough that after the failures of 1848–9 and the period of prosperity that followed, the outbreak of this general and critical crisis brought about a sharp change in attitude in the two men. In a letter to Marx, for example, Engels explains how 'in the midst of this general outbreak' he 'fell tremendously cheerful', claiming that 'the crisis will do me as much good as a bathe in the sea'. He went on: 'In 1848 we were saying: Now our time is coming, and so in a certain sense it was, but this time it is coming properly; now it's a case of do or die.'[47] Such optimisim was based upon the belief that 'a period of chronic pressure is needed to get people's blood up. The proletariat will then fight better with better *connaissance de cause* and in greater unison',[48] and a month later he noted that 'Distress has also begun to set in among the proletariat. There are as yet few signs of revolution, for the long period of prosperity has been fearfully demoralising.'[49] The role and function of crisis were given a much more realistic and moderate assessment in Marx's work, precisely because the material accumulated by Marx was incorporated into his general theory of capitalist accumulation.[50] Crisis did not become the agent of revolution, it merely provided a necessary precondition for it; moreover, crisis was recognized as a mechanism functional to the development of capitalism: it registered the barrier which capitalist social relations raised against further development of the productive forces. But it was not an absolute barrier in that breakdown was bound to follow: the productive forces *could* be further developed – *if* the costs associated with it were borne – by the individual capitalists bankrupted in its course and by the proletariat which would suffer its most deleterious consequences.

It should thus be noted that while Marx's entire theoretical system constitutes a denial of the inevitability of indefinite capitalist expansion, nowhere does either he or Engels give a purely economic theory of capitalist breakdown.[51] This does not mean that Marx was ambiguous or inconsistent in his broad outline of the development of capitalism. His view of history led him to the conclusion that the capitalist system was doomed, that capitalist productive relations would eventually cease to foster any further development of the productive forces, and that the result of this failure would be a revolutionary period of crisis, in the course of which the proletariat would overturn those capitalist relations and replace them with socialist ones.[52] And this was not a possible hypothesis. It was a historically necessary law that was bound to happen precisely because the barrier to capitalist expansion was generated in the course of its process of reproduction.[53] In this sense Rosa Luxemburg is quite correct in her assertion (against Bernstein) that the theory of capitalist collapse 'is the corner-stone of scientific socialism'.[54]

The problem of economic crisis is, then, a constantly recurring theme in Marx's writings, from *The Communist Manifesto* to *Theories of Surplus Value* and *Capital*. But Marx subordinates discussions of crises to other themes; he nowhere gives a complete or systematic treatment of the problem, which remains part of his "unfinished business". There are two main reasons for this. First, economic crisis is a very complex and specific matter that occurs under certain historically and socially determined conditions,[55] and it would therefore have been inappropriate for Marx to have provided a detailed discussion of economic crisis within those of his writings that attempted at an abstract level to provide a framework for understanding the development and structure of capitalism. This is not to say, however, that Marx did not have within his analysis of capitalism a theory that could account, albeit at a fairly general level, for the periodic outbreak of crises. It is merely to note that this theory is not the solution to the problem of explaining those crises, but is rather the framework within which the specific characteristics and peculiarities of these phenomena may be understood. The second reason follows from this, in that an adequate theory of crisis must be seen to flow from this analytical framework, must be part of a general theory of capital accumulation rather than an autonomous and external element that acts upon it.

Apart from the general characteristics of capitalist production which generate social crises and an oppositional viewpoint amongst the proletariat, Marx is quite definite in the *Grundrisse* in referring to another feature that will in particular bring about the downfall of capitalism. What he terms the law of the falling rate of profit is

> in every respect the most important law of modern political economy, and the most essential for understanding the most difficult relations. It is the most important law from the historical standpoint. It is a law which, despite its simplicity, has never before been grasped and, even less, consciously articulated.[56]

This law is crucial in that its operation signifies the point at which the capital relation becomes a barrier or a fetter upon the development of the productive forces, which 'is thereby cast off like a skin'.[57] Marx goes on:

> The growing incompatibility between the productive development of society and its hitherto existing relations of production expresses itself in bitter contradictions, crises, spasms. The violent destruction of capital not by relations external to it, but rather as a condition of its self-preservation, is the most striking form in which advice is given to it to be gone and to give room to a higher state of social production.[58]

It was thus the 'law of the tendency of the rate of profit to fall', first discussed in the *Grundrisse* and then expounded in the third volume of *Capital,* that Marx developed to explain why capitalism was subject to periodic crises which would eventually lead to its downfall. Again, though, we must note that this law was put forward not to explain each and every economic crisis in the history of capitalism, but as part of his general theoretical framework of capitalism.

Marx's theory of crisis, then, is part of his general law of capital accumulation and is to be distinguished, for example, from the form of crisis that occurred in pre-capitalist societies. These latter involved the material destruction of the productive forces – usually as the result of natural disasters, though also as a result of certain political actions[59] – while the capitalist system throws up a new form of crisis that is the result not of shortage or famine but of overproduction. That is to say, capitalist crisis is a breakdown in reproduction that is generated by the system of reproduction itself, rather than being imposed upon it by nature or by forms of political rule.

Capitalist production is oriented not towards consumption needs, i.e. use-values, but towards production for profit: the production of exchange-values and surplus-value. The forces of production (chiefly, natural resources and labour productivity) are subordinated to the needs of capital and are only used in so far as they serve the self-expansion of capital. Following from this, the general possibility of capitalist crisis may be traced back to the split that exists in the commodity, between its use-value and exchange-value. When commodity production becomes generalized, the appropriation of use-values, that is the possibility of consumption, is dependent upon the possession of an equivalent exchange-value. Where this is lacking, where the owners of commodities are unable to find customers with sufficient money capital to purchase those commodities and thus to enable the owners of those commodities to realize the exchange (and surplus) value embedded in them, then there ensues a crisis of overproduction.

Such a general possibility becomes real through and during the cyclical process of capitalist economy. But the uneven and unsteady rhythm of capitalist production moves to two different tunes: the short-term business or trade cycle, and the more long-term downward pressure on the average rate of profit, which has the effect of worsening the depressions of the trade cycle. It was Marx's discovery of the mechanism of this latter that signified a real breakthrough in the understanding of capitalism, since the trade cycle, on its own, involves no basic interruption in the accumulation process but merely a rise or fall in its rate. Only when it is influenced by more fundamental and long-term pressures does it result in a crisis that involves some form of restructuring and/or upheaval.[60]

Capitalist production has as the source of its growth and expansion surplus-value, that is the difference between the exchange-value of labour power and the productive capacity of that labour power. But equally, the productivity of labour is constrained by the fact that it is bound to the reproduction and self-expansion of capital. In order to achieve this reproduction and self-expansion capitalism must also expand this, the basis of its very existence and the sustenance for its growth. As it expands, therefore, it is forced to revolutionize the technical process of labour. There are two ways in which it can do this: by lengthening the working day as a means of increasing surplus-value (this process is known as the rate of absolute surplus-value); or by increasing the rate of relative surplus-value by increasing the social productivity of labour. There are obvious political and physical barriers to the former, and so the latter is the most significant factor in the developed capitalist economy. But the measures required to raise the rate of relative surplus-value have other, unforseen consequences for capitalist production.

We can grasp what these consequences are only if we are clear about the motivation that lies behind these changes and pressures, and these are two-fold. In reality, that is in their working out, it is the exigencies of competition that compel individual capitalists to employ the most modern machinery and techniques of production with the aim of raising the productivity of labour (and thus to reduce the costs of production); they must do this because they are engaged in a competitive struggle with each other. But this process of competition takes place in the sphere of 'many capitals', a sphere that is itself determined by a more fundamental process to capitalism, namely the relation between capital as value attempting to expand itself without limit (these limits shift as capitalism expands to embrace independent artisans, peasants, overseas territories, the nation state), and labour, the working population, the limited basis of that expansion. Capital must try to make itself independent of this its objective limitation, and in so doing living labour is replaced by objectified (dead) labour in the form of machinery.[61]

This process is, then, two-edged: on the one hand capitalism creates an expansion of the proletariat (the basis of its own expansion); on the other hand, the form that expansion takes involves increasing social productivity via the introduction of new machinery and techniques of production. From the standpoint of the capitalist system this contradictory process of accumulation presents itself as a tendency for the rate of profit to fall. The increase in the mass of capital equipment, machinery, etc. employed per worker increases: this is known as the technical composition of capital.[62] This will in turn affect the value relation between these, the organic composition of capital, which will also rise (but not so fast).[63] The rise in the organic composition of capital is the value expression of the relative increase in the ratio of means of production employed per worker: constant capital rises faster than variable capital. But since only variable capital yields surplus-value, while the rate of profit is calculated on total investments, i.e., constant and variable capital, if the rate of surplus extraction remains constant, the rate of profit must fall. This can be represented as follows:

(1) organic composition of capital $= \frac{c}{v} + s$
rate of profit $= c + \frac{v}{s}$
(2) organic composition of capital $= c + \frac{1}{v}$
(new) rate of profit $= c + 1 + \frac{v}{s}$: which is less than (1).

Obviously, the law will not express itself in absolute terms because the rate of surplus-value will change; as labour becomes more productive, so the increase in the mass of articles produced will lead to a decrease in their value, and hence there will be a fall in that part of the working day necessary to produce the wages of the workers. But this increase in exploitation has certain insurmountable limits – in particular, the working day. As that portion of the working day devoted to producing value equivalent to wages falls, the less any increase in productivity can augment surplus value. Or, conversely, the rate of exploitation has to increase that much higher to offset the fall in the rate of profit.

There are also a number of other counterveiling tendencies, each of which offsets the tendency for the rate of profit to fall: devaluation of a part of existing capital; the transformation of part of capital into fixed capital which does not serve as an agency of direct production; unproductive waste; new branches of production in which the relation of constant to variable capital is low, or where the productive power of labour is not yet developed; a lowering of taxes, reduction in ground rent, etc. Marx did little more than list these counterveiling tendencies since he regarded them as factors less important than and secondary to those he had identified as lying at the heart of the capitalist process of reproduction. Obviously they played a more important part in the actual working out of the main tendencies of capitalist reproduction, but Marx was less interested in providing a detailed description of the workings of capitalism than he was in providing an (abstract) analysis of the causes of these phenomena. Of course, it may be disputed whether Marx was justified in regarding the tendency of the rate of profit to fall as the fundamental law and all the counterveiling tendencies as secondary factors. But Marx's treatment of the matter in this way follows from his general analysis of capitalist development and the labour theory of value.[64]

The resultant indeterminate character of Marx's law of the tendency of the rate of profit to fall is actually a source of strength rather than a sign of weakness, for all Marx asserts is that the law will tend to produce effects whose character will be determined by the power relations between the classes, that is by class struggle. It is a law because capitalism must generate crises as part of its very process of reproduction, but these crises may be resolved in either of two ways; they may aid the further development of capitalist reproduction by purging it of certain barriers (but at what social cost? and only to recreate these barriers at a higher and more intense level), or they may provide the opportunity for the proletariat to turn the situation to its own advantage.

As we have noted, Marx regarded this law as vitally important to his understanding of capitalism, because it revealed that the barrier to the expansion of capitalist production lay not in some external threat to it; rather, the very basis of capitalist development is itself fraught with a central contradiction that blocks its further and continued expansion. The working out of this contradiction has two possible results, one of which is beneficial to the interests of capitalism (though not to all capitalists), while the other provides the possibility for the proletariat to raise itself to become the ruling class. In the former case 'these contradictions lead to explosions, cataclysms, crises, in which by momentous suspension of labour and annihilation of a great portion of capital the latter is violently reduced to the point where it can go on.'[65] But this is just one possible result. Another involves the violent destruction of the capitalist order and the overthrow of the rule of the bourgeoisie by the proletariat.

The law of the tendency of the rate of profit to fall, then, is a further refinement of Marx's scientific method. It shows how the negation of capitalist society can be said to be the result of a real factor inherent to capitalism, and not an ideal generated beyond it. Equally important, Marx's account of capitalism is not merely descriptive, it also generates a political imperative, for if the crises and cataclysms are allowed to persevere in their natural, objective form, that is if human agents continue to believe in their natural character, if they continue to fetishize what are essentially social relations, then capitalism will not only be ensured its historical continuity – the increasingly costly results of that continuity will be borne by human beings. Only the political rule of the proletariat can prevent this.

The Setback of 1848 and its Consequences

In directing his energies towards these new theoretical priorities that were imposed upon him in the late 1840s, and in particular in his confrontation with political economy, Marx was unable to pay as much attention to such matters as the formal element or subjective side of historical development, because these were a political and theoretical barrier to the development of what he now regarded as the most important task facing himself and the movement. And where he did deal with these (for example, on the question of the influence upon English workers of their government's rule in Ireland), he failed to integrate them within his more panaromic view of historical development.

The setbacks of 1848 gave Marx a reason to investigate in greater detail the material conditions which must serve as the basis for any long-term seizure of power by the proletariat.[66] The investigation of these conditions provided not only an explanation for the failures of 1848, to some extent it also offered a degree of compensation and comfort for them. Marx's studies yielded evidence to suggest that the success of the bourgeoisie would be shortlived and that, despite the failure of the proletariat at this particular moment, the very development of capitalist production, now that it was freed of its feudal fetters, would necessarily propel the proletariat in a revolutionary direction in the future. It is for this reason that both Marx and Engels were such enthusiasts for the triumph of capitalism at the expense of those feudal remnants that still dominated the political map of continental Europe, and so contemptuous of those nations and peoples that resisted its incursions.[67] Their support for bourgeois success was, however, double-edged. As Engels put it after the first wave of unrest in 1847:

> we do not grudge the bourgeoisie their triumph...we have no objection if everywhere they force through their purposes...Yet nothing is more clear than that they are everywhere preparing the way for *us*... than that they will at most win a few years of troubled enjoyment, only to be then immediately overthrown. Behind them stands everywhere the proletariat.

He concludes with a warning culled from Heine to his bourgeois readers: 'the hangman stands at the door'.[68] Communists thus welcome the bourgeois revolution 'as a precondition for the *workers revolution*. However, they cannot for a moment regard it as their ultimate goal.'[69]

What, then, is the model of revolution anticipated by the mature Marx? The first point to make is that Marx, though he came to share the view of Engels that the dictatorship of the proletariat could be achieved only after a period of bourgeois rule, at no point abandoned the belief expressed throughout the early period of his intellectual development, that 'of all the classes that stand face to face with the bourgeoisie today, the proletariat alone is a really revolutionary class.'[70] Recognition after 1848 that the proletariat was not as yet capable of taking power, still less of holding on to it, propelled Marx towards a deeper analysis of the conditions that would make this possible, and did not dictate any abandonment of the revolutionary mission ascribed by Marx to the proletariat.[71] The social evils of the bourgeois world still required a universal, and hence revolutionary remedy, and this remedy was only at the disposal of the proletariat, which, however, was not yet ready to prescribe it. But the central importance of the proletariat remained, for the simple reason that is is the 'special and essential product'[72] of the development of modern industry. This gives it the power to destroy existing social conditions by replacing them with with a more socially progressive alternative; the means through which to do so (centralization, urbanization and the political and general education given to it by the bourgeoisie); the desire, expressed as necessity, to do so (because of the misery of its social position imposed upon it as a recognition of an indignity); and the opportunity (afforded by the periodic outbreak of economic crisis) to do so.

The revolutionary role of the proletariat is thus mediated by two conditions: class struggle itself, and the development of production. The coincidence of these two is the key factor in bringing the revolutionary mission of the proletariat to a successful conclusion. Hitherto the underdevelopment of the latter had created a block to its success, but

Marx's analysis of the dynamics of the capitalist system led him confidently to predict an early return to the revolutionary agenda.

Conclusion

There is in Marx's writings as he makes the transition from philosophical critique to social anatomy a distinctive shift in emphasis with relation to the character of social change. Whereas in the earlier writings Marx laid stress on the capacity of human agents to become aware of and seek to abolish the social causes of their misery and dehumanization (against, for example, the elitism of hegelian philosophy and of 'critical criticism'), as a result of his interest – some might say obsession[73] – with political economy, he came to dismiss this process of practical cognition as little more than a causal response to the stimulation of economic determinants. It would be mistaken, however, to account for this shift in terms of an abandonment of Hegel for Ricardo, for as Russell Jacoby notes[74] these two positions are equally hegelian in origin and structure, one reflecting the Hegel of the *Phenomenology* in its concern with consciousness and design, the other the Hegel of the *Logic* with its account of determinism as necessity. If Marx is making a shift at all it is away from Feuerbach and his anthropological humanism. But towards what? For Althusser and his followers, just as for Plekhanov and his, it is towards a kind of Spinozist determinism in which the absurd pretensions of left-hegelianism are exposed to the indifferent calculus of cause and effect. For the Lukács of 1926 on the other hand, Marx was not in this sense a follower of Feuerbach at all but 'took over directly from Hegel', rejecting Feuerbach's transformation of Hegel's 'objective dialectics of the historical process into a mere conceptual dialectics'.[75] Thus, while Hegel treated the question of mediation in a purely theoretical or logical manner, making quite impossible any unification of philosophy and the world – save the artificial petrification of the institutions of the Prussian state – he did nevertheless seriously deal with this question. His ultimate failure was due to the impossibility at the time of achieving any such unification, because capitalist development had only just begun its task of bringing about the preconditions for such a reunification. It is in this respect that Lukács speaks of Hegel's 'magnificent realism, his rejection of all utopias, his concern to conceive philosophy as the conceptual expression of history itself'.[76] By contrast, the 'conceptual dialectics' of von Cieszowski and Moses Hess, influenced by Fichte, revert to an idealism and abstract utopianism that, despite appearance and intention, actually make the transformation of history even more difficult, based as it is upon a divorce between philosophy and history. Similarly, Feuerbach's own resolution of this problem, his critique of Hegel, goes little further, merely substituting an anthropological 'ethics of love' based on intuition and sensuousness for Hegel's categories. The substitution of God by 'species' or 'man' is in this sense a purely formal critique of Hegel, since these are not understood historically or socially, and Feuerbach's position thus amounts to little more than the substitution of idealism by pantheism. Lukács' argument is that Marx took over from Hegel what he did not find in Feuerbach, namely the conception of alienation as both appearance and objective reality, and recognized, as Feuerbach did not, that the critique of Hegel – and of alienation – cannot be epistemological or ethical but must be achieved by way of a (practical) critique of political economy. In other words, Feuerbach's critique of Hegel was incomplete and flawed by Hegel's greater appreciation of and closer relationship to the practical possibilities of historical development. It is this that accounts for Hegel's reconciliation with reality, opposition to which is bound to be a retrograde step towards utopianism unless it is based upon an understanding of reality and a perception of the revolutionary forces at work in society superior to Hegel's.

This viewpoint allows us to understand more fully Marx's intellectual development, and to avoid the error of reading into the later writings a collapse into a rigid hegelian determinism. To take but one example, the famous remark in *The Eighteenth Brumaire of Louis Bonaparte* that:

> Men make their own history, but they do not make it just as they please; they do not make it under circumstances chosen by themselves, but under circumstances directly encountered, given and transmitted from the past. The tradition of all the dead generations weighs like a nightmare on the brain of the living.[77]

This passage is not merely a shift from a philosophical to a historical perspective, but is a further reflection upon the same notion of agency. This quotation, and the one from *The Holy Family* on p.xx are two aspects of the same theory of history, and while each shares the danger that taken alone it may lead to a one-sided interpretation, read together they produce a notion of agency whereby human agency, constrained, limited and modified by determinate social-historical conditions – conditions which at any particular conjuncture may be quite beyond the direct control of actual human agents – is nevertheless the source of history and society. This also constitutes the essence of Marx's philosophical critique of both Hegel and Feuerbach; it therefore lies at the very heart of historical materialism.

The notion of agency is of course notoriously elusive, involving as it does a fundamental ambiguity in usage: an agent is 'one who exerts power or produces an effect (of things) efficient cause' but may also be 'one who does the actual work, especially one who represents a firm in business'.[78] These senses are quite distinct, the one referring to an active initiator of particular events while the other qualifies this to entertain the possibility of instrumentality, where the agent acts on behalf of another and is thus, in relation to the event in question, a passive instrument. Since Marx rarely reflected upon his own intellectual evolution, at least at any length, and because the substantive nature of his writings precluded any sustained reflection upon his previous philosophical preoccupations, there is a tardiness in his later works with regard to these, and in particular with regard to his notion of agency. For if we seek to set out an account of Marx's notion of agency purely in terms of his later writings, as the successive generations of his followers were more or less obliged to do, then we are faced with a difficult problem. For in *Capital* Marx pays very little attention indeed to agents as efficient causes, seeing them instead as largely passive, if not blind instruments of forces beyond their immediate comprehension or control, forces which determine the social conditions under which they live their lives, the social relations through which they correspond, and even the thoughts and ideas through which they encounter their environment. Thus 'individuals are dealt with only in so far as they are the personifications of economic categories, embodiments of particular class relations and class interests.'[79] These latter ('class relations and class interests') give rise to an historical movement that operates behind the back of human beings – witness Marx's favourable citation in his preface to *Capital* of a Russian reviewer: 'Marx treats the social movement as a process of natural history, governed by laws not only independent of human will, consciousness and intelligence but rather, on the contrary, determining that will, consciousness and intelligence.'[80] Nor can it be said that this derogation of human agency flows from Marx's disparagement of individualism and a corresponding concern with a collective subject, for he only begins to sketch in *Capital* the simplest of class structure – at the end of the third volume, a section only two pages in length, the manuscript incomplete.

If the legacy of *Capital* was ambiguous, the interpretation of it was not. As we shall see in the next chapter, the generation of marxists who formulated their ideas and theories upon the basis of the mature economic writings, and largely under the guidance of Engels, developed a predilection for positivism which paralleled developments in bourgeois social theories of the period and converted the dialectical concept of scientific socialism into an evolutionist scientistic socialism. An evolutionist determinism derived from Darwin became the paradigmatic *Weltanschauung* of this generation, with socialism cut into two parts: scientific research and moral ideal, the one superior in so far as it expels the other; the other the inner motivation or real human actors.

But this distinction between judgements of facts (sciences) and judgements of values (ethics) is foreign to Marx's writings, in two respects. *Capital* is permeated throughout with both a rigorous scientific methodology and an authentically moral critique: statements and evaluations are indissolubly linked. Value judgements are never autonomous or independent of analysis or empirical data; similarly, neither are statements objective in the sense that they are free from any standpoint – they are not sociological. Marx's social science, like his philosophy, is necessarily critical and thus normative, since it involves the criticism of standpoints (theories) and methods in the light of the conditions under which they emerge and the purposes they serve. The spirit of enquiry that Marx utilizes in *Capital* he inherited from Hegel, and it differs completely from the positivism that emerged in the last two decades of nineteenth-century European thought under the influence of the successes of the natural sciences.[81] Only if we understand this can we appreciate how Marx could construct a view of history in which historical determinism can co-exist and not be in contradiction with human agency. For Marx, human activity is part of a law-governed historical process: people are not to be distinguished from animals by their ability to escape this process, but by their capacity to intervene in nature and thus to effect changes in their environment. This capacity is not external to the process but exists entirely within it: no extra-terrestrial or religious intervention inspires people with the ideas necessary to effect changes, for such ideas – and the activities that follow from them – are generated by the material needs discovered by people in their struggle with nature (and with each other).

While for Hegel world history was the image and the deed of Reason, the passions and struggles of individuals merely the expression of this, manipulated by the 'cunning of Reason', for Marx the vagaries of historical development were to be explained by the interaction of humans and nature, this process providing the basis for social divisions (as well as social progress) and thus also developing the ideas and consciousness people come to possess. This study of the historical process inevitably involves paying less attention to the desires and intentions of human actors, and more to their unintended effects. This does not have to be explained in terms of an absolute setting people to work for itself, but by study of the real processes at work in history – the relations between individuals, groups and classes, and between humans and nature. In a letter of 1852[82] Marx comments that it was not he who discovered the existence of either classes or class struggle, but that his achievement was on the one hand to link classes with historical phases in the development of production, and on the other to show that class struggle necessarily leads to the dictatorship of the proletariat, this latter entailing the abolition of all classes. Marx thus achieves a more precise definition of classes and of the nature of class struggle – and thus of agency – in terms of the mode of production in which they exist and operate, while at the same time asserting the necessity of this very process. It should also be noted that this connection between the two also provides the basis for judging the relatively progressive character of any particular stage of development.

It is this that brings us back to the historical mission of the proletariat. In what sense does the emphasis Marx now places upon necessity impose itself upon the human agent which he earlier regarded as the embodiment of human emancipation and which now takes the appearance of an agent determined by the stages of development of production? Marx's future theoretical development was marked on the one hand by this question, on the other by the defeats and setbacks of the 1848 revolutions. It is in dealing with these questions that Marx came to alter his conception of the proletariat, encompassing within this new conception some explanation for its failure to raise itself to the ruling class in 1848 or soon after.

Given the defeats of those years, what options were open to Marx? First, he could have dismissed the revolutionary capacity of the proletariat and rejected wholesale his earlier philosophical works. I believe I have established that he did not do this. Two closely related alternatives were thus possible. First, the timetable for the overthrow of bourgeois rule could be rescheduled to allow the proletariat a further period of maturation. Or second, the revolutionary mission ascribed to the proletariat could be modified by placing it in historical context, alongside a more balanced appraisal of the revolutionary impulsiveness of both capitalism and its gravedigger. While these arguments are closely linked, it would, I think, be true to say that Marx generally favoured the former option over the latter, that he modified his belief in the revolutionary capacity of the proletariat chronologically, that is by the historical context through which it is mediated, and not structurally in terms of the capacity of capitalism to neutralize and disarm its opponent. It is at this point, however, that the chickens of twentieth-century marxism come home to roost and upon which the vultures of post-marxism swoop to feed. For while it may be understandable that Marx could postpone the anticipated path to power of the proletariat for two, three, or even four decades, a further century of unrealized revolutionary expectations must call into question the original conception. For history cannot be perpetually defective; there must come a point where the accumulation of 'accidents' and 'vagaries' in historical development signifies the need for a changed perspective, in which the accidental and contingent may be judged to be the normal and expected.

I will go on in chapter five to provide an account of the way in which the theory of commodity fetishism outlined in the first chapter of *Capital* may be used to provide an answer to this problem. But at this point it is sufficient to note that Marx did not himself choose to stress this aspect of his thought, for the simple reason, perhaps, that the problem of working-class revolutionary consciousness did not arise for him in the same way that it did for his successors, and for us today. Our attention must now turn to the difficulties encountered by Marx's immediate successors in their attempt to interpret marxism in the changed conditions of the late nineteenth and early twentieth centuries.

3 Georg Lukács and Orthodoxy

Philosophy and Politics

Lukács' route to Marx and reformulation of marxism was shaped by two intellectual worlds: that of academic German sociology, and the political world of socialist parties loosely grouped in the Second International. Lukács' early embrace of the former was to have important consequences for his interpretation of marxism even after the break that delivered him to communism. But his rejection of Second International orthodoxy was total and uncompromising, though equally illuminating of the particular conception of marxism developed after his 1918 embrace of communism. It is in the relation between the political practice and philosophical basis of social democratic orthodoxy that the origins of Lukács' critique lies, and which will be the subject of this chapter.

Although Kautsky, Plekhanov (and others) were wedded to a particular philosophical position, it was not this that commited them to the political practice upon which they subsequently embarked. The question of the relationship between the philosophical and political position of an individual is too complex to be cast in such a reductionist light – despite the opinions of the author of *The Destruction of Reason*.[1] Indeed, the difficulty in deriving a political position from a philosophical one may be highlighted by considering the relationship between the respective positions of social democratic orthodoxy and bolshevism, between Kautsky and Plekhanov, Lenin and Trotsky. For it is certainly the case that Lenin, and probably Trotsky also, to some considerable degree shared the philosophical viewpoints of their social democratic counterparts and yet were able to draw quite divergent political conclusions from them.[2] Whether political voluntarism was a legitimate conclusion to be drawn from a determinist philosophy is a question I shall consider later. For the moment, however, it is legitimate to question the philosophical background of orthodoxy in the context of its political practice, for the simple reason that Lukács was himself hostile to both – before and after his conversion to marxism.[3]

There still remains the question of accounting for the political direction taken by the leaders of social democracy. Was their political conduct determined by their philosophical convictions, or by the demands of the movement which they led? What was the nature of the relationship between these two factors? And what does marxism have to say about this relationship? Where the two come into conflict, for example, which takes precedence: the theoretical or the contingent (or expedient)?

Despite all the reservations one would wish to register with respect to the limited importance of leadership, and even more so of philosophy to everyday political practice, an important question remains to be answered: how was it that the party that claimed to lie directly in the tradition begun by Marx, and which was guided by Engels, came to act as it did? If its political practice did indeed diverge from the revolutionary politics of Marx and Engels, why did not its theory alert it to this divergence? And if it failed to do this, are we entitled to conclude that Engels, and possibly Marx as well, colluded – if only by act of ambiguity – in its subsequent political opportunism? Kolakowski and many other writers hold marxism partly responsible for the political practice of stalinism.[4] Is it also (or alternatively) responsible for the political practice of social democracy? And how significant was its interpretation of marxism in the trajectory of Lukács' own formulations?

The Emergence of Orthodoxy

The political practice of social democracy must ultimately, of course, be explained in terms of the social and economic conditions prevailing in the period of its preeminence, and of the particular balance of class relations in which these were expressed. These went through two stages: the era of liberalism, which may be said to have lasted from the creation of the new Reich in 1871 until the year of the death of the two emperors (William I and Frederick III) in 1888; and the era of imperialism, which coincided with the years of autocratic and personal rule of William II.[5] The rise of social democracy took place during the first of these stages; it was against the background of developments in this era that the fundamentals of its political practice and beliefs were shaped.[6]

The 1880s and 1890s were characterized by a profound change in the physiognomy of capitalism;[7] this was a period of renewed industrial prosperity coupled with social crisis. A new wave of industrialization took place, especially strong in Germany, which now came to challenge the preeminence of Britain and France as the major European powers.[8] Concomitant with this was a vast increase in the concentration and centralization of capital. The period witnessed the formation of cartels and monopolies, and the gradual replacement of liberal competitive capitalism with modern monopolistic capitalism and imperialism. As a result a change took place in the political interests of the European powers. The reliance of the monopolies upon the export of capital and the domination of the markets of the subject, colonial countries led to an intensification of the rivalry between the European powers. This change in the structure of world and European capitalism had its effect upon the activities of the workers' parties, now in the process of coming together to form the Second International, and also upon the emerging national trade union movements – all of which were drawn for the first time into the political and social life of their national polity.

Social democractic ideology had, however, largely been worked out in an earlier period when the influence of Marx's ideas came to be paramount, and in which the party in Germany grew to be a huge national organization. Engels described how Bismarck's anti-socialist laws helped forge such a party, by forcing unity upon the previously warring Lassallean and Eisenach factions of the party, but how at the same time Marx's theoretical perspective triumphed as the last vestiges of Lassalle's doctrines were purged from the party programme.[9] This was also, however, a decade of social stability, characterized by H. Stuart Hughes as 'a stuffy decade' in which the 'smugness' and 'philistinism' of upper and middle class society was complemented by a marxism that was little more than a 'peculiarly insidious...form of the reigning cult of positivism'. The effects of this period and its genesis were to persist into the 1890s, at which point marxism might otherwise have been expected to have offered a suitable weapon 'with which to combat the dominant ideology of the European middle class'.[10] Thus the ideology of social democracy was originally formulated under the distorting framework of Bismarck's anti-socialist laws, by the backward nature of German political institutions and culture, and against the background of a decade of prosperity and social stability. Social democratic orthodoxy itself, however, was later required to deal with a changed environment, in which 'social disorder, economic crisis, and institutional malfunctioning...contributed to the growth of socialist parties and to the spread of marxist doctrines',[11] but which factors at the same time posed a severe challenge to social democracy's ideology; a challenge that in the short term it was capable of resisting, but one which was later to result in its own destruction, in the division between revisionism and bolshevism.

The key word of German social democracy had always been organization. The strength of its organization and its success in wresting numerous social and economic concessions from a reluctant opponent, and indeed its apparent success in organizing the working class and promoting it to the very centre of political life, seemed to make its path to power inevitable, if not irresistible, as well as giving it a power of veto over the looming war – or so it appeared. It was in the period of imperialism, however, that all these practices and beliefs of orthodoxy were subjected to a challenge that would ultimately reveal it to be compromised politically and undermined scientifically.

The ultimate test came, as is well known, with the outbreak of the Great War on 4 August 1914, from which point the demise of orthodoxy rapidly followed. From that date the tradition linked with the names of Kautsky, Plekhanov, Jaurès and others came face to face with the challenge posed to it by the openly antagonistic, separate, and competing traditions of revisionism and bolshevism.[12] Whereas before 1914 each of these tendencies had been part of the same movement, with the orthodox centre holding the ring between the other two, the subsequent hostility and organizational separation left orthodoxy exposed to attack, and loss of influence, from both left and right.

This social and economic periodization has to be contextualized in terms of the three political features specific and unique to its history: namely the abandonment of liberalism, particularly with respect to the intervention of the state in economic and social affairs; the democratization of political institutions and the extension of the suffrage; and the economic expansion based on imperialism which was responsible for the emergence of a virulent nationalism. Thus, as Massimo Salvadori notes,

> German social democracy was the first great workers' party that was compelled to deal, squarely and bluntly, with a capitalist system whose rapid end its theory had led it to expect, which instead exploded outwards in an imperialism that rallied mass support.[13]

It is thus no coincidence that the formation of social democratic ideology took place when it did, since it was in this period that national politics itself expanded to encompass mass political parties and attempts to mobilize the support of the majority of the population: this was the age of the masses.[14] Germany was not the only, nor even the first country to experience this. What made its experience crucial and important was that it also possessed at this time something that Britain, for example, did not: a 'great workers' party'.[15] It is this combination that makes the German experience so important, for it was there that the conditions of modern capitalism came into conflict with what was the declared ideology of social democracy: marxism.[16]

But while the German party (the SPD) and its experience lay at the centre of social democracy, the International was affected by and intervened in Europe-wide politics, and it was during the 1890s that a succession of events forced social democracy to come to terms with participation in national, bourgeois politics from the inside. The Dreyfus affair, the participation of the socialist Millerand in a bourgeois government, the growth of imperialism and the growing threat of war – all these issues and the attitude adopted towards them by the social democratic parties signified a real and significant change in this period. The proletariat and its party representative were no longer pariahs. Even in Germany, whose official political life was slowest of all in recognizing the new environment and where the opposition of the social democrats to the monarchy had, in the words of the US Ambassador to the German Imperial Court, put them 'politically, militarily, and socially, beyond the pale', made them 'almost an outcast',[17] the growth of the SPD in terms of membership, votes received and Reichstag deputies made it a real – if officially unrecognized – political force.

Thus, while in the 1880s – in the period of the anti-socialist laws – the exclusion of the SPD from involvement in and responsibility for national politics put it at the head of all dissenting groups, during the 1890s the party came in from the cold, and this provided it with dangers as well as opportunities, dangers which its ideology did little to prepare it for. Moreover, at the moment opposition and isolation were in the process of being transformed into participation, so the political environment was itself being transformed from stability to instability.

Apart from these changes in its social and political environment, social democracy also suffered a major internal weakness, one that was increasingly revealed as it entered the arena of national politics. This concerned its dependence upon social forces which were independent of it but which, in the absence of any other liberal alternative, gave it their conditional, temporary support, while at the same time providing the constituency of revisionism. Social democracy was dependent upon the newly emerging trade unions, in particular their bureaucratic leadership; upon the largely non-socialist sympathizers, the 'insulted and injured', who had no other electoral alternative and who made up the bulk of its electoral support; and upon the petty bourgeois intellectuals who made up the party's functionaries and representatives.[18]

This political alignment – what Lenin later termed centrism – could not survive as an independent, discrete entity. This was not because its ideas and philosophy could not be disentangled from its rival traditions, but because the social conditions that had matured in the period of its growth, from 1871 to the turn of the century, were no longer operative; those that replaced them proved to be incompatible with its theoretical framework. In much the same way as overripe fruit is at first disguised by its skin, only for this later to split and reveal its now-decaying inner, so the crisis of the imperialist period revealed orthodoxy as a thing of the past. This is exemplified by the fate of the two individuals most closely associated with orthodoxy, Karl Kautsky and Georgi Plekhanov. The former ended up in the arms of the SPD, his authorial magnum opus on historical materialism largely ignored, and died in penniless obscurity in Amsterdam; the latter was isolated and estranged in the country he was to return to only to witness the revolution that he condemned, and which caused him to question his whole life-work.[19]

But an understanding of these social developments, though necessary, is not sufficient on its own to account for this debacle. For social democracy always prided itself on possessing a scientific doctrine, one which scientifically understood the laws of motion of capitalist society. How then can we explain its extraordinary inability to understand the period in which it operated? How was it that it was outflanked, first by the revisionists and then by the radicals?

Theory and Practice

The major problem in accounting for the political evolution of social democracy lies in the way in which it sought, within a given social and political context, to put its theoretical presuppositions into practice; in particular, how it conceptualized the relationship between its day-to-day political tasks and its desired end of the revolutionary overthrow of capitalism. This problem is, as I have said, one largely the product of economic, social and political changes that took place towards the end of the nineteenth century and which increasingly undermined the party's commitment to the revolutionary component of marxism. However, the distinction goes right back to the programme upon which the SPD founded itself as a marxist party, the Erfurt Programme of 1891, which was composed of two halves; the first, drawn up by Kautsky, outlined the general theoretical outlook of social democracy, while the other, drawn up by Bernstein, outlined its practical, immediate demands.[20]

It is important to resist the temptation of regarding orthodoxy as simply a species of revisionism, one which merely cloaked its reformism with a revolutionary theory or phraseology.[21] For there were important differences between orthodoxy and revisionism on this question. While it is true that orientation on parliament and on the political reforms parliamentary participation would make possible were crucial to orthodoxy, these are actually more symptomatic of revisionism. Orthodoxy had a much more limited estimation of the advantages to be gained from bourgeois parliaments; crucially, its politico-philosophic outlook caused it to take a view similar to the radical left: namely that capitalism would not grant reforms, could not be reformed, would continually and recurrently lurch into crises that made the conditions of life of the proletariat increasingly intolerable and forever insecure and unstable, and that would, as a result, drive it to revolution. Thus Kautsky: 'The tendency of capitalism is...to degrade the proletariat ever more and more. The moral regeneration of the working class is possible only in opposition to this tendency and its representatives, the capitalists.'[22] Orthodoxy's experience under the anti-socialist laws had led it to expect little or nothing from bourgeois democracy, indeed its continued growth in those years added to its self-confidence. Thus, reforms could not be expected from bourgeois democracy; only social democracy could provide these. Even where the state granted certain progressive measures (as with Bismarck's reforms) these would always operate to the greater disadvantage of the proletariat by giving proportionately greater benefit to the employers, signified nothing but attempts to save a sinking ship, and themselves advertised the bankruptcy of capitalism.

Plekhanov's position on this question was slightly less pessimistic, perhaps because his orthodoxy was less open to challenge in the autocratic environment of tsarist Russia. He could maintain his haughty dismissal of revisionism because the Russian movement was not dominated, as the German increasingly was, by the social weight of the trade unions. His view is revealed through his understanding of the issue that dominated the Russian section of social democracy: the connection between the bourgeois and socialist revolutions. The proletariat would support the bourgeois revolution because by so doing it would acquire the political rights that would allow it to defend its position, to obtain benefits from the bourgeoisie and thus to pursue its ultimate aim more effectively. Once having done this, the working class could obtain real and tangible benefits for itself – but only in the context of the class struggle. Reforms could not dilute the emergence of a revolutionary class consciousness. Plekhanov illustrates his point by drawing the following analogy:

> The proletariat is in the position of a person who is swimming against a powerful current; if he submits without resistance to the force of the water, he would be carried *very* far back; but he does resist; he tries to move forward and therefore the current pushes him back *not so far* as it *might*; but *nevertheless* it did *move him back*, because all the same *it was much stronger.*[23]

The dispute between orthodoxy and revisionism referred, in this context, to the exclusivity of social democracy; the former distrusting potential political allies and sceptical about the institutions of bourgeois democracy, while the latter were prepared to enter any alliance, use any means to achieve the desired reforms. Orthodoxy regarded the achievement of reforms as possible only through class struggle or via legislation which would be passed when they controlled government; other reforms were regarded as mere attempts by the capitalist system to buy off dissent and to preserve its rule. For this reason revisionism was harshly criticized as a betrayal; whatever short-term gains it might obtain would carry with them the cost of rendering the working class impotent against the increasingly aggressive demands of capitalist competition.[24]

Marx's legacy was ambiguous on this point. On the one hand he firmly advocated the central importance of the role of the proletariat in the revolutionary transfer of political power; on the other he did not rule out the utilization of class alliances, even with elements of the bourgeoisie, in that struggle. Indeed, he expressly ruled out Lassalle's notion that the non-proletarian masses form a single reactionary mass. Similarly, while Marx was himself uncompromising in his hostility to bourgeois society and the impossibility of reforming it, nonetheless he did not believe that the proletariat was – or should be – indifferent to the form of political rule of the bourgeoisie. Again, while the proletariat had no place in bourgeois society except as the exploited and suffering class, Marx did not accept the idea of the iron law of wages: he urged that workers must engage in struggles and that this would have the consequence not merely of training them in struggle but of actually 'improving their lot', would make their position in bourgeois society better than it might otherwise be.[25] Kautsky referred to the elevation of the working class through this process as 'more moral than economic'[26] and this surely signifies his scepticism with regard to the practical advances possible within capitalism.

Despite these ambiguities in Marx's political position, however, there is a fundamental difference between the attitude towards reforms achieved within capitalist society taken by Marx and by orthodoxy and the revisionists, even though the day-to-day practices of the latter could find some support in Marx's own writings. If reformism was perhaps an understandable development in the context of the socio-political circumstances of the period, it was for all that a distortion of Marx's own revolutionary politics, distorted not in the sense that Marx opposed reforms but in the sense that, in Marx's scheme of things, the struggle for reforms and wage increases provided merely the means through which the proletariat would educate itself in the class struggle, and which would result in the eventual conquest of political power. Class struggle was the means towards the end of the seizure of power, while for the reformists it was the result of these struggles that really mattered (and the wider end was superfluous and perhaps irrelevant). Thus, as he indicates in the preface to his English edition of *Evolutionary Socialism*, Bernstein was concerned above all to accentuate the everyday work of the socialist party – the *Gegenwartrarbeit* – and regarded 'the final aim of socialism' as best left to the future:

> In this sense I wrote the sentence that the movement means everything for me and that what is *usually* called 'the final aim of socialism' is nothing; and in this sense I write it down again...My thoughts and efforts are concerned with the duties of the present and the nearest future, and I only busy myself with the perspectives beyond so far as they give me a line of conduct for suitable action now.[27]

Before August 1914 social democracy was able consistently to condemn such sentiments, even though – or perhaps because – its day-to-day practice was characterized by such beliefs. The question that remains to be asked is whether the theoretical standpoint of orthodoxy contributed to its failure effectively to combat the influence of revisionism.[28] Surely its theory must have been deficient for it to have been satisfied with the Pyrrhic victories it enjoyed over revisionism, and to have ignored or failed to see the increasing divergence between its theory and practice?

Thus we must examine the politico-philosophical background to orthodoxy, to locate the particular features of its version of marxism that laid it open to the influence and eventual triumph of revisionism.

The Constituent Parts of Orthodoxy

To do this it is first necessary to define orthodoxy. As is well known, the Second International was a loose federation of political parties in which the relationship between socialist theory and the workers' movement was unusually and uniquely close. This had the consequence that there was no central organizational structure empowered to impose discipline, let alone unanimity, in matters either of theory or practice on its constitutive parts. National parties tended to reflect their own national and cultural traditions, and this to some extent militated against a dogmatic orthodoxy. Despite this heterogeneous character an orthodoxy did emerge. How and why?

The first point to make is that despite the cultural diversity of the national parties, these did not passively reflect the demands and aspirations of their respective labour movements but lent them a particular flavour, sought to integrate them into a theoretical perspective and political programme heavily influenced by the language – if not always the meaning – of marxism. These parties were not simply the political expression of the workers' movement, but were themselves political agents whose intention it was to convert the workers' movement to marxism. Such a work of conversion required the translation of marxist theory into the everyday language of the workers' movement, a process that involved making the classic works of marxism intelligible to a mass audience and met the demand that came from that mass audience – namely the demand for an ideology, for a set of beliefs which would situate and orientate its position in the world and also provide a set of signposts indicating the direction of change, past, present, and future.

Here, then, marxism came to the workers' movement and presented to it a theoretical reflection of itself. It provided a two-way translation: marxism was shown to be the theoretical expression of the workers' movement, while that movement was shown to be the essential sociological basis of marxism. A symbiotic relationship was held to obtain between the two. The problem though, as we have seen in previous chapters, was that marxism was not simply the immediate expression of the workers' movement but was the expression of what was understood to be essential (though not always apparent) to that movement, namely its revolutionary orientation. That revolutionary orientation, however, did not seem to be borne out by the social, economic and political conditions of Europe in the era of liberalism. For this reason the social democratic interpretation of its role and responsibility with respect to the revolutionary change required if capitalism was to be replaced by socialism took on a particular hue; it tended to be limited to the acquisition of state power via a parliamentary majority and the preparedness to resist by force the anticipated violent resistance of the old ruling class – the 'slaveowners' rebellion'. I take up this point further below. To begin with, though, let us examine how social democracy developed the first of these processes: the translation of marxist theory into an ideology of the workers' movement.

Two responses were forthcoming. On the one hand there were those who believed that marxism provided the essential framework for a scientific account of the mechanism of capitalist society, an historical understanding of its genesis and eventual breakdown, but that this needed to be complemented by a philosophical world outlook that would provide individuals and classes with the basis for acceptance or rejection of their (scientifically derived) position in the world. Thus marxism, which represented here the negation of philosophy, required a supplement that could be provided either by Kantian ethics, as in the case of the Austro-Marxists, or empirio-critical epistemology, as with the Russian Machists and Friedrich Adler. The orthodox view, on the other hand, was that if marxism required supplementing at all, then the philosophical writings of Engels were sufficient. These completed Marx's sociological and economic theories by giving to them a formal unity encompassing the totality of human existence.

The creation of an ideology for the workers' movement of the time therefore demanded that the scientific theory of marxism be complemented by and brought into alignment with a philosophical viewpoint that would motivate those committed to the ideology with an appropriate form of political activity. The assumption behind such a call was that while marxist science provided an objective, positive account of the laws of motion of capitalism, the source of political motivation lay elsewhere. The consequent separation of science from ethics and values is a theme common to orthodoxy[29] (indeed, common to the modern world), and is most forcefully made by Rudolf Hilferding in his preface to *Finance Capital*:

> The practice of Marxism, as well as its theory, is free from value judgements...In logical terms Marxism, considered only as a scientific system, and disregarding its historical effects, is only a theory of the laws of motion of society...But acceptance of the validity of Marxism, including a recognition of the necessity of socialism, is no more a matter of value judgement than it is a guide to practical action. For it is one thing to acknowledge a necessity, and quite another thing to work for that necessity. It is quite possible for someone who is convinced that socialism will triumph in the end to join the fight against it.[30]

There are thus three general constitutive elements to orthodox theory, each of which, as we shall see, was challenged by Lukács' interpretation of marxism. First, there is the belief that the transition from capitalism to socialism is but part of the general process of evolution of human society, one determined by the growth of the productive forces and by humankind's conquest of nature; that this process takes on the characteristics of an objective law of necessity and provides the material basis upon which all the other elements of human life rest or are constructed.

Second, there is the belief that the growth of the productive forces takes place alongside a growing centralization of these forces. This has consequences for economic management, in that capitalism is itself unable to provide an equivalent centralized machinery of administration which could harness the necessary expertise to manage a modern economy. In politics, this development puts a greater degree of power in the hands of the state bureaucracy, which steps in where individual capitalists cannot to take responsibility for the overall management of the system and which, by so doing, makes the state the fulcrum of political contest which the proletariat must control if it is to control and administer those economic forces. In other words, the state – and what is meant here is the bourgeois-democractic form of the state – is necessary to mediate between the demands of society and the economy. This is as true of socialist as it is of capitalist society.

Third, there is the belief that this process of evolution of human society is susceptible to scientific analysis, that only socialists can adequately achieve this (since they alone desire the conditions necessary for continued growth – the overthrow of private ownership), that in achieving this they are also serving the interests of the dispossessed and that the results of their efforts will be sufficient to convince any rational individual of the inevitability of socialism and the benefits which will accrue to all from it.

Orthodoxy, Evolution and Revolution

The affinity of orthodoxy to an evolutionist and determinist approach to social affairs is widely commented upon.[31] I propose to discuss the issue in relation to three further sets of beliefs: first, the matter of the party's relationship to the act of revolution; second, that of the nature of the transition between capitalism and socialism; and third, the question of the theory of economic crisis and capitalist collapse.

For Kautsky the party had no responsibility for making or even for leading a revolution: 'the revolution cannot be the work of a party but must come from the people', and the task of the party was 'not to make the revolution, but to take advantage of it'.[32] While this position was formally correct in drawing a distinction between the notion of a revolution as the transfer of political power from one class to another and a Blanquist seizure of power, it also represented and made possible another distinction, between the long-term aim of social democracy (the transfer of political power from the bourgeois to the working class) and its everyday political practice. For this latter was now absolved of any responsibility of integrating into its political tasks the organization of this transfer of power. This was made possible because it assumed that developments within capitalism were preparing the necessary groundwork for the transfer of political power: namely the transfer of social power. In this respect the model of the bourgeois revolution was not merely of limited value but was positively misleading, since the proletariat could not await, as could the bourgeoisie, the maturation of its own source of social power within the confines of capitalism.

Moreover, Kautsky's switch of emphasis from political to social revolution makes it possible for him to draw all sorts of optimistic political conclusions about the determinist character of this social revolution. As Salvadori's book on Kautsky makes clear, Kautsky's commitment to revolution did not extend to any consequence for his political practice, it merely encompassed a belief that revolution was inevitable. Moreover, that revolution need not involve an armed seizure of power: the peaceful transfer of political power was both possible and preferable, the workers would resort to force only if the bourgeois classes themselves did so upon finding themselves removed from power. Furthermore, the peaceful character of the revolution would be advantaged by the scientific provability of its inevitability and superiority, in that the demonstration of this would convince the bourgeoisie that resistance was futile.[33]

The revolution, then, was to be peaceful; it would arrive spontaneously and resistance to it would be futile: 'it is just as little in our power to make this revolution as it is in the power of our opponents to prevent it.'[34] Its arrival would of course depend upon the willingness of people to use their physical and mental powers in their own interests, but this act would be the consequence of the process of economic evolution of capitalism: 'We consider the breakdown of the present social system to be unavoidable, because we know that the economic evolution inevitably brings on conditions that will compel the exploited classes to rise against this system of private ownership.'[35]

The transition between capitalism and socialism was thus determined by two 'objective laws': the breakdown of capitalism and the periodic onset of economic crisis; and the evolution of economic conditions that will compel resistance from the workers and lead them on to revolution. This is how Kautsky described this process in the Erfurt Programme:

> The capitalist social system has run its course; its dissolution is now only a question of time. Irresistible economic forces lead with the certainty of doom to the shipwreck of capitalist production. The substitution of a new social order for the existing one is no longer simply desirable, it has become inevitable.[36]

It was precisely on this point that Bernstein directed his challenge to orthodoxy. Not only did he challenge the economic reductionism that read into capitalism the tendency to economic breakdown and read out of this the revolt of the proletariat, he also challenged whether indeed the economic forces of capitalism did irresistibly lead to its shipwreck. Against Kautsky's fatalism Bernstein registered a humanistic complaint: 'No amount of historical materialism can get round the fact that history is made by men, that men have minds, and that mental dispositions are by no means so mechanical as to be entirely governed by the economic situation.'[37] And even as Bernstein was reading into human affairs an ability to avoid the mechanical determinism of its economic situation, he also affirmed the ability of capitalism to reform its own economic conditions of existence, to introduce a rational control of its anarchic features that would have the result of easing the conditions of life of the proletariat as it made possible the space for economic and political reform.

Bernstein and Kautsky made different assessments of the possibilities of reform under capitalism, but these differences disguised an underlying similarity. For while Bernstein stressed the self-reforming characteristics of capitalist society, in particular its ability to avoid the economic and social consequences predicted for it by Marx in *The Communist Manifesto* (the tendency to immiserization, class polarization and economic collapse),[38] and Kautsky denied absolutely any such possibility, Kautsky was also prepared to acknowledge developments within capitalism that had a socialist aspect to them. For as the accumulation of capital and property increases, so 'the new system of property' is revealed as lying 'latent in the old': '[t]o substitute common, for private, ownership in the means of production, this it is that economic development is urging upon us with ever increasing force.'[39] Kautsky notes as the most essential factor in this process the economic activity of the state, whose activities, he thought, indicated to some extent the negation of the anarchy of the capitalist market, an attempt to moderate the operation of the market to fit in with the demands of both national management and the efficient management of the highly centralized productive forces.

This brings us to the second of the three elements of orthodox theory. Democracy is important to the workers' movement for two reasons. The first is that it allows it to exercise an influence over government, it is a powerful lever which can raise the proletariat out of its 'economic, social and moral degradation'; democratic freedoms are the 'light and air of the labour movement'.[40] But, second, democracy was also essential to the ability of the working class itself to control the forces of production it would inherit from capitalism. In this respect Kautsky rejected the belief that the workers could directly control all aspects of society; he rejected, in other words, the model of direct democracy about which Marx had spoken in his writings on the Paris Commune (and upon which Lenin would draw in 1917 to justify the existence of soviet power).

Kautsky rejected this model for the same reason that the elite theorists rejected it: because the development of modern society required a combination of efficiency and expertise that could only be adequately marshalled in the form of a rational-bureaucratic system of administration. Every cook could not run the state, but representative democracy could ensure that the bureaucrats who did were satisfactorily controlled, or restrained, by the political will of the majority.

This was also the viewpoint of Max Weber, as we shall see in chapter 4. What was important was not so much who made the decisions or who administered modern society, but in whose interests such decisions were made. Kautsky believed that forms of representative democracy could ensure that the interests of the masses were served, and he was strengthened in this belief by the failure of the soviet form of democracy to restrain the bureaucratic tendencies that existed in both the party and state after the 1917 Russian Revolution. However, this belief is not only a reflection of the circumstances of modern society (its size or complexity) but also directly contributes to these, in that the underlying assumption is that the masses cannot rule themselves (or society) with any degree of efficiency, so must instead rely upon experts to do so on their behalf. As we shall see, this assumption also plays a part in determining Kautsky's perception of the relationship between socialist theory – or consciousness – and the masses, in which the former represents the real interests of the latter, which the latter is by itself unable to articulate. The formulation of Kautsky's ideological viewpoint during the 1880s possibly immunized him against the critique of the functioning of the representative institutions of democracy made by the elite theorists in the two decades either side of the turn of the century.

By Contrast: Lukács

When in 1967 Lukács prepared an introduction for the long-awaited republication of those of his earlier writings which included *History and Class Consciousness*, he took care to emphasize the historical epoch in which these works were composed. His intention was, he tells us: 'to base myself on Marx and to free his concepts from every bourgeois distortion and to adapt them to the requirements of the great revolutionary upsurge of the present',[41] which he saw manifest in such events as the Kapp putsch, the occupation of the factories in Italy, the Polish–Soviet War and the March Action. The work was thus oriented from the outset on the post-war revolutionary wave and a belief in 'the imminence of world revolution and the total transformation of the civilized world'.[42]

It is important to remember, however, that Lukács had his own reasons for stressing the conjunctural limitations of *History and Class Consciousness*. While the sincerity of his later renunciation of the revolutionary romanticism of this earlier period cannot be doubted, his desire to justify his changed position leads him to seek an extra-philosophical explanation for these revolutionary writings that tends to exaggerate the directly political, conjunctural aspect of their production.

None of this is to deny that *History and Class Consciousness* did have a political aspect to it. Though Lukács' understanding of marxism is in this period essentially methodological, this itself takes on political importance when seen in the context of his concern with the possibility of reestablishing the unity of theory and practice that he had seen separated, to their mutual disadvantage, by orthodox social democracy. The outbreak of the war and the failure of the socialist parties to act upon their pre-war resolutions promising opposition and resistance to it had demonstrated the practical failures of social democracy. What Lukács now sought and intended to provide was an account of the theoretical misconceptions that had led or contributed to that practical and political failure, and this involved a reinterpretation of marxism that would free it of those assumptions and principles that had led to the discrediting of social democracy. He sought to establish, in other words, a philosophical account of those theoretical shortcomings of social democracy that had remained latent until the epoch of war and revolution had thrust onto it the responsibility to act upon its stated policies.

In this sense, Lukács's notorious claim in the essay 'What is Orthodox Marxism?' that all of Marx's individual theses could be dismissed in toto without yet abandoning marxist orthodoxy[43] is not quite so extravagant as it may seem, since it was the preservation of the marxist method that Lukács saw as the key determinant of revolutionary politics. Lukács went on to define that method in terms of the revolutionary dialectic, the possibility of uniting theory and practice with the aim of transforming the present – through the agency, or praxis of the proletariat. By such a definition marxism does not constitute a more or less dogmatic set of laws but is a guide to political practice, one that is, however, not limited to the demands and capacities of any particular situation but is based upon the relation of the present to the future. Marxism is, in Lukács' words: 'the eternally vigilant prophet proclaiming the relation between the tasks of the immediate present and the totality of the historical process.'[44]

In this essay Lukács defends marxism against those who would reject the revolutionary methodology that preserves – or rather makes possible – the link between the present and the future, and who as a consequence end up more or less willing prisoners of the realities of the bourgeois world. This applies both to those like Bernstein who explicitly reject the dialectical method and are able to announce that 'the movement means everything...and what is usually called "the final aim of socialism" is nothing',[45] as well as to those others who stake their position on the scientific status of marxism as opposed to its revolutionary method.

If marxism was to be preserved as an authentically revolutionary intellectual force its relevance could not be limited to the question of whose views were correct, who most scientifically assessed the verdict of the empirical world: Kautsky's belief that the triumph of socialism was inevitable, or Bernstein's assumption that it had become outdated by the self-reforms generated within capitalism itself. Marxism had to maintain its autonomy vis-à-vis the more ephemeral characteristics of capitalist development to avoid losing itself in the quagmire of detail that, taken at face value, could not but advertise its irrelevance and obsolescence. It could do this so long as the essential characteristics of capitalism remained, and it could detail what those characteristics are. Whether the 'proletarianization' of society or the immiserization of the proletariat was absolute or relative; whether capital was controlled by owner-entrepreneurs or joint-stock companies; whether the state pretended autonomy or took a direct role in economic affairs; whether capitalism was headed for economic breakdown or whether its self-regulating mechanisms allowed it to avoid this – all these were in some sense secondary issues: issues to be sure upon which marxists must have something relevant to say, but issues which flowed from a more essential framework of understanding, which alone determined the truth or otherwise of the doctrine itself.

The relationship between marxism and the empirical evidence of the social world is not one of subservience of the former to the latter, for the world of bourgeois social relations presents itself in an opaque manner, in the form of a world of illusions and distortions, of change and fluidity, where the appearance of things does not necessarily coincide with their truth, their essence. Marxism's scientific aspect consists in penetrating the veil of illusions thrown up by bourgeois social relations, but it cannot do this unless it is guided by a revolutionary methodology that takes as its starting point the essential problem of history, namely that of change and agency.

Lukács thus set out to reestablish this revolutionary methodology at the heart of marxism and by so doing challenged the influence of orthodoxy which operated with a view of society that by its very nature militated against revolutionary change. By separating an evolutionist conception of historical progress – based upon a Darwinian-inspired model – from the political activities of people, whose impetus was held to derive from a system of moral ethics, these writers had misinterpreted Marx's own conception of revolutionary change. More importantly perhaps, they had also provided the intellectual expression for a form of politics based upon 'the exploitation...of...fatalistically accepted and immutable laws' or for 'action directed wholly inwards'.[46]

The apparent difference between Kautsky and Bernstein lay not so much in their conception of the nature of historical change, but in their judgement as to the direction such change was headed. While Kautsky defended the orthodox determinist picture of economic decline and capitalist breakdown, making the triumph of socialism both necessary (to solve the contradictions between historical progress and capitalist social relations) and inevitable (in the sense that it was unavoidably written into the agenda of history), Bernstein saw on the contrary the triumph of conscious control, in the form of extended democracy, over historical necessity. Both were equally resigned to the determinism of the empirical world; it was the responsibility of historical actors merely to await and at best to anticipate the beneficient harvest of historical destiny, since until the facts spoke all must remain silent. Both sides of the 'revisionist debate' had fallen into the error of regarding the essence of marxism as lying in a set of scientific prognostications about the nature of capitalism, which were then complemented by a separate collection of moral imperatives that motivated either a desire for future change or an acceptance of these scientific 'givens'.

It is this fragmentaion that Lukács rejected and which led him to formulate an interpretation of marxism that reintegrated the philosophical and the economic, theory and practice, idea and reality. The severely unsettled environment of post-war Europe caused a fundamental questioning of the comfortable certainties of evolutionism and led to a reemphasis upon the role of political agency. The times had moved against orthodoxy. The factors that enabled Lukács to formulate as a response to these changes a coherent and consistent philosophical challenge to orthodoxy will be the subject of the next chapter.

4 Lukács and German Sociology

Lukács, like Marx and indeed any other writer, can only fully be understood in the context of the social, political and intellectual climate out of which he emerged. This is not to reduce the ideas of the individual to either their social or individual origins. Rather, our assessment of a writer must focus upon the interplay of personal biography and social influence to avoid manufacturing a psychologically or sociologically determined model, so that changes in orientation and perspective may be understood as both specific to the individual in question and yet reflective also of wider social circumstances. Since I am concerned here with Lukács' contribution to marxism, and in particular with his contribution to Marx's philosophy of the proletariat, emphasis is bound to be placed upon the social circumstances that shaped the particular features of his thought in this respect. This should not be taken to exclude the important biographical details or psychological characteristics that in one way or another influenced Lukács' political development.[1] Indeed it is difficult to draw a hard and fast line of distinction between individual biography and social influence; the two are bound together almost by definition, biography being the account of the travels of the individual through his or her social environment, in which particular individual circumstances and general social situation intermingle to beget a personal biography with significance beyond the individual in question.

Problems occur, however, when an individual brings about in him or herself a change of orientation or perspective that appears to indicate a rupture with previous stages of his or her thought. Specifically with regard to Lukács, this problem confronts us at the outset, in our initial delineation of his 'road to Marx', since Lukács' own account of his process of evolution casts a shadow upon the intellectual environment in which he was tutored into prominence. I have already had cause to discuss the relative merits of the continuity–discontinuity controversy with regard to Marx; with Lukács too the debate is equally important and hence open to dispute, with the added complication of Lukács' own contribution to the controversy.

Lukács committed himself to communism at the relatively late age of thirty-three when, in December 1918, he joined the month-old Hungarian Communist Party (HCP). Many factors undoubtedly played a part in his decision: his fascination with Russian culture (above all with Feodor Dostoevsky), the inspiration of the Russian Revolution and of his wife Yelena Grabenko; the collapse of the Hapsburg Empire and the apparent destruction of the old world order (with the consequent possibility of a radically new one) – these provided the historical context in which his decision was made. But what is of concern to us here is the sort of marxism Lukács was committing himself to, and this must be understood in the context of two fundamentally opposed intellectual currents out of and against which Lukács effected his road to Marx. I refer here to the new school of German sociology and the (primarily German) social democratic orthodoxy.

As we saw in the previous chapter, Lukács was never in the least attracted to social democratic orthodoxy, nor did he have any links with or participation in social democratic politics. Social democratic orthodoxy is thus of interest as a politico-philosophic backdrop against which Lukács developed his own interpretation of marxism. Lukács' intellectual roots in the period immediately prior to his conversion to marxism were sunk in the radical pessimism of German philosophy, and in particular in the new school of German sociological thought. Here, though, we encounter the problem I mentioned above, for an examination of the influence of the school of German sociology upon Lukács' thought must also take into account the views of perhaps the staunchest critic of that school: Lukács himself, who in 1954 in his book *The Destruction of Reason* [2] portrayed such thinkers as Ferdinand Tönnies, Georg Simmel and Max Weber – and also, by implication, his own early views – as part of the intellectual antecedency of fascism. How can we reconcile our claim that the influence of German sociology led Lukács to marxism with Lukács' own claim that it led to fascism?

The most obvious way of doing this is by accepting the view of Lukács' friends and colleagues of the time: that Lukács' adoption of marxism in 1918 marked a distinct and to them inexplicable break from his previous mode of thought and was an act of conversion almost religious in its effect.[3] Second, there is the view that Lukács' decision to join the HCP was analogous to Kierkegaard's 'leap of faith', that his wager upon communism flowed from his ethical conception of personal sacrifice and salvation, in which communism served as merely the vehicle in which this essentially religious and individual act could be performed.[4] In such a view Lukács' conversion to marxism is a misnomer, for this only truly came about when Lukács was able to free himself from these idealistic tendencies. This is essentially the view of the later Lukács: the influence of German sociology led him to marxism by way of its cultural critique of capitalist society, while at the same time directing him away from the vulgarized version of marxism then practised by international social democracy, but it gave to his understanding of marxism a particular distortion that he was later to discard some time after 1924.[5] Third is the view I shall argue, which is that Lukács' indebtedness to German sociology persisted through his career as a marxist, and was abandoned only at that point where Lukács also abandoned that which made his own marxist writing valuable and distinctive. Lukács' final step towards marxism is thus far less radical than his friends at the time realized and was rooted in an intellectual and political environment that affected a whole layer of intellectuals (albeit in different ways), of which Lukács is a prominent and significant example.

The Influence of German Sociology

In the preface to *The Theory of the Novel* Lukács refers to his 'youthful enthusiasm for the work of Dilthey, Simmel and Max Weber',[6] and elsewhere he notes how he came to see Marx 'through spectacles tinted by Simmel and Max Weber'.[7] His attraction to such writers was based upon their critical attitude towards the 'rationalism of the positivists', (though he was later to regard this as the prelude to a lapse into irrationalism and an apologia for German backwardness). This 'romantic anti-capitalism' was guided by the formulation of Fichte in that philosopher's reference to the 'age of absolute sinfulness' but was also determined, says Lukács, by an ethically tinged pessimism.

Distrust of the social developments brought about by capitalistic industrialization in Germany led many thinkers, in different ways, to offer a critique of such developments in terms of its inhumanity, its corrosive effect upon the human psyche and the social character of the human community that it undermined. For all such writers the undermining of *Gemeinschaft*, by means of rational calculability expressed through the pervasiveness of money, was a profoundly unsettling experience, but it was also characteristic of them that they reacted by cultivating towards it an attitude of pessimistic resignation.

From this common origin – the romantic anti-capitalism of early German sociology – two political and sociological currents developed. The first is that of sociology proper; the second is that variety of marxism developed by Lukács. What they had in common – a critical analysis of capitalistic development in terms of its cultural effects – determined their intellectual opponents (principally, the positivists of sociology and socialism), while the diverse political consequences of such views, and in particular their attitude towards marxism, determined their attitude to each other.

Lukács, for example, as we shall soon see, developed a version of marxism that incorporated or made use of many of the themes first developed by Tönnies, Weber and Simmel. This put him into direct conflict with the established consensus of social democracy and the rapidly developing communist orthodoxy, whose social theories tended to owe more to the Darwinian derivatives of Comte and Spencer than to the mandarins of Wilhelmine Germany. Weber could not so easily throw off the claim of orthodoxy made by German social democracy, so his rejection of marxism accompanied his rejection of the positivist vulgarizations of Kautsky *et al.*, though his hostility towards the political strategy followed by Lukács' German comrades also played an important part in this. Weber could muster no enthusiasm for any of those who claimed to speak for marxism – including Lukács. In his famous lecture of 1919, 'Politics as a Vocation', Weber was doubtlessly referring to his former student when he condemned the 'sterile excitation'[8] of revolutionaries who based their politics on the demands of the soul rather than the head, and after the experience of the Hungarian Commune of that year he wrote to Lukács: 'My dear friend, we are naturally separated by our political views. I am absolutely convinced that these experiments will only have one effect: to discredit socialism for the coming 100 years.'[9]

This critique of what was then 'actually existing socialism' signified the differences between sociology and Lukács' marxism. For while Lukács incorporated into marxism certain of the theses characteristic of German sociology, challenging and transforming both sociological thought and marxist orthodoxy, the German sociologists remained critical insiders to the worlds of Wilhelmine Germany and the Weimar Republic. The fate of these worlds provided the excuse for Lukács' later critique.

Lukács' Critique of German Sociology

Lukács' account of the origins of sociology at the turn of the century goes as follows. What made its emergence possible, and what gave it more than a local significance, was the changed needs of bourgeois ideology in the epoch of imperialism. Whereas the expansionary stage of capitalist development in the middle and late nineteenth century to some extent justified the evolutionist and progressive certainties of Comte and Spencer, with the coming of the twentieth century and of imperialist rivalries and political turmoil, uncertainty returned and the naturalistic analogies of economic development that had displaced the contradictory or conflictual character of social being were no longer adequate to explain the bourgeois world to itself. Social science was in need of reformulation, yet the political turmoil of the imperialist epoch made this not merely difficult and dangerous but also unwelcome to bourgeois interests. How to explain a world seemingly falling apart (or at least falling out), whose convulsions threatened to expose the contradictions upon which it lay and to reveal the social relations that made its replacement necessary and desirable? For the bourgeois the solution was to replace social science with social apologetics, but social apologetics on a new basis: hence the emergence of 'vulgar economics' and of sociology.

In the nineteenth century, Marx had examined how classical political economy had given way to vulgar political economy as the emergence of the proletariat as a powerful political force had driven a wedge between the scientific and ideological aspects of political economy, extinguishing the former because it was now in conflict with the ideological expectations and wishes of the bourgeosie.[10] This saw the transformation of political economy from a science to an ideology by means of its changed appreciation of the realities of class society, and in particular the nature of value.

At the turn of the twentieth century, a new view was called forth, one in which the economic problem was solved, or more accurately repressed, by redefining economics so that class relations were written off the agenda and passed over to the new 'science' of sociology, which in turn naturalized the alienated characteristics of the bourgeois world. Hence the birth of the two new sciences, marginal economics and sociology.[11]

This task was especially important, and indeed crucial, to fin-de-siècle Germany, for three reasons. First, as Marx had long ago noted,[12] Germany lacked any scientific economics; this made the transformation easy (because it encountered no entrenched resistance) and also necessary (to fill the gap brought about by the late nineteenth-century spurt of industrialization). Second, Germany possessed a strong current of socialism as a movement and as an influential body of ideas; this made the change desirable (to counter and undermine this influence) and particular (in the sense that it was forced to address itself directly to the issues raised by that movement).[13] And third, because Germany lacked any bourgeois-democratic revolutionary tradition this made possible the development of a dynamic sociology critical of capitalist development, substantial in terms of the issues with which it dealt yet pessimistic in terms of the possibility of resolving these issues.

The trick was turned, argues Lukács, by means of a further development in the intellectual division of labour. A new form of 'anti-marxist polemics was needed'. This was founded on the one hand by the emergence of the Austrian school of (marginal) economics, which removed from economics its concrete basis in real life and instead gave to it the less substantial basis of radical subjectivism, of psychology; and on the other by the emergence of sociology as a social doctrine that concerned itself with the issues previously the concern of political economy but now abandoned by it.

Lukács' critique of this latter school has been severely criticized for its somewhat doctrinaire attitude to social thought – the destruction of Lukács' reason, Adorno termed it[14] – and certainly the one-sided account of the German sociologists and the way in which Lukács weaves the multiple threads of sociological and philosophical thought into a single cable attached to the future Third Reich are questionable (to say the least). Moreover, the dogmatic rigidity of his enlightenment–rationalist version of marxism owes some affinity to the nineteenth-century positivism and rationalism against which romanticism and even irrationalism were partly justified responses. But equally, his analysis of the social role and importance of this new school of thought is persuasive despite its lack of subtlety, for the emergence of these schools certainly owed something to the intellectual climate at the turn of the century, a climate that was significantly different to the one two decades earlier.

The essential thrust of Lukács' argument in *The Destruction of Reason* is that in their common adoption of forms of thought derived from irrationalism, the German sociologists, together with their philosophical counterparts, created the necessary intellectual environment in which fascism could thrive and eventually come to power. By undermining belief in, and hence commitment to, such enlightenment values as reason, progress and humanity, irrationalism gave the unrestrained will an easy road to power.

Lukács thus holds the philosophical views of those of whom he disapproves as responsible for the political consequences of their attempted realization in fascism. As we shall see, this matter is as much political as it is philosophical, in that the resistance to the 'ideals of 1789' drew not only upon the German romanticist tradition but most vitally upon the more mundane experience of the supposed embodiment of those ideals in the Weimar Republic. But Lukács' understanding of fascism was not primarily historical or political; still less was it sociological. Rather, *The Destruction of Reason* was a philosophical tract that highlighted and even stressed the intellectual antecedents of the ascendancy of fascism. This might seem a somewhat perverse approach for a marxist, but Lukács' mode of operation reveals significant aspects of his interpretation of marxism, even though we might wish to question some of the political judgements he passes.

What combination of personal and political factors led Lukács to this approach? To begin with, Lukács was himself a legitimate part of the German philosophical tradition, despite his Hungarian nationality. We know from Michael Lowy's account[15] that Hungary's backwardness expressed itself in intellectual terms in a concern with and contribution to German traditions; we also know that Lukács himself from an early age concerned himself with German culture and literary life: he wrote in German and read German authors.[16] The triumph of fascism in the land of Goethe and Beethoven has been a source of rumination since 1933, and in Lukács' case the defeat of liberalism (and communism) was regarded as in no small way a self-inflicted defeat. On the one hand the sectarian agitation of the communists had alienated social democrats and liberals, and thus fatally divided the forces capable of opposing fascism;[17] on the other, the irrationalist impulse of the German intelligentsia had disarmed its ability to confront or even to resist the politically irrational appeals of the nazis to the mythical German *volk* and its claim to be constructing a new Germanic community.

Lukács thus wages a battle on two fronts: against revolutionary sectarianism (and for a version of the popular front); and against philosophical irrationalism – though these might both be said to be battles for reason and realism in (respectively) politics and philosophy. It is not the case that Lukács is unaware of the political mediations that are necessary for philosophical thought to engage with reality. But he chooses to concern himself with the philosophical implications of Germany's road to fascism for three main reasons. First, he was better qualified to assess the philosophical background to fascism than he was the political arena, which by that time he had virtually abandoned, regarding himself as incompetent in that area.[18] Second, his concern with the role of consciousness as the mediator between history and reason is a central theme running through all his writings. Third, because of his precarious political foothold in the international communist movement, any attempt to assess the political reasons for the rise of fascism could hardly fail to bring him into conflict with one or other of the political lines of the Comintern. As he was later to express it, his participation in the struggle against fascism was bought at the expense of political clarity. This was of course how Lukács justified his silence on the sectarian and bureaucratic policies of Stalin, preferring to remain an "internal" critic.[19] For these reasons I believe we are justified in following Lukács' philosophical critique of fascism's precursors. But the question then remains: is Lukács justified in the actual connections he draws between philosophical irrationalism and political fascism? And how does he justify this connection?

It cannot be based upon the personal circumstances of the writers he subjects to criticism, for despite the use made of their writings – or at least of their reputation – by the fascists, rare indeed were the actual participants in fascist politics (Werner Sombart and Martin Heidegger being the main exceptions).[20] With the possible exception of Sombart, none supported the declared aim of the fascists to reconstruct *Gemeinschaft* in the form of the German Reich but, equally, there was no common point of opposition to fascism either. The triumph of *Gesellschaft* was resented, yet for all that perceived as inevitable. As a result the more grandiose claims of the fascists were neither supported nor opposed.

At one point, however, political unanimity did emerge: on the outbreak of hostilities in August 1914. Indeed, intellectuals throughout Europe greeted the war with undisguised jubilation. This was not simply a case of patriotism, however. It was not the desire for war as a means of preserving, or serving, existing social and political arrangements against foreign aggression, notwithstanding the attempts of the politicians to justify it as such to the general populace. No, this was an enthusiasm for war that signified the possibility of changing, of improving these entities, of redeeming their unacceptable basis in sin, and reconstructing anew a human community based upon the individual made glorious again through the heroism of war. The healing of a divided community: this was what the war promised and what attracted intellectuals to it. 'It came as a relief', said Thomas Mann, from a 'horrible world' that 'crawled with spiritual vermin';[21] it promised, in the words of Max Scheler, 'a quest for unity and community in a pluralistic society' by way of a return to the 'organic roots of human existence'.[22] Such sentiments, while especially prevalent in Germany, for reasons I shall discuss below, were to be found throughout Europe. Vera Brittain wrote: 'Those who are old and think this war so terrible do not know what it means to us who are young',[23] while Henri Bergson expected from it the moral regeneration of Europe; Freud responded to it with youthful enthusiasm: 'Life has in truth become interesting again.'[24]

This Europe-wide sentiment took on a particularly virulent form in Germany for two interrelated reasons. First, its recently acquired political unity had not yet given either its population or its leaders a sense of security in their national identity. German nationhood was still something asserted rather than experienced or lived; it was something spiritual or idealistic rather than real and material. And second, it rested on fragile foundations: weak, backward, and isolated, it perceived itself as under siege from the more self-confident aggrandizements of the western powers whose success appeared to rest on their accomplished unity between material and spiritual conditions. For Germany this unity was impossible because the spiritual conditions of German thought rested not upon commercialism and the money-centred forms of life of bourgeois society, but upon the idealistic elements of pre-capitalist social relations. Indeed, it saw these latter undermined and threatened by the burgeoning expansion of industrialization which spread to Germany from the west.

In Germany then, disenchantment with the world was more complete than elsewhere. This also contained the possibility of expressing itself in a nationalist form. That it came to take this form at the outbreak of war should not lead us to simply dismiss the anti-capitalist romanticism as prototypical fascism,[25] for it registered a very real disillusion with the fruits of progress, and whatever its conservative and nationalist implications other developments were possible – indeed, many of those individuals associated with it could muster nothing but scorn for its vulgarization at the hands of the politicians.[26] Acquiescence and resignation in the face of a burgeoning *Gesellschaft* were far more common than willing participation. Lukács rests his case rather upon a more general political orientation shared by these groups of writers, of which fascism was merely the historical, and logical, outcome, given Germany's position in the world – on their common support for imperialist politics. But this was itself the consequence of Germany's relative political and economic backwardness.

Lukács is to some extent justified in his line of attack, in the sense that the essentially German character of the view of the world of those writers he is attacking is without doubt. This led them to a common orientation against the consequences of capitalist industrialization (a sentiment, incidentally, largely shared by Lukács); it also led them to support for Germany's war aims in 1914 and to a rejection of the humiliations of the Treaty of Versailles.[27] It is this latter position that is of course rejected by Lukács, and which he holds as the first step towards their accommodation with fascism. It is necessary, however, to distinguish these political positions, since the latter position is in reality – if not according to the myths manufactured by fascism's ideologues – in contradiction to the former. Germany's imperialist war aims were not merely a response to the aggressive expansionism of the west, but were also the means by which Germany's own economic expansion could continue, albeit in the name of the German *volk*.

Before I go on to examine Lukács' relationship to this school of thought, it is necessary first to note how the conditions that led to this romantic revolt led even the most enlightened representatives of Germany's middle class to support for Germany's world uniqueness and for its participation in the war. This is important because it is this connection that the later Lukács takes such trouble to establish, and to which his own example serves as a reply. Lukács illustrates his point by reference to Max Weber's political views at that time, an account of which is provided in Marianne Weber's biography of her husband.[28] In the negotiations that took place between the Entente allies at Versailles as they sought to construct the treaty the defeated Germany would be brought to sign, it emerged that they were to demand the extradition of army leaders, statesmen and the Kaiser, so as to put on trial those accused of war crimes. While at first Weber defended the direction of the war under the military dictatorship of Ludendorff and Hindenburg against what he termed the 'inappropriate yardsticks' of such a political trial,[29] he eventually came to the view that as a means of salvaging the honour of the nation (and of preserving the officer corps), Ludendorff, the Chief of Staff, should surrender himself to the allies. Indeed, Weber went to visit Ludendorff in an attempt to persuade him to make this sacrifice, and on this visit there took place an interview that touched on the meaning of democracy which is instructive in the way it illuminates how political developments at the time united in a common distortion of democracy the most widely differing political standpoints.

Weber begins his conversation by expressing his disgust at the 'direct democracy' of workers' and soldiers' councils set up by the November revolution. Ludendorff then asks him what is his idea of democracy. Weber replies: '[i]n a democracy the people choose a leader whom they trust. Then the chosen man says, "Now shut your mouths and obey me. The people and the parties are no longer free to interfere in the leader's business"'. Ludendorff then replies in a manner any general might: 'I could like such a democracy.'[30] Thomas Mann, too, was hardly illiberal in his views, yet he could write of the war that:

> it seems to me now, as if the present war...had already been waged in the purely spiritual world; as if the German spirit had already risen

> up against modern ideas, western ideas, the ideas of the eighteenth century...against enlightenment and dissolution, civilization and disintegration; as if it were in Kant that the social, the supporting, constructing, organizing German spirit had risen up against western civilization.[31]

The examples of Weber and Mann are of course not the worst that could be produced to demonstrate the unanimity of support among German intellectuals for their country's participation in the war.[32] This is perhaps why Lukács' example is so persuasive in showing how even for Weber, Germany's political circumstances could make of democratism a 'bonapartist Caesarism', the means through which imperialist policy was to be implemented. Similarly, Thomas Mann was to come to the aid of the fatherland threatened with dismantling by the ambassadors and statesmen of western civilization. In his work *Reflections of a Non-political Man* Mann reasserts against the francophile sympathies of (among others) his brother Heinrich the positive characteristics of German life that maintained some form of community, albeit hierarchical, dependent and oppressive, against the vulgar materialism and crude egalitarianism of western societies.

What lay behind such expressions of patriotism was not so much a simple defence of German conditions but a fear that Germany too was headed for the same destination as France and, especially, England, that the war was Germany's last opportunity to resist this encroachment of materialism and positivism. The attempt to summon up German spirituality in support of the war was also an attempt to summon resistance to the internal enemy of German ideas, cultural values and spiritual community which lay in the urban cities and political parties, and stressed materialism and equality as it undermined national unity. It is easy to see how such sentiments could become pro-fascist and also why they were so attractive to German intellectuals.[33]

Much later Lukács was to summarize his own political position at the outbreak of the war. In so doing he demonstrates the common point of origin between himself and the virtually unanimous intellectual climate at the time, as well as indicating the point of divergence. This is what he wrote in his 1962 preface to *The Theory of the Novel*:

> When I tried at this time to put my emotional attitude into conscious terms, I arrived at more or less the following formulation: the Central Powers would probably defeat Russia; this might lead to the downfall of Tsarism; I had no objection to that. There was also some probability that the West would defeat Germany; if this led

> to the downfall of the Hohenzollerns and the Hapsburgs, I was once again in favour. But then the question arose: who was to save us from Western Civilization?[34]

Lukács thus shared a general dissatisfaction with the existing state of affairs, but he was not about to seek the desire for spiritual renewal and regeneration of a sick culture in the triumph of any of the war participants, nor indeed in the act of war itself. War was for him merely a form of 'concentrated capitalism driven to the extreme'.[35] Moreover, due in part to his Hungarian origin, he was impervious to the appeals of Germanity: his 'opposition to the barbarity of capitalism', as he put it, 'allowed no room for any sympathy such as felt by Thomas Mann for the "German wretchedness" or its surviving features in the present'.[36] At this point his break with his former mentors was virtually complete.

Lukács did not, however, merely refuse to side with any of the pro-war factions, he also looked elsewhere for the community that his former teachers looked for in and through the war. His discovery of the revolutionary romanticism of Russia – and in particular of Russian terrorism – in the person of his wife Yelena Grabenko and through the novels of Dostoevsky, led him to an alternative perspective, to a different way of achieving cultural renewal, eventually to culminate in his affiliation to marxism, to membership of the Communist Party and to the philosophy of the proletariat.

Lukács' own path of development and changed political perspective is, then, in itself a reply to his own later criticism that the travail of romantic anti-capitalism could have only one destination: support for imperialist politics. That this was the most common result is beyond doubt, and nor is this particularly surprising, but it was not the only one or the most consistent. Indeed, Lukács' consistency was actually encouraged by his refusal to follow his mentors into enthusiasm for the war; in so far as the war enthusiasm of the masses hardly survived a week or two in the trenches (it persisted longer, of course, among those safely removed from the theatre of war itself), he was able to avoid the collapse into guilt and shame suffered by those who lived to see the realities of the conflict puncture the romantic myths at first associated with it. At this stage, then, Lukács rejected any 'reconciliation with reality': his desired community was more transcendent and spiritual than real and material. It was the *idea* of Russia and not the reality that attracted him.

It is important in the context of Lukács' later criticisms of this current of thought to bear in mind that his own understanding of the bourgeois world, and indeed even his path to marxism, were to some considerable extent a product of his own immersion in such schools of thought and that his later criticisms were in part, and by implication, self-criticisms. It will be the task of the remainder of this chapter to assess the influence of this school on Lukács and also to judge from what standpoint his self-criticisms were based.

Lukács' Marxism

Lukács' case against German sociology is based upon the link he perceives between its emergence and the realignment of bourgeois ideology made necessary by the development of imperialism: apologists of bourgeois society could no longer seek refuge in the naturalist certainties of positivism and progress, but were obliged to take account of those criticisms of capitalist development that had hitherto been dismissed as incidental to its essentially progressive character. Such an ideology signified the raising to self-consciousness of bourgeois decadence. The social world now demonstrated for all to see its basis in turmoil and inequality; its historically progressive character was brought into question by its regressive consequences and by the inability to derive from it any legitimate hope for future improvement. It was thus necessary to accommodate within the new bourgeois ideology elements of a social critique that was previously the province of marxist critics of society, but to invest in it an account of the human condition as such. Thus the dark side of human existence was no longer denied, but was given an ahistorical character: it was the manifestation of humankind's fate, not the product of specific and historical social relations.

This realignment not only gave to bourgeois ideology a new social relevance, it also provided a bridgehead within the marxist movement itself; it gave to those social critics who had until now been obliged to find a refuge within the labour movement a new outlet where they could express misgivings about modern society without the requirement that they make that critique practical.[37] Vulgar marxism thus shares with bourgeois ideology a common understanding of the world in that it mistakes 'purely historical categories, moreover categories relevant only to capitalist society, for eternally valid ones',[38] but it also plays an undermining role within the movement itself.

This change in bourgeois ideology was, moreover, especially important in Germany, which combined sharp conflict between the classes with a formerly backward but now rapidly developing capitalist economy. The 'law of uneven development' gave to Germany a highly charged political atmosphere in which rapid industrialization brought with it social changes unpalatable not only to the working classes most affected by it, but also to the intelligentsia who recorded its rise to power (and who also saw its own social prestige undermined by the impersonal mores of the money economy) and even to the pre-capitalist ruling circles apprehensive as to its consequences.

Germany thus witnessed the recreation of Romanticism. As Michael Lowy indicates, however,[39] this was a romanticism of a new type; it differed significantly from previous forms which had either sought the recreation of medieval social structures or had negatively opposed the fruits of the French Revolution and the ideals of 1789. This was a romanticism typified above all by its pessimistic acceptance of the necessity of capitalism's triumph: it accepts as fate the triumph of (western) *Zivilization* over (German) *Kultur*. This pessimism does enable it to escape the reactionary or utopian politics that usually accompanies attempts to reconstruct the idealized communality of pre-bourgeois society, yet also yields a political quietism that affects not only the romantic writers themselves but is critical of political activism per se. This is because, as Lukács repeats again and again, it mistakes the historically specific description of the modern world for a metaphysical or ontological account of the human condition.

This generally critical account of modern civilization need not, however, be limited to the political strategy of stoic acceptance or nostalgic activism. There remains the possibility of drawing out the concrete historical and social conditions that give rise to this age of absolute sinfulness and seeking the abolition of these, so that human social relationships may reestablish themselves on a new basis. This was the strategy formulated by the early Lukács and which determined first his membership of the Hungarian Communist Party, his commitment to the international communist movement and later, albeit on a somewhat different basis, his support for socialism in one country.

The pervasively restrictive consequences of the *Kultur–Zivilization* contrast may be illustrated by reference to the major political conflicts within Germany in the first three decades of the twentieth century. The typification of the imperialist conflict in terms of a contrast between *Kultur* and *Zivilization*, for example, merged with nationalism to justify – and even to glorify – Germany's uniqueness as a counter to the expansionary forces of western capitalism and its participation in the war that followed. Similarly, the democracy of Weimar was perceived by many Germans as largely an imposition upon their country of the alien values of those responsible for its war-time defeat (witness the stabin-the-back myth), while the turmoil and decadence associated with it gave sustenance to those determined to restore national pride and unity through the rejection of the overrated and inappropriate ideals of western democracy.

As we shall see, Lukács, though influenced by this debate, gave to it (or rather to its solution) a particular ambience that also signified a rejuvenation of a marxism hitherto accepted by marxists and non-marxists alike as the embodiment of modernization. Lukács' commitment to marxism and his own understanding of it can thus only be fully appreciated in terms of this polar typification that has its origins in German sociology, and in particular in Tönnies' *Gemeinschaft und Gesellschaft*.[40] The themes developed in that book explain to no little extent the nature of Lukács' commitment to marxism and of what he hoped to find as a result of his partisanship with respect to it. Consequently, it is to that book that we must turn as the first stage in our account of the influence of German sociological thought upon Lukács' variant of marxism.[41]

Influences: Ferdinand Tönnies and Communality

First published in 1887, *Gemeinschaft und Gesellschaft* initially made no impact upon the academic world until the second edition twenty-five years later (in 1912), and subsequent editions, established the reputation of Tönnies and the influence of his book. How is this delay to be explained?

Partly perhaps, as the book's English translator notes, by its unique, difficult, old German diction.[42] Partly also by its combination of German philosophical idealism and economic and legal history (hardly an inspiring combination!). Raymond Aron[43] explains it by the absence of any German academic sociology prior to the later date (Weber, for example, held a chair in political economy and not sociology),[44] but this is another way of drawing attention to the main explanation, which lies in the changed social and intellectual circumstances between the first and second editions, that is between 1887 and 1912; changes that had established Germany as a world power as they had undermined the traditional social relationships that persisted there. Traditional ways of life had been undermined and transformed: this was the underlying argument presented by Tönnies in his book, but while such a transformation was perhaps evident from an early stage in the rural culture of Schleswig-Holstein where the book was composed, by 1912 even the towns and cities could not but be aware of the nature and extent of that change and of the uncertainties that came with it. The money culture that was regarded by many – especially intellectuals – as an alien import from the west was now increasingly prevalent in German life and was evidenced in literary form by the publication in rapid succession of Simmel's *Philosophy of Money* (1900), Thomas Mann's *Buddenbrooks* (1901), Werner Sombart's *Modern Capitalism* (1902), Max Weber's *The Protestant Ethic and the Spirit of Capitalism* (1904). All these works signified a new awareness of the conditions of German economic development and a dissatisfaction with its cultural effects.

In *Gemeinschaft und Gesellschaft* Tönnies contrasts two forms of society, two ways in which individuals enter into relationships that constitute society. In *Gemeinschaft*, or community, such relationships are based upon 'mutual possession and enjoyment and also possession of and enjoyment of common goods',[45] while exchange plays little or no part in economic and social life. Relationships are based upon understanding, not contract, an understanding derived from the 'reciprocal, bonding sentiment...that represents the special social force and sympathy which keeps human beings together as members of a totality'.[46] The real foundation of such a totality is the close proximity of human contacts: 'the closeness of blood relationship and mixture of blood...physical proximity...and intellectual proximity'.[47] Here economic exchange is confined to the form of barter, which is 'fostered by manifold bonds of friendship and kinship...organically maintained, fed, and fostered by a common will'.[48]

In *Gesellschaft*, or society, by contrast, this sense of familiarity is replaced by a feeling of estrangement: 'One goes into Gesellschaft as one goes into a strange country',[49] Tönnies writes; society is an artificial construction

> which superficially resembles the Gemeinschaft in so far as the individuals peacefully live and dwell together. However, in the Gemeinschaft they remain essentially united in spite of all separating factors, whereas in the Gesellschaft they are essentially separated in spite of all uniting factors.[50]

In such a world each individual is 'by himself and isolated, and there exists a condition of tension against all others'.[51] Indeed Tönnies[52] makes clear the analogy he perceives between Hobbes' idea of the state of nature as the war of all against all, where the only constraint upon individuals is the socially reinforced obligation of contract, and the conditions of modern society.

In the first half of the book Tönnies describes the economic forms of life in the two forms of society: in *Gemeinschaft* community is essentially organic, while in *Gesellschaft* society is imposed upon autonomous individuals. In this latter the law of value distributes economic rewards behind the backs of the immediate producers, who build society only as a by-product of their central aim of furthering their immediate interests. The value form, expressed through money, imposes upon individuals a social coercion that appears impersonal and transcendent, and that distributes rewards and penalties apparently indiscriminately. *Gesellschaft* reproduces and circulates its own idea by the issue of paper money; this allows the social aggregate to form itself alongside the independence and autonomy of individuals:

> Gesellschaft...is to be understood as a multitude of natural and artificial individuals, the wills and spheres of whom are in many relations with and to one another, and remain nevertheless independent of one another and devoid of mutual familiar relationships.[53]

In the second part of his book Tönnies goes on to examine the consequences for the human will of the replacement of one form of life, *Gemeinschaft*, by another, *Gesellschaft*, and here he contrasts natural will (*Naturwille*), which carries the conditions for *Gemeinschaft*, with rational will (*Kurwille*), which develops *Gesellschaft*.[54] Work itself is also subject to change. It belongs to the natural will so long as it is done not with aversion and not desired solely on account of the end for which it is done; *Gemeinschaft* gives to work 'art...style, dignity and charm; and a rank in its order, denoted as a calling and an honor'.[55] In *Gesellschaft* however, work is divested of all these human attributes by the opposition between means and ends: work can now only fulfil the former. Merchants are here the embodiment of *Gesellschaft*: in their very speech rational will is directly expressed, in that their words are calculated for their effect and not for their truth or meaning. Rational calculation divested of all human meaning is the rule of the rational will – what works and triumphs are all that counts. Truth and human feeling must take a back seat in this world of pragmatic efficiency or, worse, they become degraded by the uses to which they are put. The rugged individual of *Gesellschaft*, says Tönnies, 'conducts himself toward all others as a merchant and toward himself as a hedonist'.[56] The contrast between *Gemeinschaft* and *Gesellschaft* is that of life to death: '[i]n contrast to Gemeinschaft, Gesellschaft...is transitory and superficial. Accordingly, Gemeinschaft...should be understood as a living organism, Gesellschaft as a mechanical aggregate and artifact'.[57] The corresponding contrast between the man (or perhaps the woman) of *Gemeinschaft* and the man of *Gesellschaft* is that of burgher and merchant, the same distinction drawn in Thomas Mann's novel *Buddenbrooks* between Thomas Buddenbrook and Hermann Hagenstrom (in which, it should be remembered, the sympathetic pathos of the author is reserved for the benefit of the former alone).

There are, however, difficulties with the approach exemplified by Tönnies' handling of the problem. The ideal-type constructions of *Gesellschaft* and *Gemeinschaft* are not intended to be simple descriptions of existing realities but tools of analysis, ideal types, against which reality is to be measured, yet it is difficult to resist the temptation to condemn reality simply for failing to measure up to this inappropriate measure. As Lukács points out in *The Destruction of Reason,* the contrast between *Gemeinschaft* and *Gesellschaft* is exaggerated by idealizing the pre-bourgeois community as it subjects bourgeois society to a critique of its life-destroying capacities. Tönnies' cultural critique 'emphasized the problematic, negative features of capitalist culture',[58] but did so in such a way that the mechanical separation of civilization and culture naturalized and thus made eternal the triumph of capitalist civilization. No society, Lukács argued in 1954, not even socialist society, could fulfil the yearning for *Gemeinschaft* if that concept is drawn in respect of the false antithesis between civilization and culture. The cultural tapesty of the past may indeed be worthy of veneration, but was itself part of humankind's progress towards civilization: the one cannot survive without the other. To demand that culture may be recreated despite the advances of civilization is 'backward looking' and 'anti-progressive'; it is to treat the problem undialectically; it is to idealize the past uncritically as the present is treated as an inadequate reflection of this distorted picture.

We might recall at this point Marx's description of feudal socialism, which he denounces for its 'total incapacity to comprehend the march of modern history'[59] that leads it to condemn the bourgeois regime from the wrong vantage point, not so much for creating a proletariat as for creating 'a revolutionary proletariat'.[60] There are indeed echoes of this approach in Tönnies, who bemoans the transformation of the 'common people' into a 'proletariat' that learns 'to think and become conscious of the conditions under which they are chained to the labour market. From such knowledge decisions and attempts to break these chains originate'[61] and would culminate in 'the end of Gesellschaft'[62] and indeed of culture itself, since their knowledge at first merely integrates them into the way of thinking characteristic of *Gesellschaft.* The common people become, just as do the educated classes and the capitalists, 'active members of the Gesellschaft', sharing 'the same attitude of mind and action'. Only their desire to share the ownership of capital interrupts the dynamic of *Gesellschaft*, against this demand *Gesellschaft* confronts an external barrier. Tönnies is thus critical of the corruption of the common people by bourgeois society and of their transformation into a rationally calculating proletariat that threatens *Gesellschaft* because rational calculation of its economic demands interrupts the growth of production and trade.

Nevertheless, despite the political implications of Tönnies' work and in particular his implicit belief in the ineluctability of capitalism, his foundational critique of capitalism is not thereby invalidated, for two reasons. First, the criticism of the inability of capitalism to create any sense of community, and the explanation of this failure developed by German sociology, penetrate to the very essence of bourgeois society; second, this itself leads to the attempt to recreate that sense of community, not necessarily through reaction or nostalgia but through the political movement that is itself – in part at least – a product of resistance to that absence of community.

German sociology, and the work of Tönnies, its founder, thus provide two key themes to Lukács' reconstruction of marxism: its critique of capitalism in terms of its effect upon the human personality and the dehumanization of social relations; and its desire to reconstitute human relations anew on a communal basis. This was not quite the position of Tönnies himself. He did not wish to ally himself with *Gemeinschaft* against *Gesellschaft*. Whilst he was very critical of the type of world created by *Gesellschaft*, he did not regard the desire to reconstruct *Gemeinschaft* as at all feasible. Rather, these were two different stages of social development – youth and maturity. The desire to relive youth was as impractical for society as it was for the individual. He was not, however, entirely pessimistic. Though the transformation of human culture into *Gesellschaft* and the state spells the doom of culture, this would only happen if 'none of its scattered seeds remain alive and again bring forth the essence and idea of Gemeinschaft, thus secretly fostering a new culture amidst the decaying one'.[63] This leaves open the question as to which social force and upon what basis such a resurrection will be based. Tönnies himself harboured great hopes for the co-operative and trade union movements, but more extreme attempts at reconstruction might claim some basis of fidelity to his hopes.

One such attempt cannot, however, stake such a claim. Tönnies was quite emphatic in his belief that the state could not be the means through which communality could be recreated, but was itself a constitutive aspect of *Gesellschaft*. It was the personification, alongside the market, par excellence of *Gesellschaft* and was thus part of the problem, not the solution to it.

To conclude this section then, we can see how Tönnies' cultural critique of capitalism, while it was based upon an ideal-typical counterposition of *Zivilization* and *Kultur* that had the consequence of formulating that critique in an ironic, detached and politically pessimistic form, nevertheless made possible a more radical critique because it was the expression of a general mood of disenchantment with the conditions of modern, bourgeois society. More than this, its nostalgic yearning for pre-capitalist *Gemeinschaft* was also the expression of a desire for communality against the atomistic individualism of bourgeois society. These themes are key features of Lukács' interpretation of marxism.

Influences: Georg Simmel and Alienation

The influence of Simmel upon the early Lukács is both more direct and acknowledged, and possibly for this reason the reaction against that influence by the later Lukács is more extreme. In an interview with Wolfgang Abendroth in 1967 Lukács commented that he did 'not at all regret today that I took my first lessons in social science from Simmel and Max Weber and not from Kautsky;[64] in his preface to *History and Class Consciousness* he describes how he was attracted to 'Marx the sociologist', whom he saw 'through spectacles tinged by Simmel and Max Weber'.[65] In 1918, in an article written on the occasion of Simmel's death, Lukács referred to his former teacher as 'the most important and interesting transitional phenomenon in the whole of modern philosophy'[66] and described *Philosophy of Money* as the foundation upon which the whole sociology of culture developed by Weber, Troeltsch, Sombart and others rested. We know that in an earlier period the author of *The Sociology of the Modern Drama* (1911) was deeply and explicitly indebted to Simmel's work – this point has been extensively covered in the literature.[67] What is of rather more concern to us is the influence of Simmel the sociologist upon Lukács the marxist. Once again, despite the evidence above, we must first assess the damning criticisms laid against Simmel in *The Destruction of Reason* – and implicitly against his influence upon the author's understanding of marxism.

It might be said that Lukács' early familiarity with Simmel's work explains his later contempt, which he expresses more forcibly than with respect to Tönnies. Perhaps also Simmel's political quietism influenced Lukács' later opinions, particularly since Simmel's death in 1918 denied him the opportunity afforded Tönnies – if that is quite the correct expression – to experience and possibly to oppose the rise of fascism. Nonetheless, Lukács has barely a kind word for Simmel, whose lapse into vitalism or the philosophy of life led him, says Lukács, to confront people with a 'pseudo-objective external life',[68] with life acting as a mediator between the two. Simmel rejected the knowability and existence of objective reality by denying that there was any objective reality independent of the subject. This led him to construct a form of radical relativism in which different forms of reality (art, science, religion, etc.) were experienced by individuals in their everyday lives as discrete entities. This undermining of scientific knowledge, or rather of the philosophical basis and possibility of scientific knowledge, 'encourages reactionary obscurantism'[69] in that it makes impossible any objective account of reality by splitting reality into different forms of life, each expressing a different attitude derived from human subjectivity and subject to no overall criteria of objective or scientific truth.

There are naturally flowing political consequences for this philosophical error, in that philosophical sanction is given to the existing state of affairs, not in the form of a direct apology but 'from the angle of the senselessness of the universe'.[70] We might observe many aspects of senselessness in the world, but without acknowledgement of the right of reason to judge and to condemn these, their existence and even their preservation are, by act of omission, justified and guaranteed. Life may be experienced as senseless, without meaning and insecure: experiences that are, to say the least, implicitly critical of their basis in social observation. Nonetheless, any critical acuteness – and no one could deny that Simmel was anything but critically acute – is dulled by the incapacity to perceive any alternative, the failure to exalt scientific reason as the standpoint against which to judge social phenomena and the acceptance of the fetish character of experience as part of the general fate of humankind. Lukács thus comes to describe Simmel as an aloof Nietzsche,[71] only not for him does the condemnation of Christianity and the Christian world lead to advocacy of the 'will to power'; instead, Simmel withdraws to a 'complacent cynicism',[72] a negative turning away from the world.

Again, though, we must ask: is this the only consequence of Simmel's views? Might it not be possible, and indeed invaluable, to historicize them? To make the social and historical connections that Simmel's philosophical position rules out of order? For if we seek to do this, other relevant questions also come into our view, together with possible answers to them. For example, the affinity between *History and Class Con-*

sciousness and Marx's theory of alienation is well known and widely discussed. But when we come to provide an account of Lukács' success in reconstructing Marx's theory of alienation from the latter's economic writings – an accomplishment quite beyond the orthodox interpreters of Marx since Engels – it is difficult to do so without invoking the influence of Simmel's *Philosophy of Money* and in particular the theory of alienation developed in the final chapter.[73]

In his preface to *Philosophy of Money*, Simmel states that his intention is to

> construct a new storey beneath historical materialism such...that the explanatory value of the incorporation of economic life into the causes of intellectual culture is preserved, while these economic forms themselves are recognized as the result of more profound valuations and currents of psychological or even metaphysical pre-conditions.[74]

Such burrowing is of course manifestly hostile to historical materialism. As Lukács remarks in 1954, by contesting the materialism of historical materialism, by separating the instances of cultural critique from their 'concrete historico-social inferences', the resulting raising to a 'universal cosmic order' of these processes robbed them of 'their concrete substance...as well as their revolutionary bite'.[75]

If we pursue this matter, not only do we acquire an understanding of Simmel's influence on the young Lukács but we can also discover the unfairness of his 1967 auto-criticisms, as well as establishing the basis for a criticism of Lukács' own later turn to ontology. For Simmel develops a theory of alienation based upon objectification: relations between people are projected into particular objects, the most important of which, because it is the most abstract and general, is money. Thus people become alienated from each other because their relationships are mediated through objects. Now, this is often taken to be the failure of *History and Class Consciousness*, that is, the failure to distinguish between objectification, the translation of human powers into particular objects, and the alienated form this activity takes under the historically specific conditions of capitalist social relations.[76] By following Hegel's own identification of alienation with objectification, the later Lukács goes on, this error was compounded just as it in turn guaranteed the book its success. The unmasking of alienation was 'in the air';[77] this fact gave *History and Class Consciousness* its audience and its influence. However, what was 'in the air' also was a desire to collapse social criticism into metaphysical pessimism. The problem of alienation 'became a central problem in the type of cultural criticism that undertook to scrutinise the condition of man in contemporary capitalism'.[78] But because such cultural criticism was undertaken beyond the purview of political economy, the consequence was a sublimation of a social critique into a philosophical problem, from sociology to ontology. In such a manner, social alienation became an eternal feature of the human condition.

The eternal feature of the human condition was objectification: on this point Hegel, Simmel, Marx and Lukács were in fundamental agreement. But while Hegel and Simmel were similar in equating this with alienation, the later Lukács greatly exaggerated, if not entirely distorted the tendency within *History and Class Consciousness* to follow this position, to equate objectification with its alienated character in capitalist society. Lukács is quite correct to indicate the neutral character of certain forms of objectification, or at least the possibility of objectification without alienation; to draw attention to the universal character of objectification as the process through which individuals externalize themselves to encompass the world. This takes on an alien character only in specific circumstances, when 'the objectified forms in society require functions that bring the essence of man into conflict with his existence',[79] and Lukács clearly thought that such a situation was specific to class societies, in particular to bourgeois society, and would disappear as they disappeared also.

Simmel, however, can find no way to break the objectification–alienation couplet, simply because, as we have seen, his specific intention was to invest his philosophy of the world with psychological or metaphysical foundations, to ontologize the economic forms of alienation. In the main body of *History and Class Consciousness*, Lukács specifically refers to this failure. In the first of only two direct references to Simmel, Lukács shows how even those (such as Simmel) who are concerned to illuminate the effects upon consciousness of reification (Lukács uses this word interchangeably with alienation) by demonstrating 'its humanly destructive consequences',[80] because they also seek to invest the concept with a profound philosophical content actually remain on the margins of the concept's existence in the 'real life process of capitalism'. He then goes on:

> Indeed, they divorce these empty manifestations from their real capitalist foundation and make them independent and permanent by regarding them as the timeless model of human relations in general. (This can be seen most clearly in Simmel's book *The Philosophy of Money*, a very interesting and perceptive work in matters of detail)...they do

> not go further than a description and their 'deepening' of the problem runs in circles around the eternal manifestation of reification.[81]

In other words Simmel reifies his own conception of reification: he makes of it an eternal ahistorical concept applicable to a society without history and without hope of improvement. This is a direct result of his failure to penetrate to the specificity of reification and the dehumanizing consequences of capitalist social relations. And this because Simmel is no socialist – indeed partly because he sees socialism itself (as did Tönnies) as another illustration of the tendency in the world of money to reduce all human qualitative characteristics to a quantitative, numerical equality. In an elitist theme common to this tradition of German sociology, Simmel unfavourably contrasts the concern of socialism with 'the degree of diffusion of desirable conditions and values' to Nietzsche's concern with 'the quality of mankind',[82] – no matter what isolated and aristocratic form this latter takes.[83]

But the point to emphasize here is that the same criticism levelled by the later Lukács against his own *History and Class Consciousness* is the same criticism made in that work against Simmel. This surely indicates that the identification of objectification with alienation is far from complete in that work, and that the 1923 Lukács *was* utilizing an historical concept of alienation. Consequently this later criticism is ill founded.[84]

As I have already indicated, Simmel's influence upon Lukács predated the latter's conversion to marxism at the end of 1918. It survived the abrupt nature of that conversion to affect the political outlook of the Deputy Commissar for Education in the Hungarian Soviet Republic, dictating his view, for example, that 'politics is merely a means, culture is the goal'[85] – by which he meant the reestablishment of human culture by means of the destruction of the reified or objective cultural practices and artefacts of modern society. But as Lukács' understanding of marxism was modified by his involvement and participation in politics, so his criticisms of this sociology of culture became more strident. The possibility of cultural renewal, the counterpart to the reconstruction of *Gemeinschaft*, appeared increasingly to the marxist Lukács a utopian illusion. First the Hungarian Soviet Republic suffered a severe and savage defeat at the hands of reaction, at least in part because the mass of the population proved inertly unresponsive to the enlightened dictats of Bela Kun and his supporters. And then came the wholesale poverty of post-revolutionary Russia and its consequent deradicalization of policy and practice (with the New Economic Policy). These factors could not but dampen down the enthusiasm of the most messianic sectarian. Lukács' first hint of disillusion (if this is quite the correct expression given his attitude to the supposed enlightened realism of 'socialism in one country') comes interestingly enough in an article entitled 'Art for Art's Sake and Proletarian Poetry', published in June 1926, in which he recognizes that the proletarian revolution had, at least initially, very little to contribute to the development of art and thus, by implication, to the rejuvenation of human life.

In such a situation a change of perspective was necessary, and was possible in one of only two ways. First, the concept of revolutionary change and the changes in social life expected to follow from it could be modified to take into account the much more moderate realities or possibilities of post-revolutionary societies. Or second, the limitations of those societies in terms of their socio-economic position in the world could call into question their representativeness as models of revolutionary change and socialist potential. In other words, the choice was between bringing the model of revolution into accord with a flawed reality, or judging reality as flawed because of its divergence from the model. The disadvantage of the first option is the possible infection of the model as a result of it being driven into such close proximity to the acknowledged flaws of reality; the disadvantage of the second is a possible lapse into an idealistic disregard of what may be unavoidable limitations imposed upon theoretical aspirations by empirical reality. The advantage of this latter position, however, is that it preserves as a powerful critical tool the model of revolution and revolutionary change as the means for developing the potential for human development and change, against which the claims to feasibility of all realities may be judged. The advantage of the former is that it allows the maintenance of political loyalties and obligations, forged in specific social and historical circumstances, to survive changes in such circumstances. It is hardly surprising then, that a philosopher turned politician should opt for the former approach, should stay with the movement rather than insist upon doctrinal absolution and, further, attempt to discredit that doctrine by drawing attention to it as idealistic and irrelevant.

Lukács' 1967 self-criticism is a consequence of this political decision and his philosophical critique is based upon a (for him) more fundamental political loyalty. His concern to differentiate objectification and alienation is of course philosophically correct; however, it also follows from his concern to shield the regime and movement to which he felt a great loyalty from the radical critique inherent to his own anticapitalist concepts and theories. By weakening the penetration of his theory of reification, by establishing areas of existing reality beyond its compass and by dismissing the theory as an ahistorical abstraction, the honour of actually-existing-socialism is preserved. The fact that the younger Lukács' initial expectations were not rewarded, that the Soviet Union was unable to realize those expectations invested in the proletarian revolution, turned him away from the political strategy which demanded such high standards and towards an ontological reconciliation with reality. Because his hopes for cultural renewal were dragged through the dirt of post-revolutionary Russia, he came to the conclusion that theory, not fact, was in error, that to expect such a renewal was a utopian aberration based upon the idealistic counterposition of the absolute sinfulness of the old world and the heavenly beauty of the new. When reality demonstrated the unreasonableness of the demands made of it, it was time to listen, and listen Lukács did. Instead of retreating to the pessimistic and stoical acceptance of such a fate (the stance adopted, let us remember, by Weber, Simmel *et al.*), Lukács reconciled himself instead with the theoretical possibility of neutral objectification, the belief that such indeed was occurring in the Soviet Union and that such objectification did not contradict – except possibly temporarily – the essence of individuals and their quest for freedom.

Lukács' political alignment caused him to move away from what he now came to term his idealist vision of a conflict and gulf between various pairs of antinomies that he previously expected to be overcome in and through the act of revolution: subject and object, life and cultural forms, subjective and objective culture, freedom and necessity. All these were to be solved by the accession to power of the proletariat. When upon the assumption of power of the bolsheviks it was found that they continued to co-exist, Lukács sought the explanation not by investigation of the social and political peculiarities of soviet society and its inheritance from tsarism – which might reveal its inapplicability as a model for socialist revolution – but by reading into his perception of the nature of the revolution the same unbridgeable gap between concept and reality to be found in Simmel's theory of alienation. What led Simmel to a tragic world view led Lukács to a world view equally tragic, but to which he gave the title of realism.

The importance of Simmel's theory of alienation has other more substantive aspects and can be shown to have influenced Lukács in two important ways. First, it led him to reconstruct Marx's labour theory of alienation from his economic writings, and in particular *Capital*. This was his response to what was at the time 'in the air': the unmasking of alienation. And second, it led him to extend the theory beyond the immediate processes of economic production to all the areas of social life, that is to culture in general. This two-fold influence set the seal on Lukács' original contribution to twentieth-century marxism; it gave to his work an emphasis on alienation and consciousness and a concern with relating the subterranean socio-economic conditions of life that generate these to the wider aspects of human culture, without suffering the vulgar consequences of economic reductionism.

Simmel's concern to extend the economic forms into the wider currents of human existence (that is, to psychology and to metaphysics) was achieved at the cost of robbing them of their 'concrete substance' and 'revolutionary bite'. Lukács wishes to carry out a similar task without these drawbacks, yet without reintroducing economic reductionism. We shall see how he attempts this in the next chapter. In the meantime I propose to discuss briefly Simmel's own theory of alienation and to assess the value of the 'very interesting and perceptive...matters of detail' that first attracted Lukács to them.

There are two aspects to Simmel's theory. The first is the matter of the corrosive effect of the money economy upon human social relations. As we have seen, this is a theme that also occurs in Tönnies. Here the cold impersonality of the money economy reduces the social estimation of all human values and characteristics; these become (literally) valueless unless realized as commodities, at which point they lose their qualitative nobility and are debased to the same level as all other marketable goods and services. Prostitution here serves as the typical model, showing how the power of money not only corrupts the most personal and intimate of human capacities but reduces all values to the same level – that at which the market alone ascribes worth.

The second aspect is the changing balance between subjective and objective aspects of life, and the gradual and inexorable development of reification. Here the process of objectification in economic life is seen as but one aspect of the general character of modern life, in which money is the means by which reification is brought about. Simmel writes:

> The process by which labour becomes a commodity is thus only one side of the far-reaching process of differentiation by which specific contents of the personality are detached in order for them to confront the personality as objects with an independent character and dynamics.[86]

Simmel also draws our attention to the growing gulf that lies between subjective and objective culture. The division of labour and the development of specialization give a tremendous boost to the quantity and degree of refinement of the things which determine and surround our lives ('tools, means of transport, the products of science, technology and art').[87] However, the culture of the individual suffers at the same time a degree of degradation and devaluation that seeks recompense in the form of the commodities he or she is able to purchase, but which has the result of further devaluing human development and uniqueness by further increasing dependence upon the objective and universal (market) culture: '[e]very day and from all sides, the wealth of objective culture increases, but the individual mind can enrich the forms and contents of its own development only by distancing itself still further from that culture.'[88] Simmel refers to the development of national newspapers as an example of this process; while their existence testifies to the increase in the information and culture available to society, they do so on a mass basis that has the effect of destroying the refined individuality of the smaller number of people hitherto linked together by more individual, personal (and by implication, human) means of communication. Another example: the development of machinery greatly aids the social productivity of labour and allows an increase in the social consumption of goods and services, but at the same time it deprives the worker of that essential sense of fulfilment that the artist feels when producing, alone, on a more or less individual level, a definite and specific artefact. Moreover, the demands of machine-minding make irrelevant the individual, human characteristics of workers by removing from them the necessity and desire even to understand the significance of the work they undertake.

The power of this objective culture over individuals is widespread and may be shown in many ways to explain how we surrender our individuality and humanity to the objective basis of an alienated culture. The cult of the computer, new technology and robotics, the technological basis of popular culture and its manifestation in television; the manufactured or synthesized artificiality of much modern music – these demonstrate not only the power and influence of objective culture but also our willingness to accept and even to worship that power. That their triumph is achieved in the name of progress, science or modernity serves also to condemn their critics to the cul-de-sac of so-called reactionary luddism.

A contemporary writer who draws on many of these themes is Christopher Lasch. He shows[89] how developments in modern society have devalued and undermined such human characteristics as mutual dependence, self-improvement and even intelligence, as the power of objective culture makes available the goods and services previously provided on a social basis by families or communities, but in such a way that dependence upon the market or bureaucracy is intensified to the point of near slavery.

There are problems with such analyses, however. First, there is the polar juxtaposition of what went before with what now is: to present such a contrast is to invite either an idealization of the past – the glorification of the experience of (others') poverty – or the one-sided condemnation of what now exists, in this case the welfare state. Second, there is the matter of the political consequences of such an approach, which can be to despair of the present and its capacity to effect radical change when contrasted to the glorious experiences of the past, or else to withdraw from the struggles of the present, particularly when they are located in areas such as the welfare state which necessarily pose complex tactical problems for socialists. Again, though, this tactical difficulty can be overcome neither by abandoning the legitimate criticism of the bureaucratic functioning of such institutions nor by setting unacceptable conditions for support, for example by failing to support struggles that do not offer a positive alternative vision of social provision.

The significance of this digression and of Simmel's theory of alienation lies in the basis it provides for an understanding of the genesis and structure of Lukács' own theory of reification. Before I go on to examine this in more detail it is worth summarizing the major points of influence exerted upon it by the romantic anti-capitalism of German sociology.

Conclusion

Lukács' theory of reification is an amalgam of Marx's notion of commodity fetishism, Simmel's theory of alienation and the notion of rational calculability common to German sociology in this period but associated in particular with the work of Max Weber. Lukács is of course much closer to Marx in stressing the socio-economic centrality of the labour theory of alienation than he is to Simmel's elevation of alienation to a metaphysical aspect of the human condition. Nonetheless, under the influence of Simmel, and partly as a result of his desire to escape the economic reductionism of orthodoxy, Lukács is also concerned to show how this process of the construction of social life, which has its origin and basis in labour, comes by way of the commodity form to dominate – and indeed to structure – all aspects of social life; even, as we shall see, those which appear independent and autonomous of it.

In setting himself this task, Lukács treads a dangerous path. On the one hand he wants to avoid the identification of objectification and alienation that led Simmel to his tragic world view; while on the other, he wants to stretch the role of commodity production to all areas of social life and thus avoid the necessity of utilizing the troubled base-superstructure metaphor. This approach carries with it the danger of reductionism, of reducing spheres of non-economic social activity to their origins in economic relations by systematically emptying them of their non-economic aspects; it also carries the risk that by extending the antinomies of culture to life in general it makes these antinomies eternal aspects of the human condition, beyond resolution in any conceivable form of social organization, including socialism.

The second major theme of Lukács' theory of reification is the idea which again finds its origin in Simmel and Weber, namely that society is mediated through forms of consciousness which in bourgeois society take on reified aspects. This also touches upon another major component of his social theory, the notion of totality which he conceives, in common with Hegel and this time in opposition to Simmel and Weber, as a historical process of a coming-to-consciousness. Totality is derived in an ideal sense from Tönnies' conception of *Gemeinschaft* and from the hellenic influence upon German philosophy, but it is to be reconstructed in communist society upon the basis of its antithesis towards and the *aufhebung* of bourgeois society. There is also, at least in Lukács' earlier marxist writings, a tendency to regard the partisanship of communist organization as itself an example or perhaps a prefigurement of this new human community.

Finally, again derived from the critique of culture developed by Simmel, Weber and Tönnies, there is the idea that the all-encompassing jurisdiction of Gesellschaft requires a *total revolution* to liberate humanity from the 'iron cage' of rational or objective calculability. Lukács contra Weber and Simmel saw this as a feasible result of a real and concrete revolutionary process, because of the view he shared with Marx concerning the revolutionary and emancipatory capacity and social role of the proletariat.

5 Alienation, Reification and Commodity Fetishism

As a preliminary to an assessment of the substantive contribution to marxism of Lukács' theory of reification, two things are necessary: an account of the genealogical derivation of the concept and of its relationship to the theories of alienation developed by Hegel, Feuerbach and Marx; and a differentiation between the similar and in many ways complementary terms of reification, alienation and commodity fetishism. Only after these tasks have been accomplished is it possible to judge what Lukács' theory contributed in an original way to marxist philosophy and how it may be of use in an analysis of the modern world.

I begin this chapter by interrogating the terms alienation, reification and commodity fetishism in an attempt to discover what the users of these terms were attempting to contribute to social theory, both substantially and relatively (to each other). This necessarily raises at the outset the particular problem of the relationship between Lukács' theory of reification and Marx's theory of alienation or commodity fetishism.

As is well known, the work in which Marx's theory of alienation is most fully developed – the *Economic and Philosophical Manuscripts* of 1844[1] – was unknown to Lukács when he developed his own theory of reification in 1923.[2] It might thus be said that Lukács merely anticipated this work of Marx and that his theory of reification is a remarkable feat of philological reconstruction, but hardly unique or original. And indeed it must be said that in *History and Class Consciousness* Lukács uses the term reification throughout to cover meanings that include alienation as well as the more specific sense of reification, suggesting that his theory might well be incorporated within Marx's own, more original theory of alienation. This would, however, be an innaccurate assessment, for while Lukács does indeed presuppose Marx's theory of alienation and while his reconstruction of this is remarkable in being drawn from the available economic writings of the mature Marx, he nevertheless invests in the concept of reification a specific meaning that makes an original contribution to marxist social theory and which at the same time overcomes many of the philosophical inadequacies of marxist orthodoxy.

Lukács takes Marx's theory of alienation – or more specifically his theory of commodity fetishism – as his starting point and makes two unique contributions to marxist theory. The first is the reestablishment of this theory as the central pivot of marxist social theory, demonstrating the important role it played in Marx's thought up to and including the 'scientific economics' of 1867 and beyond. This he does by careful and selective quotation from these works, showing how Marx's philosophical concerns underlay the myriad of economic fact, observation and criticism that orthodoxy had taken to be their sole content. Second, because Lukács deals explicitly with issues that for various reasons lay dormant within Marx's published writings or were at best unclear, and because Lukács' background lay in a species of interpretive sociology, when he came to integrate his own ideas with his understanding of marxism he not only brought about a new perspective on Marx's thought but contributed a new sense of social critique, one sharpened by the continued developments within capitalism since Marx's death.

Theory of Reification

The explicit basis of Lukács' theory of reification lies in that section of the first chapter of *Capital* entitled 'The Fetishism of Commodities and the Secret Thereof'.[3] For Lukács explicitly, but implicitly for Marx also, commodity fetishism is the concrete and material form in which alienation is instantiated in bourgeois society: that is, alienation takes a real form as commodity fetishism. This latter occupies a prominent place in Marx's account of the structure of capitalist society and in Lukács' reinterpretation of Marx, because it is the means through which alienation is given an economic or productive basis, it is the specific means through which human alienation is structured in bourgeois society. Fetishism – the worship of an inanimate object irrationally ascribed magical powers[4] takes on a peculiar character in bourgeois society in that it is directed towards an interchangeable multitude of very real objects (commodities) whose principle characteristic is precisely their equivalence and exchangeability with money, and it is drawn towards the conjunction of the social means by which these commodities are created and the consequences of these means upon the resources and capacities of the human community.[5]

As I. I. Rubin points out,[6] Marx's theory of commodity fetishism provides the key to the economic works of Marx in general and to the labour theory of value in particular: '[t]he theory of fetishism is, per se, the basis of Marx's entire economic system and in particular of his theory of value.'[7] Commodity fetishism is the specific form in which alienation and/or reification are realized or instantiated in bourgeois society, it is the new term by means of which Marx concretizes what thirty years previously he had written of in terms of estrangement and alienation. It is the economic structure of society that generates commodity fetishism, though as we shall soon see this by no means confines its jurisdiction to overtly economic matters (as opposed, for example, to philosophical, political or religious aspects of society). The difference between this concept and alienation and reification, then, is a difference of abstraction: commodity fetishism is the specific and concrete form taken by alienation/reification in capitalist societies.

Why, then, did Marx abandon use of the one concept and replace it with the other? Rubin argues that Marx's abandonment of the concept alienation was deliberate and conscious and that this was part of his development towards 'a different world of ideas ... from Utopian to Scientific Socialism ... from negating reality in the name of an ideal to seeking within reality itself the forces for further development and motion'.[8] There is some truth to this, but this is not the whole truth. Marx did express himself differently in *Capital* than in the notebooks that constituted the *Economic and Philosophical Manuscripts,* and he was analysing social matters at different levels of theoretical abstraction. But this is not to say that one mode of analysis excludes the other, that Marx's concretization of human alienation in terms of commodity fetishism entailed the rejection of the former as an idealist execrescence. As Kolakowski points out,[9] by regarding the latter concept as a continuation of the former we are able to understand that the specific determinants of exploitation analysed in *Capital* are not the negation but the culmination of Marx's earlier notion of dehumanization; likewise, the social contradictions he identifies between exchange and use values, and the domination of the former over the latter, express the enslavement or estrangement of human activity to a non-human purpose.[10] Continued use of the alienation concept carries with it one further advantage. By drawing our attention to the human essence of which the modern individual is an alienated expression and away from the feeling of necessity which the process of reification itself falsely draws us towards, it allows us to draw upon a vision of human potential that is not immediately apparent if we confine our field of vision to everyday reality. The concept of alienation provides us with a normative standard of social critique that highlights the dehumanization of bourgeois society, that exists whether or not the individuals who compose it recognize their lives as degraded or debased. Indeed, one of the most valuable contributions made to social theory by Lukács rests on this very point: the concept of reification itself provides an explanation as to why people fail to recognize the dehumanization to which their lives are subject in bourgeois society.

Discussion of the relationship between reification and alienation also provides a way of drawing attention to the way in which Lukács' account is able to develop points from Marx's theory that were opaque, if not to Marx then certainly to many of his followers. The most important of these concerns the nature of the relationship between the objective and subjective conditions of social existence, or, as this has become known, that between the base and superstructure or the economic base and ideological superstructure. The point to note here concerns the underlying factors that make this dualism an important problem for marxist theory in the first place, Lukács' position being able also to account for the difficulties the two major tendencies of marxist interpretation – vulgar reductionism and sophisticated eclecticism (or autonomism) encounter in attempting to deal with it. In fact, Lukács' account provides a way of rejecting the approaches of both because it perceives the problem in a different way.

Lukács' concept of reification follows Marx's concept of alienation in distinguishing between the objective conditions of its existence – the creation of a world of objects alienated or estranged from their producers – the subjective consequences of this structure upon the human psyche and the ability of humankind to understand the world it inhabits. In this respect it is useful to define alienation in relation to the underlying state of reality and the way that this reflects (or fails to reflect) the philosophico-anthropological conception of humankind and reification as the consequence of this state of reality upon human consciousness. Clearly this distinction is a subtle one and cannot be made at the level of reality itself, since the two aspects correlate with one another so that it would be impossible for one to exist without the other; it is heuristic not ontological. For purposes of social analysis however, it is a necessary and important distinction to make precisely because reality is itself structured by such a rupture. Further, it allows us to appreciate the drawbacks of approaches that in running the two concepts together suppress one or other side of the couplet. While it is certain that an adequate understanding of reality must grasp both the objective and subjective conditions of human existence, the way in which reality presents itself to the human individual is by way of a structured rupture between the two. As we have seen in the section on Simmel earlier, the social world has seen the increasing encroachment of objective culture upon human life, a development that has led bourgeois thought to 'enter into an unmediated relationship with reality as it was given' and which in turn leads it to regard bourgeois existence as 'an eternal law of nature or a cultural value enduring for all time'. As Lukács notes, this 'means that history must abolish itself'.[11]

Lukács provides a new outlook on this problem. For him, alienation and reification are irrevocably united in the structure of bourgeois society simply because for him, and for the philosophical tradition in which he was schooled, society is mediated through forms of consciousness and thus any attempt to divide reality into two parts – the objective or subjective, economic or psychological – is bound to lead to an incorrect philosophico-political outlook, to either contemplative quietism or idealistic voluntarism. If society imposes itself as an objective structure upon humam consciousness, then true human activity (praxis) is impossible; if, on the other hand, human volition is the key, then moral regulation is the sole restriction upon human activity. Lukács wishes to unite these two aspects of human society, but realizes that the first step in so doing is to recognize that it is the structure of bourgeois society that causes the rupture between them and that it is necessary to bring this society and thereby also this rupture, to an end.

Such an approach has consequences that raise important questions; the development of a theory of ideology, for example, is dependent upon taking a position on this question. I will elaborate later in more detail upon Lukács' metatheoretical account of ideology and defend it against those who would assign priority to a more empirical, worldly grounded approach to the study of ideology. This will allow me also to show how Lukács' theory of reification provides the key to understanding the ideological subversion not only of social consciousness but of social science itself by the conditions of life of bourgeois society – by referring, as does Lukács, to that area of social thought seemingly most abstract from and therefore presumably most immune to this process of corruption, namely classical German philosophy.

Alienation and Ideology

In his discussion of alienation Adam Schaff introduces a useful distinction between alienation, which he defines as the relation that pertains between a human agent and the products of his or her activity under specified social conditions, but which occurs objectively and autoalienation, which he defines as the subjective phenomenon of the human individual's estrangement from society.[12] This distinction has the advantage of correctly following Marx's understanding of alienation as an objective phenomenon, of which individuals may or may not be aware, that it is the form in which the structure of bourgeois society presents itself to the individuals who compose it and is not to be reduced to the individual thoughts or feelings of the individuals concerned.[13] Thus we do not assess the alienated character of a society by examining the psycho-social consciousness of individuals, whether they feel themselves to be at one with themselves or with society, or even whether they exhibit behaviour which we might somehow describe as alienated; we look instead at the objective structure of that society to see whether it allows the free expression of what we regard as essentially human characteristics and behaviour. We might profitably contrast this view with that presented by Robert Blauner in his book on alienation,[14] in which he compares various forms of work organization in terms of their ability to increase or decrease the workers' sense of alienation – the implication being that these forms could then be adjusted to allow workers the maximum sense of personal achievement in their work situation. The problem with such an approach is that because it isolates certain particular phenomena from the social environment that nourishes and determines them (in this case forms of work organization), and because it restricts itself to the exhibited consciousness of individuals, it mistakes the immediate form of alienation for its real structure. In fact, the expressions of alienation given by individuals, either directly or by attribution, are just that: expressions of an underlying structure of alienation which must first be grasped if these expressions are to be correctly evaluated. These expressions are the effects of alienation, not its cause.[15]

This is not to deny that there is a necessary connection between the objective structure of alienation and individuals' and classes' conscious experience of its effects. But even here a further level of mediation is necessary before we descend (or ascend, according to your methodological persuasion) from social structure to the consciousness of individuals. We must first assess the consequences for consciousness in general of this structure of alienation before we can go on to see how the consciousness of individuals is affected by it.

Schaff's article is least satisfactory on this point. Because he resists the temptation of what he refers to as the 'metaphysical speculations'[16] of defining this subjective aspect of alienation in terms of individual's self or species estrangement, he confines himself to an empirical approach which refers to the disappearance of traditional social bonds and the corresponding collapse of existing systems of values. While this approach may be of some value, it carries with it the danger of slipping into a variety of psychopathology analogous with Durkheim's concept of anomie, where concern is directed to the problem of social interaction or control rather than, as is the case with the concept of alienation, to the barriers to the exertion of human capacities and values.[17] I do not wish to argue that concern with the sociological aspects of alienation is misplaced, nor to deny its claim that the alienation of the modern world is evidenced by the collapse of community and social ties. What I am concerned to argue is that in the concern to deal with alienation empirically (or non-metaphysically), attention has wrongly shifted away from the more metaphysical concerns of the younger Marx – from, for example, his conception of human essence and of what might constitute a truly human society.[18] This is not to advocate the creation of blueprints to describe what a future society would look like,[19] but to set out what the human condition would require of any society created to serve its interests.[20]

The questions must then arise: why has this empirical tendency been so powerful, on what basis does it justify this denial of a non-empirical backdrop and is it correct to dismiss this latter as metaphysical speculation?

The case against the view I am advocating goes as follows. Whilst it may be true that Marx's theoretical development was to some degree shaped by his origins in post-hegelian philosophy, it was also marked by a rupture with this heritage, a rupture achieved in two stages. First, under the influence of Feuerbach's inversion of the hegelian dialectic, Marx prioritized the materialistic or naturalistic character of humankind over the metaphysical-transcendental character of the 'absolute spirit'. This led Marx to his investigations into political economy, to the social and material preconditions of human alienation (what Feuerbach referred to as humankind's species-estrangement) and these investigations proved adequate on their own to account for both the unsatisfactory nature of existing bourgeois society and the historical developments that had led to it but which in the future would lead from it. This marked the second stage of Marx's rupture with hegelian philosophy, the stage at which Marx broke also with Feuerbach and with all talk of species extrangement. Thus the philosophical basis upon which Marx's own development had proceeded was now rendered redundant; indeed, it was positively harmful in that it diluted the scientific rationality of the new approach by encouraging a quasi-romantic vision of authentic individuals that also weakened Marx's emphasis on class divisions. In such a view, we do not need to know that human life is in contradiction to its species-essence, it is enough merely that it is in contradiction with the here and now of bourgeois society. The future of marxism lies, therefore, in developing the scientific-objective account of the capitalist mode of production and the internal contradictions that create the conditions for its eventual overthrow; supporting this, where necessary, with an account of the *ideological* means through which the exploited are convinced that such a society is the best they can realistically hope for. Such indeed has been the travail of orthodoxy since Marx's death: study of the economic structure of bourgeois society was the predominant characteristic of marxism from Marx's death until the first two decades of the twentieth century; since then the setbacks of the socialist movement have led to a greater concern with those ideological mechanisms which have supposedly corrupted the revolutionary zeal of the proletariat.[21]

Following Lukács, I argue that such an interpretation of ideological mechanisms, for all of the insights it may yield as to the flexible vitality of civil society, is flawed by its one-sided empiricism and, moreover, can never be properly integrated into the objective account of the social structure. Instead, as has become increasingly obvious in the recent past, it subverts this account – at least in so far as this retains a revolutionary commitment to change – into a species of evolutionist pragmatism.

The de facto disjunction between the objectively defined real basis of capitalism, its basis in exploitation, immiserization, crisis, war and imperialism and the subjective experience of this by the disadvantaged has led many marxists either to disregard the experiences of the masses as irrelevant, as something that is itself determined and will also in the future be changed by the objective structure of capitalism (in which case change is inevitable anyhow), or else to regard this subjective experience as evidence of working-class rapprochement with capitalism.

The advantage of Lukács' approach is not merely that it takes seriously the ideological mechanisms of bourgeois society, in particular their effect upon working class consciousness, but that it integrates these insights into an analysis of the structure of capitalism that rejects any notion of inevitability. The working class is impregnated with bourgeois forms of thought not only because the bourgeoisie has at its command superior instruments of ideological domination, but because the very structure of capitalist society, and especially the dehumanization of the labourer into a commodity, itself engenders an outlook (albeit contradictory) that can safely accommodate itself to such a process and that makes these instruments of ideological domination superior in the first place.

Such an assessment of Lukács' contribution is contrary to the views of, among others, Jorge Larrain,[22] who advocates the superiority of Gramsci's work on ideology because of its greater concern with the component parts of consciousness: the agents of ideology (the intellectuals) and the material institutions through which ideologies are produced and disseminated. This view of Gramsci would apply also to Lenin, for he too showed a greater concern with the institutions through which the bourgeoisie could influence the ideas of workers.[23] As Larrain notes, however, Gramsci and Lukács were in fact dealing with the problem of consciousness at two different levels.[24] I am not advocating the abandonment of the approach shared by Gramsci and Lenin; I am seeking to put this approach into (its more limited) context by challenging the view that Lukács' concern with the more abstract philosophical origins of consciousness is at the expense of an adequate understanding of ideology and that the former is to be replaced by the latter (as Gramsci is alleged to have done). In his book *The Real World of Ideology*, McCarney argues against those critics of Lukács who share the modern sociological conception of ideology, which seeks to discover its meaning by examining its manifestation in the ideas or actions of concrete individuals, groups or classes in given concrete circumstances.[25]

Lukács' approach to consciousness does not commence from the ideas in people's heads, or with the institutions that disseminate the ideas intended for people's heads and then proceed to create a theory of ideology. On the contrary, it attempts to integrate into his understanding of the objective character of bourgeois society an account of the consequences for consciousness of bourgeois society in its totality, which is mediated before it may be embodied in particular ideas or ideologies by consciousness in general or, more accurately, by the consciousness of the two main classes of bourgeois society: the bourgeoisie and the proletariat. It is for this reason that it is mistaken to read into Lukács a concern with ideology as currently understood and then to criticize him for only providing a partial treatment of this conception of ideology.[26] Lukács' treatment of consciousness follows a descending escalator of abstraction, starting from the inhuman, alienated character of bourgeois society, leading to the reified forms through which this world imposes itself upon the consciousness of the main classes of that world and only then leading to the concrete ideologies of specific groups or individuals. Lukács' method is thus to proceed in the same way as did Marx: from the abstract to the concrete and not vice versa.

He combines this with an absolute antipathy to all psychological forms of social understanding.[27]

Of course, such a view is open to the criticism that its abstraction makes it of rather limited utility in understanding how people, and especially workers, come to think and to act as they do. Certainly, the theory of reification on its own would have little to say about, say, the voting habits of British workers in recent years. However, more specific arguments are themselves incomplete without some account of why workers apparently think, act and vote against what might be construed to be their real interests. Might it not be that a limited perception of alternatives – something which it is the function of representative democracy to accomplish – makes them especially vulnerable to ideological manipulation? And that this is part of, or partly to be explained by the phenomenon of reification?

Reification and Ideology

Reification is the chief characteristic of the bourgeois world outlook. In the next chapter I will analyse the dynamics of its dissolution; for the present I intend to explicate the concept in terms of its origin in bourgeois social relations and account for its near-universal predominance in that society – in the sciences that attempt to analyse it and even in the labour movement that is in (some form of) opposition to it. The concept is not, however, ideological in the non-scientific sense that it refers to the misconception of reality held by individuals, since this conception is an accurate reflection of the way in which reality appears to them. In other words, to become dominated by a reified outlook is not necessarily to misinterpret the world, it is not to suffer a false consciousness that requires merely a more concrete awareness of reality to be overthrown. It in fact finds verification and support in the concreteness of reality and this explains the extent of its dominance. Just as Marx's critique of religion was expressed in terms of the need to overturn the world whose spiritual aroma was religion, so here too the world of reification will not be destroyed merely as a result of a challenge to the reified ideas that are its expression.

As I have already indicated, Lukács begins with Marx's discussion of commodity fetishism in the first chapter of *Capital*, but this serves as merely the starting point for an account of the commodity structure of capitalism in general as the basis for his social theory and also incorporates insights gleaned from the work of Simmel and Weber. What attracts Lukács to Marx, however, or at least to that particular section, is the way in which Marx depicts the effects of the commodity structure upon consciousness. What takes place, let us remind ourselves, is a two-fold process. First, the social relations of production and of life in general are expressed not as inter-human relationships, but are mediated through things, through commodities. Second, that expression takes on a fetishistic character in that the productions of social activity and of the brain take on an independent, determining character, opposite to and opposed to its human origin. Hence Marx's analogy with 'the misty enveloped regions of the religious world'.[28]

The concept of reification, then, lies at the very centre of Lukács' critique of bourgeois society, of bourgeois thought and of its influence upon and within the socialist movement. It is the system of reification that is the constant target of his critique, whether in the form of the revisionist worship of legality, Kant's notion of the thing-in-itself, or the commodity form itself: all these are criticized as human (or, more pertinently, class) constructs that reflect the pseudo-objective manner in which bourgeois domination manifests itself, by themselves taking on an objective character seemingly independent and autonomous of the wishes and intentions of historical actors. They appear as brute facts of life, a 'second nature'[29] to which human beings have no alternative but to accommodate themselves. Any theory of society that treats such phenomena as they immediately present themselves cannot but be locked into this framework of domination, cannot but be compelled by the inner necessity of its methodology to mythologize and regard as eternal this its true essence – the bourgeois character of the social world – and thus itself become part of the ideological armoury of that world. Lukács therefore draws our attention to the way in which bourgeois society not only creates, shapes and controls the objective structures of social power, but how it instantiates itself into social thought itself; indeed, how social thought becomes part of the objective structure of social power as it takes on this appearance of objectivity.

The very success of capitalism and its continued existence are to be explained not solely in terms of the objective structures and institutions of social and political power, but also in terms of this ability to shape the way in which its world is perceived. This is not in the crude sense of disguising or disregarding the facts of exploitation, inequality and oppression, but in the sense of foreclosing any alternatives to these, in regarding them in such a way that they become unavoidable burdens of human existence. Just as obedience to law is the call sign in the natural sciences, so it is too – if this method is applied – in the social world, only here it carries with it thoroughly debilitating political consequences. The price of obedience to law in the social world is to maintain and preserve the social world as it presents itself to us; it is to surrender our capacity to shape that world to our desires; it is to have our desires shaped by that world; it is to reify that world into a creation that shapes us rather than one that we shape ourselves.

It is clear at this point that Lukács' methodology is coloured by a radical distinction between on the one hand the natural and social sciences and on the other essence and appearance, and whose intention is precisely to pierce the immediate appearance of the social world to its subterranean essence, a task which, once achieved, puts back onto the agenda of history the capacity of human agency. It is also true, however, that such an approach carries with it certain difficulties, one of the most important of which is that social change appears to be the result merely of a change in consciousness. It is on this that Lukács is criticized by many commentators as an idealist,[30] that in regarding the domination of capitalism as the result of a false consciousness instilled by some means or other into the working class, the only logical conclusion can be that this false consciousness has merely to be reformed for capitalism to be annulled. The strength of this criticism is boosted by certain remarks made by Lukács in *History and Class Consciousness*: 'the fate of the revolution (and with it the fate of mankind) will depend on the ideological maturity of the proletariat, i.e., on its class consciousness';[31] 'knowledge brings about an objective structural change in the object of knowledge';[32] and 'the act of consciousness overthrows the objective form of its object.'[33]

The critical conclusion often drawn from these remarks is, however, quite unfounded. For the intent of Lukács' writings at this time was to defend an account of revolutionary change made impossible by the determinism of orthodoxy and by the rationalism of the enlightenment. When Lukács refers to a change, or a reform of consciousness, he does not see this as a matter of critical reflection taking place inside the heads of individuals (on the enlightenment model), but as part of a practical-political process of revolutionary change. It is precisely the unique character of proletarian class consciousness that it is both practical and, if it is to be successful, revolutionary: it must transform the wider reality that maintains the structure of ideological domination that in non-revolutionary epochs imprisons the proletariat in passive quietism. It must, in other words, effect a revolutionary overthrow of its own conditions of existence; in this sense, the knowledge so produced is both practical and self-knowledge as well as knowledge of an object.

Furthermore, the whole point of the exercise in 1923, as it is today, is not to ask how and by what means the bourgeois class is able to resist the demands of the exploited – these means are obvious and increasingly visible – but to ask why the exploited so very rarely make radical demands of the bourgeoisie. To ask this question is not to deny the importance of the means of repression, of the monopolization of socially legitimate violence by the state, but is to examine the effects upon consciousness of these and other mechanisms of bourgeois rule. It would be wrong, therefore, to characterize the reified ideology of bourgeois society as a false consciousness in the sense that it has no basis in reality, or that it distorts reality. On the contrary. As we shall see, the reified consciousness of bourgeois ideology enjoys as its basis the very real and concrete basis of bourgeois society, it corresponds to *this* reality, expresses and reinforces *its* conditions of existence. But for Lukács, as indeed for a whole current of German philosophical thought, there is a deeper and more fundamental reality than the immediate facts of everyday life; the development and processes of history are the true reality against which the content and meaning of any individual moment or epoch are ultimately to be judged. As Lukács puts it, 'the developing tendencies of history constitute a higher reality than the empirical "facts"'.[34] We need merely add at this point that for Lukács these developing tendencies can only be seen from the standpoint of the proletariat.

Lukács wants to develop and to extend this analysis on two levels. He wants to draw out the wider implications of the commodification of things to incorporate all aspects of life in bourgeois society – this he calls the objective side of the concept. But he also wants to deepen the analysis of the effect of this upon the consciousness of those who live in such a world – this is the subjective side. These two factors are mutually reinforcing; it is essential to Lukács' argument that the subjective side has increasingly been encroached upon and captured by the 'mystical illusion' of a 'phantom objectivity' that disarms the capacity of consciousness to resist. In other words, the ability of the commodity structure to penetrate society in all its aspects and to mould society in its image causes the stance of the human subject to change and also to come under the sway of this stultifying structure. The system of commodity production not only constrains and determines society in the sense of providing a set of limits beyond which it may not depart, but itself comes to constitute, to become instantiated in the whole of society. It is not just that society cannot afford to ignore the material foundation of its existence – commodity production – but also that the system itself impregnates with its essence all the seemingly autonomous or separate spheres of society. The commodity truly becomes the universal category, affecting both the objective evolution of society and people's stance towards this; it, the commodity, becomes, in Lukács' words:

> crucial for the subjugation of men's consciousness to the forms in which this reification finds expression and for attempts to comprehend the process or to rebel against its disastrous effects, and liberate themselves from servitude to the 'second nature' so created.[35]

The commodity structure causes the very activity and labour of the individual to become 'something objective and independent of him, something that controls him by virtue of an autonomy alien to man',[36] and this is extended beyond the immediate process of production to encompass all spheres of social life, with the factory system serving as the image of society that intrudes everywhere.

This factory analogy is important, for it is this that expresses not only the exploitation of the proletariat but also the utter degradation of humanity itself.[37] It is here that the qualitative human and individual attributes of the worker are progressively eliminated – through the division of labour, the establishment of labour time as a physical fact, the alienation of the direct producers from production and the domination of dead over living labour. It is here too that the fragmentation of the object and tasks of production leads to the fragmentation of the subject, where human qualities become perceived as mere sources of error or disequilibrium, as barriers to the efficient application of machinery.

The reification of bourgeois society places human subjects into a pre-existing and self-sufficient system that operates and functions independently of them, and to whose laws they seemingly have no option but to conform. The drastic curtailment of valid choices or interventions, political or otherwise, into this machine-like system demands an attitude not of active involvement, still less of critical rejection, but of passive contemplation. As mechanization and the division of labour produce social atomization, so the triumph of objectivity produces passivity and contemplation, introduces not the age of the masses but rather the age of the mass spectator, of mass society – the civilization of the crowd.[38] This is the pervasive and corrupting state of affairs of bourgeois society: the impersonal commodity structure captures all areas of social life, transforms them so that everywhere its laws come to be regarded as 'natural' and beyond challenge; the forms of social life become petrified into timeless models of human relations in general; and, moreover, this applies even, or perhaps especially, to social thought, to attempts to understand this reality.

Reification, then, is the creation of a 'second nature' or a 'phantom objectivity', so called because the structure of commodity production takes the appearance of necessity akin to that of nature. The subjective consequences of this lead to the estrangement and alienation of human beings, whose relationships with each other and with society can only take place through the mediation of things,[39] through the market, and to their deactivation as political agents, as citizens. Before going on to examine the many and various ways in which this second nature sinks ever deeper into human consciousness, it is well to detail the ways in which it is able to so achieve domination.

According to Lukács, the prime mover in this state of affairs is the division of labour and the specialization that accompanies it. This has a dehumanizing effect upon the worker because a split takes place in the character of labour, between labour that is performed to satisfy a portion of the total needs of society and that which satisfies the direct needs of the worker. While the needs of bourgeois society are satisfied by means of the division of labour, the dominance of the objective structure of commodity production disregards as inessential the human needs of the worker, which are met only indirectly, as a by-product of the wages paid for his or her labour. Division of labour forces specialization onto workers so that any potential they may have for a more rounded, polytechnic, intellectual development is stunted; moreover, the character of labour is now subject to the coercion of the market and its personification in the employer, so that the only needs recognized by this system of production are those that may be met by the economic exchange made possible by the payment of wages.

The relation of workers to their labour is thus mediated through things, as indeed is their relation to the rest of human society. Indeed, the very structure of the wage system signifies this fact, in that the unequal exchange[40] that takes place between the worker and capitalist appears equal to both sides of the contract; workers' capacity to labour – their labour power – is treated as a thing, as something alien to and separate from them, as something that may be detached from them, as something to be exchanged and sold at whatever price is attainable. Having detached this essential characteristic from the direct producer, it can then be transformed into an objective social power that then becomes the means through which this unequal exchange is reproduced to become the social norm. All of this is of course what Marx's theory of alienation was developed to explain. What Lukács adds to this is an extension beyond the immediate processes of production to a social imagery in which the fate of the worker expresses the fate of the whole of society. Lukács comes to Marx's theory of alienation by way of the latter's theory of commodity fetishism and then integrates this with elements drawn from Max Weber's notion of rationalization.

Rationalization is an instance of the sort of thinking associated with specialization and its most typical form, namely bureaucracy. Compartmentalization of human affairs and the rigid domination of means over ends – which latter can be formulated only in terms of a totalizing vision of human society – produce a social universe of specialities, in which all radical options are foreclosed or disregarded. It is true of course that there were commodities in pre-capitalist societies and indeed that these societies were subject to a division of labour. Lukács' recognition of this signifies his rejection of any tendency towards the reactionary romanticism of the feudal socialists castigated by Marx in *The Communist Manifesto*, or to the political reactionaries of German academia in Lukács' own time. The point for Lukács is that commodity fetishism made only an 'episodic appearance'[41] in pre-capitalist societies and that its character in bourgeois society is both qualitatively and quantitatively different, in that here it must 'penetrate society in all its aspects and...remould it in its own image'.[42]

This subversive characteristic of commodity fetishism has two major consequences. First, it brings about the destabilization of the solidified social relationships of pre-bourgeois societies. The increased importance of commodity production gives it greater weight in social prioritization and enables it to subvert resistance to it by virtue of providing a more productive and usually more efficient, means of gratifying human wants and desires. Second and crucially, it has the gratifying effect of covering its tracks, of rendering invisible the changes it has brought about. It is able to do this because the means it employs to satisfy human desires – commodity production – involves a division of labour and degree of specialization that tend to undermine any image of social totality that people might once have had, replacing these with a universalistic image based upon compartmentalization and fragmentation. Paradoxically, commodity production is more universal than the forms of direct exchange associated with pre-bourgeois societies, yet the form of its universality is that of division, diversity and individualization. This explains why immediate resistance to it is greater at its outset, when 'the personal nature of economic relations was still understood clearly',[43] and when this recognition could be used as a beach-head of resistance, as an alternative vision of ordering human economic affairs, in favour of which support could be mobilized amongst those threatened by the changed economic circumstances of commodity production.[44] This fact has another important implication, one that has not gone unnoticed in the literature on the stability (or otherwise) of bourgeois society. For Lukács' account of commodity fetishism is quite clearly specific to the conditions of life of advanced capitalist society and because of this it could legitimately be said to pose a problem for marxism, since proletarian revolutionary politics, where this has arisen, has done so not in the conditions of advanced capitalism but only where capitalism was newly emerged and where its conflict and competition with precapitalist forms of economic and social life weakened its social dominance. The conditions to which Lukács refers and upon which Marx expected the purity of the class struggle to be most fully developed, have in fact yielded disappointingly non-revolutionary forms of proletarian politics.[45] By contrast, in the newly industrializing societies militancy has been far greater. I will return to this point later. It is sufficient here to note how the particular characteristics associated by Lukács with societies dominated by commodity production have made possible the emergence of what we now refer to as 'western marxism', a version predicated on the combination of unrealized revolutionary expectations in the west and the surprisingly more revolutionary developments in the less developed countries, where in the latter the outcome of such revolutions has been equally disappointing.

Lukács: Political Influences

The conditions that brought about this paradoxical state of affairs lie at the centre of Lukács' analysis, in that the concept of reification is developed precisely to explain why, despite the universalizing characteristics of commodity production, social images continued to depend upon compartmentalization and lead to a refusal to acknowledge the real historical character of bourgeois society and to draw the relevant conclusions from engagement in the class struggle rendered unavoidable by it. Politically, however, Lukács is obliged to register a qualitative distinction between different forms of revolutionary situations, between those expected to take place in the typical features of a fully developed bourgeois society where the commodity truly is the 'universal category',[46] at which point reification assumes decisive importance for both the objective evolution of society and for people's stance towards it, and those which take place before this stage is reached, where particular circumstances make revolution possible but also make its socialist character questionable.

It is probable that the origin of this contrast lay in the different outcomes of the Russian bolshevik revolution and the Hungarian revolution of 1919, between the achievements of the USSR and the failure of the Hungarian Commune, though if this is so it is at least probable that this involves an exaggeration of both the successes of the former model and the pristine proletarian character of its strategy. Lukács' model of revolution was implicitly critical of the Russian revolutionary experience in terms both of the nature of the society that it overthrew and hence also the nature of that revolution. For commodity production was not universal within pre-October Russia; the revolution was an amalgam of working-class urban socialism and peasant agrarian populism and it was not at all clear to Lukács at the time (nor indeed to many others) whether the shaky foundation of this alliance could survive for long the testing conditions of post-revolutionary society. This dilemma was, however, to become increasingly obvious over time, in particular to those responsible for attempts to preserve this alliance. This meant that theories which were critical of the physiognomy of the Russian Revolution were doubly unwelcome, since they not only challenged the heroic self-image of the makers of that revolution but were a challenge from the left that brought into question the alliance on which the revolution and the stability of the society that followed it, were based. On the one hand such theories had something to say about the political experience of post-revolutionary Russia and the difficulties of maintaining the proletarian–peasant alliance without making concessions to the latter that weakened – if not threatened – the socialist character of that society. On the other hand, they posed a challenge to those who held that the Russian experience was a model to be followed and adopted elsewhere. In other words, Lukács' model of revolution posed a challenge, whether he realized it or not, to both the New Economic Policy[47] and the so-called policy of bolshevization of the Comintern.[48]

Kautsky and social democratic orthodoxy had also raised the question of the relevance of the Russian experience to the social and political circumstances of western Europe. However, their views were discredited, at least in the eyes of those committed to revolutionary socialist politics, by their failure to provide effective opposition to the war and by their willingness to trade revolutionary for governmental aspirations. Lukács' views, like Luxemburg's, were less easy to characterize as bourgeois revisionism, since they were motivated by different considerations: namely the desire to establish political principles that were untainted by either bureaucratism or opportunism.[49] It was perhaps for this reason that the denunciation of Luxemburg and Lukács – and indeed of the whole current of the so-called ultra lefts – was so virulent.[50]

If socialist revolution was dependent upon the universal existence of commodity production, that is upon the prior universalizing mission of bourgeois society to achieve its own perverse form of social harmony, then where this was absent social unity could only be held together by mechanical means, by class dictatorship. Such indeed was the unambiguous position of the bolshevik leadership, though not perhaps of the less politically acute Lukács. The latter had seen the policies of the Hungarian Soviet Commune come to grief on peasant indifference and opposition to the universalist mission of the Hungarian Communist Party, in particular its nationalization of the land.[51] And while Lukács had long abandoned (if indeed he had ever shared) what Lenin called the idiocies of Bela Kun,[52] he had not yet been prepared to apply the criticisms he had of the Hungarian experience to Soviet Russia, where the success of a different strategy disguised an essentially similar social and economic situation.

Lukács' concept of reification, then, is developed to explain the difficulties of revolutionary activity in developed bourgeois society and is thus by implication critical of revolutions that occur in different, possibly more favourable circumstances, where capitalist development is as yet incomplete. Some commentators have taken this to be yet another instance of his idealism, his rejection of the political exigencies of any given set of concrete circumstances in favour of the creation of an ideal-type revolutionary situation against which these are to be measured. And such indeed is the logic of his position, though it should be remembered that this is only by implication: Lukács himself remained unconscious of it. Illusions in the bolshevik regime were both widespread and understandable in 1923; its later degeneration – to which at most points Lukács gave his support – should serve to cast doubt upon them. For the essential point is this: either the bolshevik revolution was entirely typical of the sort of revolution envisaged, expected and worked for by marxists, in which case its degeneration must remain a constant possibility in any revolutionary movement; or else it was not typical, in which case the revolutionary movement may retain its discrete charm. This latter position only remains idealist in so far as it fails to specify the material circumstances in which a typical revolution might take place and this is not a failure that can reasonably be levelled at *History and Class Consciousness*. For Lukács does there detail the sort of environment in which socialist revolution is a possibility. Whether, on the other hand, he adequately explains how such a revolution may be brought about is a question that will be taken up in the next chapter.

Lukács and the Proletariat

The first section of the essay 'Reification and the Consciousness of the Proletariat' is in fact a detailed analysis of that sort of society, in which Lukács sets out an account of the social conditions which make revolution necessary (to overcome the contradictions and dehumanization of bourgeois society) and which at the same time make it extremely difficult. Machine industry, rationalization, bureaucracy, the division of labour, fragmentation and specialization: all of these cause damage to the human condition, damage that may be remedied only by breaking in a radical way with the societies which they characterize. But these factors also lead to a dimming of humanity's critical faculties and yield illusions about the limited extent of its capacities that are no less illusory because they are a necessary reflection of a particular reality. This veil of illusions is rendered necessary and universal because thinkers confine their ruminations to the surface phenomena of which they are examples; they 'remain on the surface and make no attempt to advance beyond its [capitalist society's] objectively most derivative forms'.[53] The consequence of remaining on this level of surface phenomena, in which the specialization of skills destroys every image of the whole, is that thought is itself locked into a series of compartments in which the law-like determinism within is complemented by a series of autonomous, haphazard and largely unexplained links without. Economists, for example, know how the price of a commodity is determined, but cannot explain why the factors that cause fluctuations in the price themselves alter over time – except, that is, by recourse to other disciplines (to history, to politics, to psychology, or whatever). This sort of thought is acceptable as a snapshot of a static and inert society but unacceptable in a dynamic historical society where description must at every point be supported with explanation. Lukács' image of capitalist society, that it 'rests on the interaction between a necessity subject to strict laws in all isolated phenomena and the relative irrationality of the total process',[54] draws attention to the fundamental inadequacies of bourgeois thought, which describes where it should explain and which he condemns by drawing the analogy with the critic who, upon learning that the world rested upon an elephant, asked upon what the elephant stood and was satisfied with the reply: a tortoise.

The inability of bourgeois society to generate an adequate scientific analysis of its own workings is instanced by its failure to develop an account of law and by its refusal to concern itself with economic crisis. This is not the fault of particular individuals, but arises from the structural impossibility within bourgeois society of developing the historical and critical outlook necessary to solve the theoretical issues raised by its social circumstances. The revolutionary bourgeoisie had, in the person of Voltaire, declared: 'Burn your laws and make new ones,' and when asked, 'From whence can new laws be obtained?' had replied: 'From Reason.'[55] But this itself was now in dispute. The rationalism created in the course of the bourgeois epoch was now incapable of formulating new laws, because the real basis for the development of such changes, namely the power relations between the classes, 'becomes hazy and vanishes into the sciences that study it'.[56] Lukács goes on: 'a radical change in outlook is not feasible on the soil of bourgeois society',[57] even in that branch of thought concerned, as the particular sciences are not, to formulate a comprehensive overall knowledge.

This point explains why the second part of the reification essay deals with classical philosophy, in that this is the discipline that comes closest, in intention if not in result, to formulating a totalistic outlook on human life and activity. It is the highest expression of bourgeois thought; its failure signifies the failure of bourgeois thought itself and the need to develop an alternative standpoint. Lukács' discussion of classical philosophy is undertaken first to discover the insights it discovered but could not build upon and, second, to expose the failure of bourgeois thought at its highest and not its lowest point.

Throughout his discussion of classical philosophy Lukács repeats the point that what is at question is not the inability of individual philosophers properly to account for the facts of social life, but that this failure is 'the intellectual expression of the objective situation itself which it is their task to comprehend'.[58] As he puts it in the very first sentence of his account, 'Modern critical philosophy springs from the reified structure of consciousness'[59]; consequently he does not set out to provide a history of philosophy but rather 'to sketch the connections between the fundamental problems of this philosophy and the basis in existence from which these problems spring and to which they strive to return by the road of the understanding'.[60] One would think that for a marxist and in particular for one of Lukács' methodological persuasion, this would indeed qualify as a history of philosophy. Nonetheless, Lukács' sense of modesty does not restrain him from setting out the progressive encounters classical philosophy makes with what he sees as the central problem raised by modern social conditions: namely the relationship between the modern conception of rationality and what he calls the irrationality of facticity.

Lukács' argument is that modern rationalism, for all its superiority over medieval dogmatism, is nonetheless unable to overcome the gulf it definitionally introduces between the subject of knowledge and the objects of that knowledge, between 'us' and the facts. Rationalism is useful in developing the *forms* of philosophical engagement but cannot disguise its indifference to the *contents* of that knowledge, to facticity. Kant's notion of the thing-in-itself represents the acknowledgement that for all its detailed and general analyses of the phenomena of existence, there nevertheless remains a residue about which nothing at all can be known: the so-called noumena. The basis of this failure can be traced back to the very issues which raised modern rationalism beyond the dogmatism of theological philosophy These are fourfold: first, the continuity of all phenomena; second, the demand for immanent rather than transcendental causal connections between them; third, the demand that mathematical or rational categories be applied to all phenomena; finally, the parallel evolution of philosophy with the exact sciences.

Modern philosophy thus seeks no external vantage point, no archimedal point of transcendence against which to measure phenomena, but rather truth and meaning in the concepts themselves; knowledge can only be knowledge of something we ourselves create; dogmatic or religious creations must remain unknowable. The necessary consequence of this approach – which has its origin in cartesian scepticism – is to cast systematic doubt upon everything but the knowing subject; it is to doubt the possibility of our constructing knowledge of objective facticity.[61]

This notion sits uneasily alongside the triumphant successes of the natural sciences in the era of bourgeois rationalism. Kant was to epitomize this dilemma. The concept of the thing-in-itself was his way of accounting for the apparent success of the exact sciences in constructing a body of knowledge with respect to objects that manifestly were not the creation of science. The contradiction between this success and the basis of modern rationality, which held that knowledge could only be self-knowledge, was resolved in two ways: by restricting the province of knowledge to the concepts and categories generated by it (hence Lukács' disparagement of its indifference to facticity), and by accepting the discrete discourses of the individual sciences. The distinction between the knowledge-creations and the concrete objects upon which they are based and about which they are supposedly informative, is thus retained at the cost of the latter, in themselves, remaining unknowable.

Scientific specialization is hence able to justify itself both coherently and pragmatically. It develops concepts and categories that raise it above the status of pure empiricism; its practice yields tremendous practical advances to humankind's interaction with nature. It cannot, however, integrate these partial advances into a unified world outlook; it is condemned to retaining an essential scepticism with regard to basic philosophical questions. The rationalist model of knowledge can successfully overturn the dogmatism of theology, replace transcendental escapism with scientific experiment and thus claim credit for the advances science is then able to bring about. But this model cannot be applied as a model of knowledge in general; its weakness derives from attempts to translate a particular model of scientific method, namely that one generated in opposition to theological dogmatism, into a general model appropriate for knowledge as such.

Lukács refers to mathematics as the very epitome of an exact science, where the knowledge generated is definitionally true because it is itself the creation of that branch of knowledge. The material basis of the real world is not, however, amenable to the same sort of scientific methodology and a comparable degree of certainty, because its existence does not await our scientific understanding: its objectivity is ontologically distinct from the 'objects' of mathematics, formal logic or philosophy.

The special sciences in their emulation of this scientific model create the illusion that they are producing a similar kind of truth, and philosophy in its lack of concern with this process adds to that illusion. However, because the underlying base of the special sciences 'is permitted to dwell inviolate and undisturbed in its irrationality ("non-createdness" "givenness")'[62] all that results is a methodological purity and a 'refusal to understand reality as a whole and as existence'.[63] Lukács concludes by noting the double tendency of bourgeois thought:

> On the one hand, it acquires increasing control over the details of its social existence, subjecting them to its needs. On the other hand it loses – likewise progressively – the possibility of gaining intellectual control of society as a whole and with that it loses its own qualifications for leadership.[64]

We should note at this point that the basis of Lukács' critique of the bourgeois world view is simultaneously its idealism and its positivism. It is idealist in the sense that it accepts true knowledge can only be attained with respect to objects that we ourselves create; on the other hand, it is empiricist in its acceptance that the special sciences can themselves produce knowledge without any successful integration with philosophy, with existence or with facticity. Classical philosophy has aided this by its retention of 'the – dogmatic – assumption that the rational and formalistic mode of cognition is the only possible way of apprehending reality'.[65] This successfully led it (unconsciously) to question the knowledge productions of the special sciences in the sense that they do not yield knowledge of the objects in themselves, but it prevented this dogmatism from going on to develop its 'true antidote, namely the practical'.[66]

In the next chapter I will discuss the details of Lukács' own solution to this problem, namely his notion of dialectics, totality and the standpoint of the proletariat. Here I am concerned to note how the methodological basis of bourgeois thought is reciprocally influenced by its reified character.

For Lukács, as indeed for the current of anti-naturalism that surged through central Europe from the 1890s,[67] it was essential to introduce a distinction between the natural and the social sciences, partly because of the widespread tendency to explain human activity in terms of naturalistic analogies (social darwinism, the evolutionism of Spencer, the organicism of Durkheim, etc.) and partly because of a recognition that the scientific enterprise, for all its practical successes, was nonetheless compromised by its retention of a philosophical incompleteness that made possible both a profound scepticism with respect to the status of the knowledge so produced and a reversion to a materialist version of theology, to pantheism (cf. Spinoza). If scientific knowledge was restricted to the phenomenal forms, with the noumenal left untouched by it, this required a metaphysics to account for the latter, one which might yet be another alias for theology.

Lukács' commitment to the view that knowledge must be in some sense self-knowledge, or knowledge about objects of our creation, registers his complicity in the notion of rationality generated in opposition to theological metaphysics by the 'bourgeois' rationalists. This metaphysics had held that the world and its objects were the creation of God and that consequently knowledge was irrevocably coupled with faith. This transcendental knowledge was rejected in favour of an immanent knowledge, that is to say knowledge that draws its source from the object of study itself. This latter model proved incomplete in that it failed to account for wider questions with regard to the world, for which it had no answers and which thus allowed the void so created to be filled by a further development of metaphysics. This was only possible, however, because of the running together of two types of scientific enterprise, the natural and the social. The modern or bourgeois notion of rationality was, strictly speaking, only appropriate to the social world, to the creations of humanity: only here could full and complete knowledge be said to be existent. In the natural world scientific endeavours were limited to 'experiment and industry', to attempts at exploiting objects and laws already in existence; speculations about origins, nature and reality were here unanswerable except in the restricted sense of how these objects and laws presented themselves to us. The noumenal realm that lay behind them was unknowable in the scientific sense.

A dual disadvantage was thus manufactured. First, the social sciences were naturalized, their objects and laws endowed with a similar ontological objectivity to the objects and laws of the natural sciences. The realm of human creativity was falsely perceived as part of the world of nature, human laws perceived as natural ones, human restraints perceived as natural ones, and so on. Second, the natural sciences were themselves wrongly assimilated into a view of knowledge that raises the problems discussed by Kant and which undermine their claim to scientificity.

At this point we can take up again Lukács' theory of reification, since his criticism of bourgeois rationalism concerns its naturalization of the social world, its transposition of the methods of natural science to the human world and its consequent reification of the objects and laws of bourgeois society. The revolutionary methodology Lukács seeks to reestablish at the centre of marxist analysis is his alternative to the dominant scientific method of bourgeois thought: that based upon the model of the natural sciences. This latter model has even permeated into the workers' movement, where its tendency to reject 'the idea of contradiction and antagonism in its subject matter',[68] says Lukács, makes it attractive to revisionism and whose desire to define a given area of intellectual discourse in such a way that contradictions and/or antagonisms are absent has obvious political connotations. Indeed, their presence can then be passed off as an indication of error, or of the intrusion of concerns external to the matter at hand.

Lukács takes bourgeois economics as an exemplary demonstration of this point, as an example of a social model flawed by its methodological premisses. So-called positive economics, with its desire to expunge from itself all explicitly stated value judgements, manages at the same time to exclude from its subject matter all those questions that involve dysfunctional factors or political and moral choice – these are simply purged from the discipline, regarded as problems of politics, sociology or philosophy.[69] A similar process may be observed in all the separate and distinct spheres of social science, where what is gained in technical expertise as a result of this division of labour is gainsaid by the construction of a systematic structure of human thought and activity that excludes all effective political intervention, simply because nowhere is the total structure of society made the subject of critical analysis. All the questions most relevant to human society are systematically avoided, and in the name of science and the pursuit of objective truth (or perhaps one should simply say useful knowledge) there is created a structure of ideological power that oppresses critical thought.

Lukács sees three fundamental problems with the application of the natural scientific method to the human world. First, in encouraging the separation of distinct spheres of technical expertise it diverts attention away from the more general concerns of human life and society: specialization breeds a kind of theoretical tunnel-vision. Second, the objects of analysis in the natural sciences – inanimate objects or primitive forms of life – are fundamentally different from the objects of analysis of the social or human sciences – the social characteristics of humanity. The problem is thus not only that discrete spheres of human affairs are created such that their totality cannot be subject to dispute but, in addition, the manner of comprehending human affairs is based on a conception of the human subject as a passive and contemplative object. There can be no room in such a mode of thought for an adequate conception of human agency. Finally, the end result of such an approach is an empiricism that elevates the given appearance of the world into the basis and origin of science itself, whereas, as I have already had occasion to note, the character of bourgeois social relations makes the penetration of appearances a decisive characteristic of any science worthy of the name.[70]

Lukács' rejection of empiricism draws upon three important influences: his pre-1918 ethical rejection of a corrupt and corrupting world; his attachment to a Weberian *verstehendsoziologie*, which itself formulated, if not an alternative, certainly a check upon the immediate knowability of social facts; and the critical aspects of marxism. The confluence of these produced certain methodological consequences that affected and structured his attempt both to understand and to change that world, and which cannot be dismissed merely by referring to the unsatisfactory nature of any one. Lukács is led to a version of philosophy, or of science, radically different from the empiricist tradition which, in its influence upon the workers' movement, had led to what Lukács considered to be unacceptable political applications. If we pursue Lukács' rejection of empiricism a little further we will see why he regards this as so necessary to the development of a marxist 'science'.

One of the main points of divergence between Lukács' views and the methodology of the natural sciences, at least in the popular representation of it,[71] lies in the understanding of the role and function of facts in science. Lukács identifies five key weaknesses in the natural-scientific treatment of facts: it tends towards empiricism in its worship of facts, or the distillation of facts by means of observation, abstraction or experiment – theory becomes merely the means of accurately ascertaining the truth that resides in the facts; in the human sciences it passively accepts the domination over human potentialities and abilities of these facts; it ignores the definite historical character of facts; in particular, it ignores the definite historical epoch in which these facts are generated and which therefore in some sense determines them; and finally, it fails to distinguish any divergence between the essence and appearance of the facts.

Lukács' position ought not to be read as some kind of idealist rejection of facts per se, for only a year later he was to write a short book on Lenin, praising the latter's ability to formulate a 'concrete analysis of a concrete situation'.[72] What Lukács challenges is the status attributed to facts, their interpretation, the view that the study of facts is both necessary and sufficient for the creation of knowledge. In this respect he stands full-square in the tradition of classical German philosophy in asserting the primacy – though not necessarily the independence – of theory over facts, as a necessary consequence of the disjunction between the empirical content of the world (facts) and its reality. Also apparent here is the influence of Rickert, Windelband and Weber, in the drawing up of such a methodological distinction between the natural and the human world.

Lukács thus calls into question the applicability of the natural-scientific method to the study of social conditions and to the generation of social facts. He does this because such a method is incapable of integrating the facts of social life into a totality, an overall conception of reality without which it is impossible for 'knowledge of the facts...to become knowledge of reality',[73] because it compartmentalizes the world into a series of specialized forms of activity and accompanying schools of knowledge, and because it fails to question the structural-historical derivation of facts.

On this point also Lukács criticizes what he terms 'vulgar materialists', because they 'do not go beyond the reproduction of the immediate simple determinants of social life...they take the facts in abstract isolation, explaining them only in terms of abstract laws unrelated to the concrete totality'.[74] They are unable to mount an effective challenge to this dichotomy between the brute facts of everyday life and the abstract explanations of those facts. Indeed, both these orientations to the world – uncritical positivism and critical idealism – are, as Marx pointed out in 1842, two sides of the same coin.[75] If the facts are given, then whether they are justified or criticized in terms of an abstract theory they remain given, the oppressive nightmare weighing on the brain of the living.

The same problem of the applicability of the natural-scientific method to the social sciences underlies Lukács' critique of Engels' treatment of the problem of Kant's notion of the 'thing-in-itself'. According to Engels[76] the answer to the supposed unknowability of the thing-in-itself lay in the application of experiment and industry to the object: it is this that makes the object, literally, ours:

> The most telling refutation of this as of all philosophical crotchets is practice, namely, experiment and industry. If we are able to prove the correctness of our conception of a natural process by making it ourselves, bringing it into being out of its conditions and making it serve our own purposes into the bargain, then there is an end to the Kantian ungraspable thing in itself.[77]

According to Lukács however, this is simply a misunderstanding of Kant. For the generation of knowledge about the thing-in-itself does not answer Kant's belief that such knowledge, however practical, concerns only the appearance of the object and does not penetrate to its essence. Indeed, if it were Kant's position that nothing could be known of the object, then this would be absurdly false, in contravention to the advances in the natural sciences of which Kant was a keen follower.

The point is that Engels regards the thing-in-itself and the thing-for-us as opposites, whereas they are actually necessary correlatives. Knowledge of the object, the thing-for-us, does nothing to alter the objectivity of the thing itself, and the activity of experiment and industry likewise in no way transforms the thing-in-itself into its true opposite, namely the thing-for-itself. Knowledge of one object by another, or even by a subject, merely replicates the dualism that Kant takes as his starting point and it is incorrect to regard the production of such knowledge as praxis in its true sense. Moreover, such practice is but the reflection of capitalism, ensuring as it does the subsuming of the human subject under the domination of the object. The observer does not here really act – even though he or she might think that that is what is happening – but on the contrary is acted upon; such practice as does take place goes no further than 'the correct observation and calculation of the objective working out of the natural laws of society'.[78]

In his *Anti-Dühring* of 1880 also, Engels fails to appreciate the heart of the dialectical method, the 'most vital interaction, namely the dialectical relation between subject and object in the historical process':[79] a result, Lukács argues, of his misguided attempt to apply the dialectic to nature, where, in the absence of a subject, such an interaction is impossible. Lukács thus again makes the distinction between the social or human sciences, where the dialectic does have a role to play, and the natural sciences, where it does not and cannot. This is a consistent theme in Lukács' thought in this period, as is his denial of the applicability of the non-dialectical scientific method of the natural sciences to the human world and his stress on the political and methodological consequences of such attempts.

Of course, it might equally be argued that in making such a distinction Lukács in fact surrenders more ground than he thinks to the objectivists, since he leaves a whole swathe of human affairs – the investigation of the natural world – outside and beyond the critical jurisdiction of the dialectic. This is the point made by Gramsci, who criticizes Lukács thus:

> If his assertion presupposes a dualism between nature and man he is wrong because he is falling into a conception of nature proper to religion and to Graeco-Christian philosophy and also to idealism which does not in reality succeed in unifying and relating man and nature to each other except verbally. But if human history should be conceived also as the history of nature (also by means of the history of science) how can the dialectic be separated from nature?[80]

As I have indicated earlier, Lukács came later to accept such criticisms and to recognize the importance of the category of labour as the means through which the relation of humanity and nature could be brought into some kind of unity, but he did so in line with the orthodox viewpoint, by reverting to the 'experiment and industry' objectivist model of Engels. While Lukács refused the embrace of the absurdities of the dialectics of nature, which made of the dialectic a dogmatic imposition upon the methods of science, in reacting against what he now came to regard as his earlier idealism he came to denigrate the category of the subject within the act of labour and thus reinforced the belief that the production of knowledge, like the production of things – and, indeed, reality itself – consisted in the generation of laws which are 'impenetrable, fatalistic and immutable'.

The danger of such a view is that the necessity of the processes of material production come to be seen as an econonic determinism counterposed to the political activities of the proletariat. From such a viewpoint the revolutionary act of insurrection must appear as it did to Bernstein and many others, as a Blanquist interruption of the general and normal course of events, for the simple reason that for the individual, reality appears as a world governed by eternal laws of nature in which only two types of political orientation are feasible: accommodation to those laws through, for example, the development of technology, or action directed inwards of the Kantian type. Both are consequences of the dilemma of (individual) impotence, itself a consequence of the analysis of social affairs in terms of economic fatalism. By falsely separating 'economics' from 'politics' and by explaining the latter as a mere determination of the former, the way is left open for an economic determinism that far from guaranteeing the eventual triumph of socialism, by virtue of its reductionist account of reality and ignorance of the importance of agency actually makes its realization impossible.

6 Lukács, Revolution and the Party

I promised in the previous chapter that I would go on to examine Lukács' proposed solution to the static and dogmatic methodological basis of bourgeois thought that he analysed in terms of reification. This chapter presents, therefore, an account of Lukács' proposed alternative to this, namely his notion of dialectics, totality and the standpoint of the proletariat. In the course of this analysis I will have cause to discuss whether or not Lukács' attraction to the revolutionary capacity of the proletariat was a conjunctural appeal determined by the historico-social circumstances of his epoch, or a trans-historical philosophical commitment; the precise nature of Lukács' reaffirmation of the works of the early Marx; the character of the relationship between Lukács' philosophical interpretation of the reified social relations of bourgeois society and the alleged capacity of the proletariat to penetrate and to revolutionize these. This latter point will involve discussion of the role party organization plays in Lukács' thought as the form of transmission between this philosophico-revolutionary mission and the practical and concrete tasks of the proletariat. I will discuss this aspect of Lukács' thought in terms of a comparison with Lenin's account of the role of party organization.

In chapter 4 I had cause to criticize Lukács' estimation of *History and Class Consciousness* made in his 1967 preface to that work, where he overemphasizes the political/conjunctural determinants of the book in order to retrieve for himself a reconciliation with the limited achievements of 'socialism in one country'. Here I want to demonstrate that whether or not Lukács was himself influenced at the time by the wave of revolutionary militancy that broke out throughout the advanced capitalist societies in the post-war period, the importance of the book - the philosophical questions it addressed, as well as its proposed solutions to these – in fact transcends these circumstances, just as it transcends and offers solutions to the pessimism of the present. Rather than riding the waves of historical change, the book, properly understood, offers a buoyancy that shields from both violent turbulence and becalming immobility. Lukács' revolutionary dialectic, the uniting of theory and practice by the aim of transforming the present through the agency of the proletariat, is, in a phrase, the marxist method that *History and Class Consciousness* makes its own, even as it returns to the themes of the early Marx, rescuing marxism from both the quagmire of ephemeral detail and the overladen determinism of the reified consciousness of bourgeois society into which it had fallen. By so doing, marxism as a political theory is given an anchor point from which it can escape fatalism, the product of both the overly deterministic philosophy of orthodoxy and the exigential opportunism of reformism. In other words, Lukács provides a third way for modern marxism, diverging from orthodoxy and reformism and thus illuminating, albeit in a fundamentalist light, an emergent western marxism.

All this of course begs the question: how does Lukács' revolutionary dialectic work?

Totality

As we have seen in the previous chapter, Lukács' dissatisfaction with the unmediated character of (bourgeois) social thought led him to an analysis and critique of its reified character. He is thus required to confront this immediacy, this divinity of the factual, with a methodology and a practice that can transcend it. This he locates in the proletariat and its authentic political practice, that is to say Lukács' characterization of marxism lies in his adoption of the standpoint of the proletariat.

To begin with, Lukács observes a fundamental chasm between the triumph of rationality and necessity in each particular sphere of social life (and theory) – as these come to instantiate the particular form and content of commodification – and the overall irrationality of the system as a whole.[1] While he is undoubtedly influenced by Weber's conception of bureaucracy and the consequent construction of an 'iron cage' of rationality out of the materials of specialization, this contradiction between localized rationality and universal irrationality is also an extension to universal significance of that dichotomy traditionally located by marxism, between the planned, organized rationality of the factory and the anarchy of the market.

Lukács' own approach in this matter takes as his starting point the notion of totality,[2] a category altogether absent from Weber's thought. It is the structure of commodity production that gives determination and shape to each particular enterprise, each of which in turn is both the instantiation of that system as a whole as well as being necessary to it. There is an interactive relationship between each individual part and the whole: the latter determines and gives shape to the former, while itself being dependent for its maintenance and development upon the former's ability to camouflage this, its reality. Each separate department of specialization, to all intents and purposes autonomous and independent, develops skills in a direction that destroys every image of the whole, of the totality. Each department, each science, turns its back on the wider problems of the total social nexus and its position in and relation to it and becomes, in Lukács words, 'a formally closed system of partial laws'.

The result of this is two-fold: a deactivation of the subject and a naturalization of the object. The function of knowledge is stripped of its dynamic character; the scientist merely discovers or is made aware of the necessity and determinations of reality; the domination of specialization and the consequent loss of totality; the freezing of immediate factuality and the consequent absence of dynamism; an uncritical methodology – all these mark the passive and contemplative relationship of humanity to the world engendered by this method.

The alternative methodology Lukács advocates against this fragmentary and hence disarming approach is what he calls the dialectical conception of totality.[3] Only this approach dissolves the characteristically reified structure of bourgeois thought by making possible an understanding of reality as a social process in which human agency plays a more crucial role than the mere contemplation of external events.

He would, of course, be claiming too much were he to assert that the concept of change was ignored by other social theories, but for him the concept takes on a particular slant that assumes nothing less than revolutionary significance. The sort of change for which Lukács is concerned to provide the philosophical justification is not limited to the 'interaction of otherwise unchanging objects' but is nothing less than 'a change in the form of objectivity itself'.[4] This conception of change is different, first because of the presence of a social agent active in the very processes of social and historical change, and not merely a passive recipient of externally generated historical events; and second because in the very act of history, that agent destroys the false objectivity that had hitherto kept it the prisoner of a particular reality. Knowledge of reality which was at first merely the classification and recording of external data thus becomes transformed into human self-knowledge, that is knowledge about the structures and events created through the intervention of human agency and knowledge that through its very generation brings about a fundamental change in its recipient, who is brought to a level of social awareness that punctures the false objectivity that previously paralysed its will and capacity to act. It is, moreover, the social conditions of life that make this situation both possible and necessary, that bring about the rise to self-consciousness of social life. This is the unconscious achievement of bourgeois society: it makes individuals truly social where before they were not; and it creates the specific social force that can, and indeed must, survey the whole of society as its own, that can truly claim to constitute social knowledge as self-knowledge. In Lukács' words:

> for the proletariat the total knowledge of its class situation was a vital necessity, a matter of life and death; because its class situation becomes comprehensible only if the whole of society can be understood; and because this understanding is the inescapable precondition of its actions. Thus the unity of theory and practice is only the reverse side of the social and historical position of the proletariat...the proletariat is at one and the same time the subject and object of its own knowledge.[5]

We can thus see that Lukács' discussion of scientific methodology has a specifically political significance, in that his advocacy of the revolutionary dialectic not only provides the basis for criticism of alternative models of scientific method, but is at the same time a philosophical justification for the possibility of revolutionary change and the rise to social power of the proletariat. By uniting theory and practice in the praxis of the working class and by using the category of totality to avoid the ideological influence of bourgeois thought, this method has resulted in a relationship to reality that is both critical and active and that provides a pole of reference by which to demarcate orthodoxy from heresy. It is therefore from the standpoint of the proletariat, its class struggle and its development of a revolutionary consciousness, that Lukács sees embodied the essence of the marxist method.

This method has not, however, been the dominant or even the most usual method adopted by marxists; far more frequent has been the appeal to science or to the role economics plays in reality and in marxist thought. Lukács takes up these views at several points in *History and Class Consciousness* with the intention of highlighting their weaknesses and their proximity to bourgeois thought.For example, in the essay 'The Marxism of Rosa Luxemburg', Lukács develops his position by contrasting it with those 'vulgar marxists' (among whom he does not include Rosa Luxemburg) who see the primacy of economic motives, and not the category of totality, as the distinguishing feature of marxism and the hallmark of science.[6] Once again Lukács reiterates the vital importance to marxism of the hegelian dialectic – Herzen's 'algebra of revolution' – and argues that it was the situation of that dialectic within an overall totality that marked Marx's break with hegelianism, not the simple transposition of matter over idea, of materialism over idealism (which had in any case already been achieved by Feuerbach). The totalizing point of view permits the reestablishment of the unity of theory and practice, absent from Hegel's philosophy except in mythological form, as well as from hitherto existing materialism, because it denies the separation of being and thought.[7] It can do this for two reasons: first, because of its location of a mediator between being and thought – the universal class that can unite subject and object; and second, because the discovery of this historically located mediator links the present to the future and thus puts an end to the limitations which the past imposes as a burden upon the present.[8] There is of course another fundamental criticism of bourgeois thought that has consequences for those who typify marxism as an economic science, and that is its concern with the individual as the focal point of social thought and action. Because bourgeois thought 'judges social phenomena...consistently from the standpoint of the individual',[9] says Lukács, it is thereby unable to puncture the 'appearance of a world governed by the eternal laws of nature'.[10] It is only from the basis of a class viewpoint that the appearance of reality can be penetrated to its essence, to its reality and thus be in a position to seek its transformation; only the aggregate has the capability of achieving this. From the standpoint of the individual such a feat is made literally incredible by the dominance of the normal course of events – whether these are described in economic, political or ideological terms. That is to say, individuals are in normal circumstances stymied by those circumstances, their range of action constrained and limited by their lack of power. The consequence of such a viewpoint is that the act of revolution cannot be understood as anything more than 'an isolated act cut off from the general course of events',[11] a judgement similar to that Kautsky made of the forthcoming war in 1914.[12]

We have already seen how Lukács challenged the interpretation of Feuerbach as a materialist thinker in the marxist sense, how the absence in Feuerbach of a dialectical approach to materialism made his philosophy quite unsuitable for the development of historical materialism. In this respect Lukács' critique of reification deals precisely with this tendency to regard materialism, the economic motive, or whatever, as the primary force operating upon and determining human activities as if by a law of nature. In Feuerbach's case it is as if individuals were rescued from the domination of their own religious sentiment only then to be imprisoned again in the uncritically regarded prison of human sensuousness. Similarly, the tendency among some marxists to regard the demonstration of economic motives as sufficient explanation of social phenomena (while enjoying some degree of truth) is incomplete, since the economic movements in society do not in themselves generate the sort of revolutionary change Lukács for one is in favour of.

This point may be illustrated by reference to two articles by Gerry Cohen and Tony Skillen,[13] both of which challenge the view that economic interests will inevitably lead the working class towards socialism. These articles demonstrate that the economic fact of exploitation does not necessarily lead the working class towards a collective solution to the ills that it endures, but may instead simply reinforce the individualistic ethic of capitalism. Instrumental calculation, says Skillen, is insufficient to compel a socialist consciousness – for this a socialist ethic is required, since it is precisely by appeal to instrumental calculation that workers are persuaded to accept, for example, that wages are too high, that strikes are self-defeating and that blacklegging, avoiding disputes and bowing to authority are ways to improve their lot in life. The influence of these sorts of beliefs is undoubtedly affected by the overall industrial and political climate, being more prevalent at some times than others, but it is a universal barrier to socialist ideas.

Cohen seeks to define in his article the precise nature of proletarian exploitation in capitalist society and comes to the view that collective unfreedom (of the working class) co-exists with the possibility at least of individual freedom. He goes through the usual objections to collective unfreedom and socialist objections to the idea of individual freedom and concludes that for at least some members of the working class the possibility exists for some form of individual solution to the economic exploitation that remains for the class as a whole – through 'rising' to the petty-bourgeois shopkeeping class (the example Cohen uses), through trade union officialdom, the education system, or whatever. The economic and aggregate importance of this escape route may be rather minimal, but its ideological importance is crucial.

One would wish to register some reservations with regard to the effectiveness and reality of these individual 'solutions', and certainly Lukács never believed that such a means of escape was possible.[14] Despite these reservations, however, two important points retain their validity. First, despite evidence to the contrary, the perception of the possibility of such individual means of escape is an important counterbalance to the denial of such means and advocacy of the necessity for a collective solution. Second, despite this, the fact remains that for the class as a whole (and thus for those who analyse society in class terms) such individual means, even were they found to exist, are irrelevant to the problems caused by the conditions of life of the mass. As Eugene Debs expressed the matter, the point for socialists is to 'rise with the working class and not above them'.

There is thus a paradox: whilst capitalist production is the source of the class struggle that leads to both the creation of the proletariat and the possibility of its own transformation, it is also, and at the same time, the central point of the domination of labour and the working class by capital.

It is important to understand that these social factors limiting the appeal or efficacy of socialist solutions are not artificial impositions upon the normal processes of capitalist development but are essential to its social reproduction, and it is thus necessary to recognize the limitations of that process of development: that it will not of its own accord create the political force that will overthrow it. The notion that society is governed by extra-human laws, whether these justify the eternal existence of capitalism or indicate its inevitable demise, is a self-validating intellectual construction rejected both by Lukács and by Marx.[15] Such a notion is encouraged and strengthened by the conditions of life in capitalist society; it is also perhaps the primary guarantee of the ideological hegemony and continued reproduction of that system of society.

It is opposition to this belief that lies at the heart of Lukács' critique of social democracy, for he sees in the reflective attitude towards the 'laws' or 'facts' of capitalism the basis of passivity and opportunism, the strategy of adaptation to such laws or to action 'directed inwards'. An inability to regard society dialectically, that is in terms of the development of a revolutionary consciousness among the working class, leads necessarily, given the economic determinism that explains capitalism's great success, to an attitude of resignation and defeat. In contrast to this view of economic fatalism Lukács champions the 'economic' views of Rosa Luxemburg which, despite her predilection for a 'breakdown theory' nevertheless deal with capitalism as an historical totality rather than a category 'in general'. Her approach treats capitalism and the problems of the capitalist epoch as an essential unity. Imperialism, for example, far from being the chosen policy of a degenerate ruling class is the result of the problems and difficulties of capitalist accumulation. It is a further manifestation of the integration within capitalist society of all spheres of human life: economic, political, ideological and now military.

A sharp distinction is therefore drawn between two views with regard to the emergence of socialism. On the one hand there is the approach shared by much of social democracy that stresses the element of continuity between capitalism and socialism, regarding the success of the latter as guaranteed by the economic developments of the former. Thus expansion of the productive forces, the concentration and centralization of capital, the spread of capitalism to encompass the whole world, the erosion or destruction of all vestiges of pre-capitalist social relations, the increased involvement of the state in economic affairs – all these are held to indicate how socialism develops inside and within capitalism, just as did bourgeois relations within feudal society and will, given time and by avoiding premature outbreaks of conflict, lead necessarily to its supersession.

On the other hand there is the view favoured by Lukács and by Luxemburg – and the parallels with Lukács' criticisms of the worship of objectivity should here become obvious – which places far greater stress on the requirement to transform the very nature of these objective developments. This requires the active and conscious agency of the major productive force itself – the proletariat – but this role will not be one of gratefully accepting the benefits of these developments. Rather it involves subjecting them to a further process of revolution, so that not only are they taken out of the hands of the bourgeois class, not only is the process of socialization (itself an objective development within capitalism) taken a stage further, but in and through the process of revolution the proletariat actually seizes control of these objective processes, subjecting them to its dictates, making them its own. This leap, this change in the course of social development puts an end to 'the self-reproduction of the capitalist relation and gives the self-reproduction of society another, new direction...for the first time mankind consciously takes its history into its own hands'.[16] This is not merely in the sense that it acts upon history, but that by so doing the 'objectivity' of bourgeois economic and social laws is abolished; the 'economy' loses its self-contained autonomy, is abolished and through the revolutionary act the proletariat breaks the 'enslaving hold of reified relations over man and the hold of economics over society'[17] and creates an economy – if it may be so called - that is nothing more than the 'servant of a consciously directed society'.[18]

The Proletariat

Lukács' starting point, then, is not an empirical analysis of society but the political problem of transforming society – or more accurately it is to subsume the analysis of society under the historical imperative of changing it. This task cannot be achieved except by embodying theory and practice in a mediator that can transcend the limitations of both dull objectivism and utopian aspiration. This mediator is the proletariat.

To support his view Lukács refers back to Marx's early writings to emphasize the crucial and indeed central role played by the proletariat in marxist thought, how it is at one and the same time both a material force rooted in reality and a force striving for the overthrow or transformation of that reality. Its revolutionary potential, its capacity to bring about such a transformation, is given not by its adherence to ideas or to a philosophy conceived independently of it, nor does it flow inevitably from reality itself; it requires a union of these two factors. Lukács quotes Marx thus: 'it is not enough for thought to strive for realization, reality must itself strive towards thought.'[19] This is the essential pre-condition for the unity of theory and practice, embodied – or actualized – in the proletariat, whose ability to assert itself in society flows from and in turn reinforces its capacity to understand society, and its own position within it, as a whole. The proletariat, then, mediates between those polarities that if left unmediated paralyse the development of change; it mediates between present reality and the future, between material existence and philsophical critique.

Lukács does not restrict himself to a notion of proletariat as a material force denuded of that spiritual or intellectual aspect which is to be located in philosophy. The importance attached to the proletariat lies precisely in its mediating function between reality and ideas about reality. It brings the latter down to earth and by so doing subjects both to a radical and democratic critique, overcoming the dualism of utopian intention and material impotence by embodying within itself not only the concentrated miseries of capitalist exploitation but also the epistemological capacity to understand its situation and to recognize the necessity to change it. The proletariat is located in material reality but, in addition, philosophy, or rather true philosophy (i.e. marxism), is in turn located within the proletariat. To assert itself the proletariat must understand society and its own position within it; to understand these correctly is the prelude to asserting itself over them. In consequence, 'the class becomes both the subject and the object of knowledge'.[20]

That this was no arbitrary imposition upon Marx's own conception I have demonstrated in chapters 1 and 2, where I expounded Marx's views concerning the historical compulsion propelling the proletariat to emancipation via the 'steeling school of labour' and the self-abolishing consequences of its function as 'dehumanization which is conscious of its dehumanization'. From this point of view the social tendencies that propel the proletariat to struggle and revolt are dependent, if they are to enjoy a successful outcome, upon the proletariat achieving both a true appreciation of its role and function within capitalist society, and of its ability to remedy this through political activity.[21] Philosophy, or knowledge, is thus not so much put at the service of this part of reality but becomes part of reality itself, the demiurge of this revolutionary power and the new reality it is about to impose upon the old.

There is, though, a major difficulty with regard to this position, a difficulty that remained latent, and therefore unexplored, in Marx's time but which came to assume central importance for marxists at the turn of the century and one to which Lukács directed himself. For while the revolutionary force, the proletariat, is actual, in that it is a real and concrete material force located in reality, it is not yet real, it is not yet conscious of itself as a revolutionary force – and until it becomes so philosophy is not yet at one with the world, or even with its own material embodiment – nor can it be so until the revolutionary process, understood in terms of both substantive political change and proletarian self-enlightenment, brings it to this state. For Lukács, just as for Marx, the need for a unity of theory and practice through the mediation of the class struggle of the proletariat was the key task for those who seek radical change, with theory performing the role of guide to the praxis of the working class: it is 'essentially the intellectual expression of the revolutionary process itself'.[22] But until this is achieved the relationship is bound to be subject to the stormy vicissitudes of class struggle, with failure and compromise drawing it ever wider apart. In the absence of a mass movement Marx was not called upon to address himself to this problem (which is not to say that elements of his work may not aid any such analysis), but the changed historical and political environment by the time Lukács came to prominence as a marxist brought about a distinct shift in emphasis between them.

For since the death of Marx in 1883 capitalism had survived a further forty years of development, an epoch of development, moreover, that was as cataclysmic as that earlier period eulogized in *The Communist Manifesto*. Capitalism had taken itself literally and metaphorically into the twentieth century; it had survived the Great Depression and expanded to encompass the whole world; it now exploited intensively and extensively and this new form of imperialism had heightened all its previous antagonisms, raising them to a world level. The wondrous expansion of the productive forces had culminated in the great imperialist world war, itself a mark of the great crisis towards which the system had lurched and from which it was now attempting to extricate itself.

The bolshevik revolution had revealed what lay beyond the precipice of disaster and precisely because of this the crisis of capitalism was now also a crisis of marxism.[23]

Despite the decades of economic development in which the working class had taken tremendous strides – socially, politically and organizationally – it had, with the single, possibly unique exception of Soviet Russia,[24] been unable to take successful advantage of this world-wide crisis. The imperialist war had hastened and made final the hitherto latent splits and divisions within the socialist movement, but nonetheless the relative weakness of the communist parties and the continued influence of social democracy created a central problem for marxists of this period, and indeed ever since. Revolutionary consciousness had not been generated by a century or more of economic development and socialist agitation, nor by the political and economic crisis signified by the world war. How were marxists to respond to this failure?

Having himself attached so much importance to the epistemological and revolutionary role of the proletariat as the ultimate arbiter of the truth of marxism, Lukács must also come to terms with this unexpected perpetuation of capitalism. The self-derogatory comments of his 1967 preface to *History and Class Consciousness* have led many to perceive the book as merely a reflection of the revolutionary crisis of 1919–23 and it is certainly true that Lukács regarded capitalism as close to overthrow at the time. But while this perhaps explains Lukács' sudden and unexpected recruitment to the Hungarian Communist Party in November 1918, and the investment of his hopes and expectations in the revolutionizing potential of the proletariat, it would be quite wrong to manufacture a conflation of revolutionary epoch and revolutionary theory. Although it is true that the revolutionary conditions at the time made possible and encouraged the theory of proletarian revolution developed by Lukács in this period – and similarly by Marx in the period of the 1848 revolutions – these do not exhaust the matter and we should not fall into the genetic fallacy of explaining the book's importance in terms only of its generation. The particular character of, and also the conclusion to, that period play an equally important role in requiring an account not only of the revolutionary potential of the proletariat but also of the barriers to that potential. Consequently, Lukács' theory of revolution was but part of an overall social theory cognizant of the barriers to as well as the assailants of revolutionary change; this fact gives the book a relevance and contemporaneity it would not have were it simply the reflection of a political conjuncture no longer existent.

In the light of a further period of capitalist development since the book's appearance, it has often been pointed out that Lukács' own attempt to bridge the gap between revolutionary potential and actual consciousness was a failure. It has also been argued that in seeking to establish a link between the two, Lukács was merely constructing upon the 'messianic sectarianism' of the time an idealist-subjectivist social theory that could not but run aground at the first indication of capitalist stabilization (as indeed happened) and thus end up as an apology for an objective state of affairs over which it had no control or purchase. Lukács eventually came to this view himself, offering in 1967 an explanation for his failure to construct a bridge between reality and the future. He draws our attention to 'the disappearance of the ontological objectivity of nature', to 'an overriding subjectivism', to a 'relapse into idealistic contemplation' – all of which arise, he argues, because in the work 'the purview of economics is narrowed down because its basic marxist category, labour as the mediator of the metabolic interaction between society and nature, is missing.'[25] What is left is 'an attempt to out-Hegel Hegel...an edifice boldly erected above every possible reality'.[26]

Lukács' hindsight-aided view of his early work is shared by Lucien Goldmann, who regarded the 'reality-horizon' perceived by Lukács in 1919-23 as 'almost an apocalyptic vision' that now 'has value primarily as an ideal concept, not as a practical reality'.[27] Should we share this view and regard *History and Class Consciousness* as an important historical document whose political views were determined by the unrealized (and unrealizable) revolutionary expectations of the time and which consequently no longer have any direct relevance? This view is shared by most commentators on Lukács. Members of the 'Telos' group, for example, saw the revival of interest in Lukács in the west as part of the (shortlived) resurgence of militancy of the 1960s, the demise of which led them to a reassessment of Lukács in terms of a 'cultural critique' that, though an important characteristic of Lukács' thought, taken on its own (that is, outside the compass of his revolutionary thought), denies to his thought as a whole its marxist character. The means by which they seek to achieve this reinterpretation of Lukács, by way of a critique of his bolshevism and its degeneration into stalinism, is a method shared with Victor Zitta's book[28] which not only distorts the revolutionary essence of Lukács' own thought but also conflates into one movement the quite distinct emphases, traditions and methods of bolshevism and stalinism.

It is my contention that *History and Class Consciousness* must be judged not in terms of the immediate political situation that existed at the time of its origination, and certainly not in terms of the psychological attitude of the author, but according to the problematic to which it was a contribution, which was: given the practical-revolutionary mission of the proletariat, and the theoretical-practical status of marxism itself, what are the internal barriers to the realization of this dialectic? More simply, what are the factors that prevent, or hold back, the creation of a revolutionary consciousness and politics among the working class?

It is true that Lukács' attempts to indicate how revolutionary class consciousness may be brought about is the most contentious part of the book, based as it is at times upon a belief in economic breakdown – for example, when he remarks that

> the class consciousness of the proletariat...does not advance according to mechanical laws...its true essence can only become visible in its authentic form when the historical process imperiously requires it to come into force, i.e., when an acute crisis in the economy drives it into action.[29]

and at other times upon a typically bolshevik appreciation of the role of the revolutionary party. For the moment it is enough to note that this problem is one common to all marxists who sought and seek to apply the revolutionary dialectic to the non-revolutionary conditions of western Europe.

In essence, Lukács offers an account of this process that is in most respects similar to that advocated by the Communist International in its early years. It is the changed outlook and orientation of that body after 1923 that account for the belief that Lukács' views were a theoretical heresy. What the early Lukács and the early Communist International shared was an attempt to account for and overcome the difficulties faced by revolutionaries in the conditions of western Europe; both sought to inject revolutionary theory and practice into a non-revolutionary situation. It is on this point that further evidence is accrued of Lukács' supposed idealism. His 'ideal-type' model of revolutionary class consciousness is said to be independent and autonomous of all possible realities, while the consequences of the absence of such a consciousness in reality are such that his theory takes on a religious aspect, expressed in terms of a withdrawal from the world and a complementary worship of the divinity of the theoretician or party.[30] The problem is, of course, that revolutionary class consciousness does not, indeed cannot, exist as a thing until the moment of revolution itself: it is not until then an 'empirically given', even of a minority, but part of a process of self-activity and struggle by means of which the proletariat constitutes itself independent of the system of capitalist production. The absence of a revolutionary current among the proletariat creates the basis for a process of substitution and bureaucratization within the party that seeks to instantiate that current, and this historical fact or tendency appears to discredit or to cast serious doubt upon the very notion of a revolutionary party engaging in political practice in non-revolutionary conditions.

The essential point is that neither Lukács nor Marx before him thought that it was encumbent upon them to abandon the advocacy of revolution as soon as this was taken off the immediate political agenda as a realistic expectation. Instead, Marx explicitly, and Lukács implicitly, sought to analyse and to explain the reasons why this state of affairs came about, why revolution failed to appear or failed to succeed.

The failure of many marxists to resist the ambiguous verdict of history, to accept the non-revolutionary facts of the modern world rather than to integrate these into a fuller account of the nature (and capacities) of bourgeois society, leaves them at the beck and call of history, akin to Spinoza's free stone, conscious only of the direction in which it is, or they are, thrown. Lukács was himself, for various reasons, also unable to withstand the social and political pressures of the communist movement after 1923 and made a 'tactical retreat' to his own 'reconciliation with reality'. But in *History and Class Consciousness* he left a tribute to the high point of the post-war revolutionary wave, incorporating both advocacy of the necessity of revolution and an awareness of the barriers to its achievement.

Lukács takes as his starting point his understanding of marxism as involving the uniting of theory and practice through the political agency of the working class and its development, through history, of a revolutionary class consciousness – but he then goes on to examine and to analyse those features of capitalism that disarm and weaken that process. Because the failures of pre-war social democracy and its distortion of marxism are one of the main points of analysis in the book, it also anticipates later judgements of the 1919-23 crisis, which account for the failure of socialism in terms of the location of a prime weakness of the working-class movement: the existence within it of 'bourgeois' modes of thought, expressed through the influence of social democracy. Thus Lukács notes in *The Changing Function of Historical Materialism* how 'the view of history favoured by the vulgar marxists has...been a decisive influence on the actions of the workers, parties and on their political theory and tactics.'[31] This point follows on from his recognition of the need to challenge revisionism and utopianism, to realize at the same time that their vulgarization of marxism is a consequence not so much of personal failings as of the widespread ideological influence of bourgeois thought.[32] This provides us with the key to the whole text, which is concerned with the distortions within marxism caused by the influence of bourgeois thought, the weaknesses and shortcomings of bourgeois thought in general and its debilitating role within the working-class movement. And also, as we shall soon see, the role played by party organization in attempting to remedy this situation.

The Party

In Leszek Kolakowski's stimulating (if prejudiced) account of the development of marxism,[33] he makes much of the discovery that Lukács' revolutionary dialectic is in accord with his commitment to communism and his advocacy of the role of the (communist) party. This should not, however, generate the surprise it might, for two reasons. First, Lukács' understanding of the role and function of the party was not limited to that stalinist version imposed by the 'bolshevized' Comintern after 1924. Second, the importance of party organization follows logically upon Lukács' notion of the revolutionary dialectic – which Lukács takes from Marx as much as from Lenin. For if, as Lukács and Marx say it is, the function of the proletariat is to mediate between existing society and the revolutionary future and if also, as they also both recognize, the proletariat is itself a product of the historical process, the question then arises: who mediates the mediator?

Let us remind ourselves at this point that our use of the term proletariat does not follow as a point of fidelity to Marx or to Lukács, but is used to symbolize an important distinction that is too often put aside, or else dismissed as idealist. For while the working class is always with us, an empirical existent, the proletariat is a politico-social category whose reality is in a state of becoming; it is, in this sense, the essence of the actual and existing working class, whose purity is diluted in two ways: sociologically, by the existence of those who work but are not part of the central processes of capitalist accumulation (i.e. non-productive workers); and ideologically (or philosophically) by workers whose consciousness does not corespond to their social position.In other words, to speak of the working class is incorrect and incoherent, for the term disguises a multifarious variety of social interest and circumstance, political standpoint and participation, ideological viewpoint and commitment. To attribute any mission at all to such an entity would be futile, easily falsifiable and would fly in the face of a pluralistic variety and disharmony within that class. This is not to retreat into a pluralistic agnosticism;[34] for all this variety there is a common point, the exploitation of the labour process in the interests of the capitalist system of accumulation, and this introduces into this cacophenous toing and froing periodic and systemic outbursts of unifying class struggles, which affect first one section of this class and then another.[35] That is to say, the existence of class struggle affects unevenly the consciousness of the working class; its vanguard is ever changing as it responds to the vicissitudes of the class struggle.[36] In such circumstances a mediator is required to hold together and to impose upon those different sections of the same class a united opposition to its opponents, to draw together and to make conscious the history of its struggle and to formulate the strategy and the tactics that will best serve its long-term interests. This mediator is vested in party organization.

The nature of the relationship between evolutionist reformism and revolutionary vanguardism seems on first examination to depend upon the nature of representation – the reformist party represents the unorganized and non- revolutionary majority; the revolutionary party the militant and revolutionary vanguard or minority. In fact however, the difference resides in something more fundamental, namely the theoretical notion of class itself. If the role of party organization is merely one of representation, or even the mobilization of representation, then the prospects are bleak indeed for the revolutionary vanguard; if the party represents the mass of wage workers, then so long as these wage workers remain wedded to the existing social conditions the party must also be reformist, whether it is able to admit to it or not. Moreover, since the working class is itself moulded by capitalism, which meets most of its needs for most of the time (even if it also creates most of those needs)[37] the working class will tend to accept for the most part the structural limits of capitalist society. Opposition will take the form of a 'trade union consciousness' that will seek to further the interests of sections of the class while remaining part of the prevailing economic ordering of society, and this will set the seal upon the limitations of the majority of the class for most of the time.

Capitalism creates the objective conditions for socialism, the proletariat above all. But it does not do this in a unilinear, smooth and gradual manner. The proletariat is formed in a particular way; involved, it is true, in its own creation and reproduction, but nonetheless the object as well as the expression of the movement of capitalism. Capitalism defines the class but it first defines the individual, the cause célèbre of marginal economics: atomized, cut off from the wider social body and thus particular and narrow. It is this historical subject that emerges as a working class and thus it is not sufficient for such a class or for a party representing its interests merely to represent or even to seize political power: to be able to go beyond such a coup d'état and to build a new form of classless society, this class must also change itself, it must engage in a process of auto-suppression. And the party charged with this task must engage in the very creation of such a class; it must, in part at least, create the class it is to lead to power.

The proletariat is the universal class that may abolish all class divisions, but it emerges from a working class that expresses and resumes the entire mechanism that regulates capitalist society. It represents human labour as a commodity and is thus in its immediacy the very essence of capitalism, its most faithful expression. It does not have an objective existence as a revolutionary class except through the mediation of revolutionary class consciousness. Until it changes itself it is no more than a possibility: fragmented, sectional and subaltern. Only in and through this act of revolutionary class consciousness can the proletariat liberate itself both from the ideology and control of capitalism and from the sectionalism and fragmentation given it by its role in capitalist society. This is so because capitalist rule is based not primarily upon the ideological manipulation of the working class but on the basis of the actual day-to-day workings of the economy and society. These have the effect of causing the internalization of commodity relations and the reification of human relations.

Thus the proletariat is not in its immediacy capable of achieving full revolutionary class consciousness. Its class consciousness develops under capitalism,[38] but it cannot develop fully except by passing through the liberation of revolution, by participating in the festival of the oppressed. Until then it is stultified by its very role and function in capitalist society and the extent of its limitations are symbolized by the nature of its demands: organization against the distribution of resources via the market, rather than the elimination of exploitation itself. Hence the problem is not one merely of consciousness. The very formation of the proletariat does not create a pure proletariat but rather, because this is a historical process, it gives rise to a host of structural and historical differences between groups of workers and so develops the stratification of the working class.

All of this is to say that the working class is not, even during periods of militancy, capable of generating a revolutionary consciousness as a mass; elements within it may well do so at particular times under particular circumstances, but its transformation into a revolutionary force requires a mediator that will take it beyond the immediacy of its life experience. This then raises the contextual importance of Lukács' book since it reveals the other debate within which Lukács was intervening, namely the debate on the question of party organization which had been initiated at the turn of the century but which at that stage had been located primarily at the level of political strategy and tactics. Lukács' second great achievement in *History and Class Consciousness* (his first had been his appreciation of Marx's treatment of the role of the proletariat as an essential element of his revolutionary dialectic) was to provide a philosophical justification for the realpolitik of bolshevism. This is not to say that Lukács followed the bolshevik line at the time – the influence upon him of the 'ultra left' and the already-emergent tendency to bureaucratism in the Comintern provided key points of difference for Lukács. Rather, Lukács' work then was based upon a theoretical (and at times abstract) appreciation of the issues contemporarily the focal points of political debate. Perhaps the tragedy for Lukács and for the book was that it appeared at a time when the political conjuncture was no longer receptive to it: the European revolutionary movement faced setbacks at home and away and the response of the Comintern to these setbacks put the seal upon Lukács' uncompromising book.

Let us then seek to locate *History and Class Consciousness* in the context of the organizational debate initiated by Lenin in 1902 with his publication of *What Is To Be Done*?

As with all of Lenin's writings, *What Is To Be Done*? has to be understood in the specific terms and circumstances of its origination.[39] The book is no philosophical treatise but deals at length with the particular circumstances faced by socialists attempting to organize in tsarist Russia at the turn of the century. Importantly, there was no revolutionary workers' party at that time – though a founding conference had taken place in March 1898.[40] The socialist movement, such as it was, consisted of small scattered groups, composed mainly of intellectuals whose contact with the working class was minimal (if increasing) and who survived (or perished) under conditions of police repression and clandestinity.

There are three crucial themes, important for our purposes here, that may be identified and abstracted from Lenin's book: the question of theory; the relation between trade union and socialist politics; and the relations between spontaneity and consciousness. The relevance of the following points of comparison between the Lenin of 1902 and the Lukács of 1923 lies in the similar political situation faced by each: both represented a theoretical position marginal to the existing working-class movement, developed on Lenin's part by his opposition to narodnism and economism and on Lukács' by opposition to orthodoxy and revisionism. Each, therefore, had peculiar reasons for stressing the importance and distinctiveness of their particular form of theory and of criticizing the resistance to theory in general and the particular variant of it adopted by their opponents.

Whereas Lukács' orthodox opponents were themselves well known as the purveyors of marxist theory to the working-class movement, Lenin was faced with a political situation in which theory, as well as the role of intellectuals, was much more problematic. The tradition of the narodniks and the spontaneous militancy of the Russian peasantry had led to the delusion that intellectuals had only to submerge themselves into the lower orders in order to further the revolutionary movement.[41] It was against this tradition that Plekhanov and Kautsky had raised the standard of marxist theory; it is hardly surprising therefore if we should find echoes of their theories in Lenin's own work. In fact Lenin's vitriolic polemic against the trend of economism (which stressed the economic trade union struggle rather than the political revolutionary struggle, of becoming involved or immersed in the day-to-day struggles of the workers rather than the development of a political programme) takes over, as we shall see, large parts of Kautsky's own interpretation of theory.

Lukács' own advocacy of the standpoint of the proletariat places him comfortably in the marxist tradition discussed here in chapters 1 and 2, but Lenin's view expressed through his newspaper *Iskra* came under fierce attack from the economists precisely because it failed to stress, as they did, the class character of their programme and party. Instead, they argued, it exaggerated the importance of theory and ideology and thus flattered and feted the intelligentsia by giving undue weight to the supposed common antagonism of all classes and strata to the autocracy. For the economists, revolution involved class struggle, therefore the activity of those who aspired to revolution had to be subordinated to the support of such struggle as was taking place: the class struggle between workers and their exploiters.

Lenin for his part, however, pointed to the narrowness of certain forms of struggle and argued that for these struggles to be transformed into a revolutionary movement, theory was necessary: 'without revolutionary theory there can be no revolutionary movement'[42] and 'the role of vanguard fighter can be fulfilled only by a party that is guided by the most advanced theory'.[43] Lenin was not arguing for abstention from (trade union) struggles, but was asserting that any intervention in these by socialists should be sufficiently theorized so that an awareness of their limitations could be made by socialists to the workers involved and so that they could be generalized to embrace the wider, general and international struggle for socialism. The workers' movement needed theory, knowledge of its own social conditions to guide it in its struggles, for without socialist ideas workers would remain under the sway of bourgeois ideas, unable to progress beyond their immediacy. The fact that economic struggles were decisive did not mean that such struggles could assure the proletariat of final victory: for this a political revolution and proletarian dictatorship was necessary. I will deal with this point further below. At this stage it is important to stress that Lenin's advocacy of a revolutionary theory was based upon the supposition that it developed independently of the working-class movement.

The question of the origin of socialist theory is at the same time the question of bringing socialist politics to the trade union struggle. In this Lenin quotes favourably a long passage from Kautsky's commentary on the programme of the Austrian Social Democratic Party, a passage Lenin refers to as 'profoundly true and important'[44] and which is worth citing here in full:

> Many of our revisionist critics believe that Marx asserted that economic development and the class struggle create, not only the conditions for socialist production, but also, and directly, the *consciousness* of its necessity. And these critics assert that England, the country most highly developed capitalistically, is more remote than any other from this consciousness. Judging from the draft, one might assume that this allegedly orthodox-marxist view, which is thus refuted, was shared by the committees that drafted the Austrian programme. In the draft programme it is stated: 'The more capitalist development increases the numbers of the proletariat, the more the proletariat is compelled and becomes fit to fight against capitalism. The proletariat becomes conscious' of the possibility and of the necessity for socialism. In this connection socialist consciousness appears to be a necessary and direct result of the proletarian class struggle. But this is absolutely untrue. Of course, socialism, as a doctrine, has its roots in modern economic relationships just as the class struggle of the proletariat has and, like the latter, emerges from the struggle against the capitalist-created poverty and misery of the masses. But socialism and the class struggle arise side by side and not one out of the other; each arises under different conditions. Modern socialist consciousness can arise only on the basis

of profound scientific knowledge. Indeed, modern economic science is as much a condition for socialist production as, say, modern technology and the proletariat can create neither the one nor the other, no matter how much it may desire to do so; both arise out of the modern social process. The vehicle of science is not the proletariat, but the *bourgeois intelligentsia*: it was in the minds of individual members of this stratum that modern socialism originated and it was they who communicated it to the more intellectually developed proletarians who, in their turn, introduce it into the proletarian class struggle where conditions allow that to be done. Thus, socialist consciousness is something introduced into the proletarian class struggle from without (von Aussen Hineingetragenes) and not something that arose within it spontaneously (urwüchsig). Accordingly, the old Hainfeld programme quite rightly stated that the task of Social Democracy is to involve the proletariat (literally: saturate the proletariat) with the *consciousness* of its position and the consciousness of its task. There would be no need for this if consciousness arose of itself from the class struggle.[45]

Now this raises important questions. For if Kautsky and Lenin are correct then the revolutionary class would appear to be not the proletariat but the discontented, declassed intelligentsia; the former acting merely as agent for the latter, only superficially its own self-emancipator. This conclusion surely follows from the positivist view of science and theory encapsulated within it.

Lenin's inadequacy and it is one which Lukács' book remedies, is his poor appreciation of the social grounding of social consciousness. For Lenin the domination of bourgeois ideology lies in the simple reason that it 'is far older in origin than socialist ideology, that it is more fully developed and that it has at its disposal *immeasurably* more means of dissemination'[46] that is, domination is imposed from without, as its socialist opponent must do. Lenin goes on to add that

it is often said that the working class *spontaneously* gravitates towards socialism. This is perfectly true in the sense that socialist theory reveals the causes of the misery of the working class more profoundly and more correctly than any other theory and for that reason the workers are able to assimilate it so easily, *provided*, however, this theory does not itself yield to spontaneity, *provided* it subordinates spontaneity to itself...The working class spontaneously gravitates towards socialism; nevertheless, most widespread (and continuously and diversely revived)

> bourgeois ideology spontaneously imposes itself upon the working class to a still greater degree.[47]

In fact, rather than being autonomous of social life, theory and especially social theory, is and must be intimately related to, influenced by and based upon social conditions: socialist theory specifically by the activity of the working class.

I have shown in the previous chapter that for Lukács this dualism is rejected and replaced by a notion of consciousness that is generated by the very system of commodity production which imposes upon workers a style of life (the exploitation of the labour process), a structure of power (in which they are powerless) and a (partial and fragmented) outlook on life that all contribute to the creation of a reified outlook – the ideological enslavement of the working class. Lukács thus defines his understanding of class consciousness in terms of the social being of life: this is not a relationship of separation but of identity; theory is not separate and apart from being, nor is consciousness. Each are part of a complex reality; the appearance of bourgeois society makes this seem otherwise but the underlying reality, understood dialectically, is an interrelated totality.

To take this further: the task for socialist theory is not to penetrate proletarian consciousness from somewhere beyond but to become part of that consciousness. And it cannot achieve this if it is the creation and still less if it is the possession of an alien stratum of privileged, albeit alienated intellectuals. Furthermore, though the theoretical practitioners of marxism have in the main been members of the bourgeois intelligentsia in their origins, they have all broken from such a background and radically transformed their relationship to and involvement in working-class political practice. It would be incorrect to portray this relationship as one of externality.[48]

However, for Lenin and on this point Lukács is in agreement with him, the relation of party to class is, as a vanguard, no longer simply one of composition but is now one of ideology. Lenin's argument that the working class on its own can only aspire to a trade union consciousness leads him to question the representativeness of mass workers parties which may only express this lower level consciousness and to define the revolutionary socialist party in terms of its ideology, its possession of the marxist ideology that will allow it to represent not the mass of workers as immediately given but their historically determined class interests. Thus the composition of a party has far less significance in determining its class character. This does not mean that Lenin sought to substitute intellectuals for workers, nor that he saw in the former the embodiment of socialist consciousness, but rather that he saw that embodiment as the party, which could mediate the two, in which the distinction between intellectual and worker would disappear, both to become components of a centralized, disciplined organization. But to achieve this it was necessary to be clear about the precise nature of the relationship between the socialist politics of the revolutionary political party and the trade union politics of the economic class struggle.

Lenin's purpose in *What Is To Be Done*? then, is first to assert the importance of socialist theory. He then goes on to develop a notion of theory defined in opposition to the economic struggles generated by capitalism. Whilst these latter are vital and essential to the socialist movement, they are not sufficient on their own for the generation of a socialist consciousness, nor do they amount to socialist political practice.[49] They require the complement (not replacement) of a wider struggle;[50] to achieve this the horizons of the class conscious worker must be extended beyond the immediate confrontations with his/her employer to encompass a political struggle against the regime itself and an understanding of the interests and values that unify the regime and those that may be used to undermine it.[51]

Lenin's argument is that what he refers to as the trade union struggle cannot on its own lead to a revolutionary socialist consciousness because it is based upon a partial, sectional perspective of society, involving particular groups of workers in struggle against a particular employer. The global understanding that is a basic prerequisite for a socialist consciousness cannot emerge of its own accord from such a sectional struggle but must be consciously introduced from without.

This leads to Lenin's third and possibly most crucial theme – that of the relationship between spontaneity and consciousness. It is here once again that we may locate significant weaknesses in Lenin's argument, weaknesses that were contradicted by his political practice but which were corrected at a theoretical level by Lukács.

In *What Is To Be Done*? Lenin asserts the absolute and vital necessity of a political party steeped in revolutionary theory as an instrument of political centralization, a party which is faced with the task of combining partial struggles and linking them with a general struggle for political power, with the ultimate aim of challenging the institution of political centralization possessed by the ruling class : the state. It is by no means clear, however, that this argument must carry with it the idea that the working class cannot on its own rise above a trade union consciousness, or that the class struggle must be artificially inseminated from outside with a dose of socialist theory. At certain times political struggles have resulted in working-class movements spontaneously throwing up forms of struggle that have quite clearly gone beyond any notion of trade union politics and have attempted to impose a general perspective of social change upon society. Revolutionary movements have emerged without the midwife of a vanguard party amongst the Chartists, in the Paris Commune, in Russia in 1905 and again in 1917, and in Hungary in 1956. Such historical examples must cause us to question the rigidity and the undialectical distinction made by Lenin between spontaneity and consciousness.

Again, the problem largely follows from the conception of theory held by Lenin. Because the party alone was held to have the capacity to understand the laws of social development and the historical mission of the proletariat and because it must be organized separate from the actual, empirical consciousness of the working class, it is but a short step to regarding that empirical consciousness as a barrier which must be overcome and never as a source of inspiration. The party is completely independent and thus can justify, by virtue of its scientific knowledge of society, itself as the sole source of political initiative.

This substitutionist tendency is indeed a permanent and insuperable danger in bolshevism, for in counterposing socialist consciousness and the immediate reality of working-class struggle the problem of Jacobinism is thereby raised, a position where the working class becomes simply an agent of the party's plans. There is little sense of any organic unity between party and proletariat in *What Is To Be Done?*, where Lenin stresses the distinction between socialist politics and those of the day-to-day struggle. It is thus necessary to distinguish between the positive contribution of the book and the negative, one-sided and mechanical conclusions often drawn from it.

Lenin has rejected the notion of the party representing the class in favour of a vanguard organization, this latter being necessary because of the stratification of the working class, the cyclical variation of the class struggle and the political centralization of the bourgeois state. Only a party which relates at all times to the most active and militant members of the working class, which offers leadership to those struggles that take place and which attempts to generalize, to draw socialist politics out of the class struggle, can avoid falling into the routinism and passivity that strengthens bureaucracy, for the simple reason that the party must relate to a working class that is generally and for much of the time passive and acquiescent. Only such a party can develop an active and politically conscious membership as a guarantee against bureaucratic manipulation. Only such a party can put into practice a political and ideological selection of leaders, who owe their position to their political and not their bureaucratic function. Only such a party, basing itself on the knowledge that the objective conditions for socialism are present, can take advantage of revolutionary situations and construct bridges between the old world and the new. Such a party does not passively await the revolution but builds and prepares for it so that when revolutions do occur – and when they do they are not usually organized and planned by the party – that party can make such a revolution more effective, increase its chances of long-term success. The vanguard party makes permanent by giving an organizational form the lessons that the masses learn through their action and experience. It contributes continuity to cyclical struggle, socialist consciousness to day-to-day struggle. It consolidates and enriches the higher consciousness achieved by the mass of workers through struggle. And only such a party can effectively challenge the centralized coercive apparatus of the state in any revolutionary struggle, by unifying and centralizing the political opposition of the masses.

However, such a form of party organization carries with it the danger that the aim of such activity is overtaken by its method, that the organizational separation of the party, originally intended as an aid to the development of a revolutionary consciousness amongst the proletariat as a whole, becomes itself a self-sustaining means of political activity, an end in itself. The early history of the Soviet Union provides evidence of such a process. The development of stalinism involved the substitution of the party for all the representative functions and institutions of the proletariat and the forcible removal of any alternatives to it, in an environment where such a method afforded possibly the only means for the regime, and the system it represented, to survive. As we know, the regime did survive, but was in the process transformed into something quite different from the original conception of its founders. Success here was not paralleled with truth: on the contrary its success was achieved at the expense of the truth which it claimed to embody.

It is at this point that Lukács' work becomes pertinent, since he provided a philosophical justification for a form of political organization which drew upon the writings and experience of Lenin and the bolsheviks but was not restricted to them. Lukács enjoyed the privilege not only of observing the revolutionary events of post-war Europe; he also straddled both perspectives – the backwardness and revolutionary upheavals in Russia and his native Hungary as well as the possibly more typical experience of Germany and Austria. And his own theoretical orientation gave him a unique opportunity to draw together a theory of revolution that based its theory of party organization upon an understanding of the role played by the proletariat in bourgeois society, as well as being the force striving for its revolutionary transformation.

Lukács' account of party organization, though illuminated by the experience of the bolsheviks, was not restricted to that example alone, but rather embodied a synthesis of that experience (together with others available to him) with the theoretical approach to marxism he had already developed. Lukács thus provides not a political handbook for bolsheviks but a marxist philosophy that integrates the specific experiences of bolshevism into a cohesive theory of revolutionary class consciousness.[52] The importance of party organization lies not in its political efficacy alone but in its relationship to theory: it is the embodiment of theory as well as of its critique. Lukács criticizes orthodoxy because of its divorce between theory and practice, because 'it was able to commit itself to many things in theory without feeling in the least compelled to bind itself to any particular line as practice'.[53]

Moreover, the vicissitudes of class struggle discussed above, and the influence of bourgeois ideas amongst workers, mean that the reaction of workers to the crises to which they are periodically exposed is invariably 'much less violent and intense than the crisis itself'.[54] Therefore it is an error to expect that any natural law of capitalism, including that which generates crises, will lead to its downfall.[55]

Capitalism will not drive itself to destruction nor will opposition to its destructive tendencies lead to its replacement unless those individuals who suffer its effects and who offer resistance to it are able and willing to subordinate their individual wills 'to that collective will that is destined to bring real freedom into being...This conscious collective will is the Communist Party'.[56] The party allows class consciousness to develop before and in anticipation of events, rather than after them, so it can consciously determine events rather than being formed by them; it is thus the concrete mediation between man and history.[57]

Despite comments about the matter of discipline and 'the active engagement of the total personality'[58] that bring to the mind of the modern reader somewhat unpleasant images, Lukács does build limitations into the activities of the party, limitations that are absent in that phenomenon we customarily refer to as stalinism. Lukács' dialectic between party and class has a clear focus; this is not the organizational strength of the party but the class consciousness of the proletariat.[59] Further, this is synonomous for Lukács with the process of revolution itself; since this involves the party in a process of political engagement with the aim of establishing 'the highest possibility *objectively* available at a given point of time, as represented by the autonomous organization of the conscious vanguard',[60] this requires it also to embody a spirit of collective solidarity based upon self-criticism, self-correction and theoretical development.

In his book on Lenin Lukács notes that this theoretical clarity 'always culminates in the concrete analysis of a concrete situation'[61] and gives the following justification for Lenin's concept of organization:

> Lenin's concept of organization therefore means a double break with mechanical fatalism; both with the concept of proletarian class consciousness as a mechanical product of its class situation and with the idea that the revolution itself was only the mechanical working out of fatalistically explosive economic forces which – given the sufficient 'maturity' of objective revolutionary conditions – would somehow 'automatically' lead the proletariat to victory.[62]

The party opposes to this the following task: '[i]t must unite the spontaneous discoveries of the masses, which originate in their correct class instincts, with the totality of the revolutionary struggle and bring them to consciousness.'[63] Lukács is thus clear that party organization represents a fundamental break with the 'mechanistic and fatalistic vulgarization of marxism'[64] that had been the target of his polemical edge in *History and Class Consciousness* and this for theoretical as well as practical reasons Indeed, even at the point where he emphasizes the role such party organization plays in the period of the transition to socialism it is clear that its guide is and must always be 'proletarian class consciousness'.[65]

Lukács' core contribution to marxism is itself concerned primarily to contribute to the task of developing a proletarian class consciousness to the maximum extent possible within prevailing circumstances. This requires organizational embodiment, but this latter is not sufficient to its creation, for it must seek to create this, to paraphrase Marx, in circumstances not of its own choosing but in ones given and transmitted from the past. Moreover, the tradition of all the dead and defeated generations weighs like a nightmare on the brain of the living; the 'midnight of the century'[66] has not yet passed and the diminished expectations of the later Lukács, themselves largely the product of the unacknowledged transformation of the political movement to which he continued to pay allegiance, should not blind us to the radical and liberating vision of the century's primary advocate of the revolutionary mission of the class-conscious proletariat.

Conclusion

> An Oxford professor meets a former Ph.D. student and courteously inquires what he's working on these days. 'I'm writing a book,' says the other, 'on the survival of the class system in America.'
>
> 'Really, how fascinating. I didn't think they had a class system in America.'
>
> 'Nobody does. That's how it survives.'[1]

I hope it has been the consequence of this book that the above joke succeeds in its irony. I have not sought to vindicate the claims made for the proletariat by marxism but to explore what these claims are and how they might be judged. I have thus spoken primarily of marxism and only indirectly of the proletariat. If what I have said of marxism is correct, and I believe this to be likely, then marxism as a philosophy of history may be a truth but it might at the same time be, in Merleau-Ponty's memorable phrase, 'a truth that failed'.[2] The version of marxism which I have outlined is predicated upon a set of beliefs about the proletariat, beliefs which are primarily of theoretical import but which also carry with them empirical referrants. I have sought to challenge the empiricist interpretation that challenges marxism's claim to validity because of the failure of these empirical referrants, by calling for a critical assessment of what is really real, that is by rejecting the kingdom of the factual. The essentialist message of Marx and Lukács (and I do not use the term in a pejorative sense) requires a mediating function between the theory and the factual: this it seeks to provide by itself conjoining the theoretical and the practical.

Until recent times the demise of class politics appeared to be vitiated by its vitality as part of the anti-colonial struggles of the third world, its institutional embodiment in the Soviet bloc and its continuing, if weakened position in western European polities. Hence the apparent uniqueness of the United States in respect to its labour movement. Whilst I would not wish to dismiss entirely the historical and cultural specificities that affect all political movements, modern times have at least had the positive virtue of giving to us the opportunity to dismiss the spurious claim to marxist partisanship, in any meaningful sense, of the nationalist movements of the third world, the bureaucratic backwardness of the Soviet bloc and the parliamentary trade unionism of the western European labour movements. Some, but not all of such movements may have their origins in class struggles and class politics, but their position with respect to the standpoint of the proletariat, in the revolutionary sense outlined by Marx and Lukács discussed above, stands compromised by other, more pressing priorities. Where this leads us is to a position of considerable clarification, to a more realistic appraisal of the possibilities available to us in the present, but also to a notorious dilemma signified implicitly in the above joke.

Class divisions may persist, class inequalities may widen, the class nature of the bourgeois state may become increasingly explicit, but if for whatever reason this has little or no effect upon the consciousness of the proletariat, then do not these truths become enveloped by the satiating dreams of the (wilfully) unenlightened? Does not the failure of the proletariat to realize those universal ends to which it is directed signify an essential error of vision and lead to attempts to realize the myth elsewhere? Again, to refer once more to Merleau-Ponty, does this not indicate the necessary degeneration of all revolutionary movements which cannot preserve as regimes what they promised as movements: 'revolutions are true as movements and false as regimes'?[3]

Here, though, it is necessary to confront the understandable but flawed desire to read truth as if it were a guarantee of success. According to Russell Jacoby[4] it is this tendency that allowed the triumph of leninism/stalinism over western marxism, indeed which saw the latter retreat before the apparent successes of the former. If marxism is predicated upon the supposed revolutionary mission of the proletariat; if that proletariat has either refused, declined or failed in that mission, does this ipso facto mean that marxism is false? Not necessarily: it may have failed, but failure is not the same thing as error. What is of utmost importance is whether or not that failure can be accounted for in terms that do not contradict its truth or meaning. Marxism has two possible means of confronting this need. First, historically, it may account for any particular conjunction of circumstances that led to its defeat.[5] However, whilst such an approach is important in revealing strategic and tactical errors, miscalculations, imbalance of forces or whatever, it is also inadequate as a full explanation, since marxist political philosophy would wish to assert that history contains within itself tendencies that will ultimately (whenever that may be) annul such contingency. Of course, it might be said that this will indeed happen sometime ahead. But I think that at some point a historical balance sheet has to be read, and so far must hold such an assessment to be in deficit. This kind of argument must be supplemented, not replaced, by an addition to the theory that places the barriers to revolutionary achievement a little higher than the contingencies of circumstance. It is in his theory of reification that Lukács provides such a theory, in providing an account of the way in which capitalism, as part of its very process of accummulation, also creates structures of thought and understanding that are themselves replications of the society from which they arise. Partial, separate, divisive, autonomous, and yet somehow part of an integrated system: such is the mode of thought and way of life characteristic of bourgeois society. Because no one sees the system as a whole, the totality, so the system may continue to survive.

But, yet again, the rebuttal arises: if this be the case, what is the way beyond it? If society is condemned to sets of partial understandings that aggregate to total misunderstanding, where is the way forward? Or does history stop there (here)?

Here we must turn to two things: to Marx's theory of alienation and to Lenin's theory of the party, both of which must be contextualized in terms of the rhythms of capitalist accumulation. The point of Marx's theory of alienation was not merely to detail the misery and estrangement into which people had fallen, but to contrast this with their essential humanity, out of which would grow resistance to such a system. Again, there is no guarantee of success but there is a guarantee of resistance and Marx thought that the particular life experience of the proletariat would privilege it as the embodiment of such resistance and also frame the context in which it would be compelled to overcome the limitations imposed upon it in its daily experience. Lenin for his part, as a result of the particular experiences of organizing as a revolutionary in tsarist Russia, developed a form of organization that reflected the needs of such a class engaged in such an endeavour.

It fell to Lukács to integrate all these strands of thought and activity into a coherent whole, cognizant of both theoretical and practical needs. His *History and Class Consciousness* is often referred to as the single major contribution to marxist theory since the death of Marx; this must be judged to be correct, even though we must acknowledge at the same time that marxism thus loses the institutional shields that have for long protected it from the need we appear to have to judge things from the point of view of their success. Truth does not necessarily, always or even usually prevail – strength prevails over weakness and Lukács' work offers to the proletariat the means through which its weaknesses may be overcome, the means through which, shorn of dependence on representatives, it can reassert itself as a revolutionary class and assume the revolutionary mission of changing the world as it changes itself, of demonstrating the truth of Marx's words that 'in revolutionary activity the changing of oneself coincides with the changing of circumstances'.[6]

Notes and References

Introduction

1 Perry Anderson, *In the Tracks of Historical Materialism*, (1983).
2 See also Alex Callinicos, *Making History: Agency, Structure and Change in Social Theory* (1989).
3 *MECW* IV, p.93. See note 22 to chapter 1.
4 Karl Marx, *The First International and After* (Harmondsworth: Penguin, 1974) p.82.
5 *MECW* XI, p.103; *MESW* p.96.
6 *Capital* I, p.27.
7 See the discussion in Perry Anderson, *Arguments within English Marxism* (London: Verso, 1980) chapter 2, and further in chapter 2 here.
8 See the argument put forward by G.A. Cohen in the first chapter ('Images of History in Hegel and Marx') of his book *Karl Marx's Theory of History – A Defence* (Oxford: Oxford University Press, 1978).
9 See Richard L Schacht, 'Hegel on Freedom', in Alasdair MacIntyre (Ed.), *Hegel: A Collection of Critical Essays* (1972), also included in his *Hegel and After: Studies in Continental Philosophy between Kant and Sartre* (Pittsburgh: University of Pittsburgh Press, 1975).
10 G.W.F. Hegel, *The Philosophy of History* (New York: Power Publications, 1956) p.20. Hegel begins this section by noting that 'The question of the *means* by which Freedom develops itself to a World, conducts us to the phenomenon of History itself' and that this process of History is characterized not so much by aims and virtues but by 'Passions, private aims, and the satisfaction of selfish desires' which reject the limitations that would safeguard history from evil, vice and ruin. In other words, this means by which history is motivated operates to realize ends external to them, ends given, in Hegel's opinion, by the idea (in the form of the state).
11 G.W.F. Hegel, *Hegel's Logic* (Oxford: Clarendon Press, 1975) p.205. This advance requires science to overcome 'the spectacle of a contingency losing itself in vagueness' (p.205). Science, in other words, must distinguish essence from appearance, and consists of the penetration of the latter to the former.
12 Hegel, *The Philosophy of History*, p.27.
13 Cited by Lucien Goldmann, Is there a Marxist Sociology?, *International Socialism* (1968) 34, pp.15–16.

14 Lucio Colletti, for example, has argued this point most forcibly in his essay Bernstein and the Marxism of the Second International, included in his *From Rousseau to Lenin* (London: New Left Books), 1972. See also his introduction to *Karl Marx, Early Writings* (Harmondsworth: Penguin), 1975.
15 *MESC*, pp.395–6.
16 *Ibid.*, p.155.
17 For example, Andre Gorz, *Farewell to the Working Class: An Essay on Post-Industrial Socialism* (London: Pluto Press, 1982).
18 *MECW* XL, p.628.
19 *MECW* IV, p.37.
20 In The Poverty of Philosophy, *MECW* VI.
21 Witness the differing temper of Merleau-Ponty's analysis from *Humanism and Terror: An Essay on the Communist Problem* (Boston: Beacon Press, 1969), through the political essays included in *Sense and Non-Sense* (Evanston, Illinois: Northwestern University Press, 1964), to his final abandonment of marxism in *Adventures of the Dialectic* (Evanston, Illinois: Northwestern University Press, 1973).

Chapter 1: Karl Marx and the Discovery of the Proletariat

1 These articles are all to be found in Volume 3 of *MECW*.
2 The journal was banned in Prussia, warrants were issued for the arrest of Marx, Heine and Ruge, and Marx became a political refugee. Marx's adoption of communism also led to his break with Ruge; see David McLellan, *Karl Marx His life and Thought* (London: Macmillan, 1973), p.98.
3 Rubel refers to the 1843 Introduction as the 'germ of the future Communist Manifesto', Maximilien Rubel and Margaret Manale, *Marx Without Myth: A Chronological Study of his Life and Work* (Oxford: Basil Blackwell, 1975), p.40.
4 *MESW*, p.182.
5 *Ibid.*, p.181.
6 All quotations: *MECW* V, p.236.
7 *MESW*, p.183.
8 *MECW* III, p.181. David McLellan's translation catches somewhat better the flavour of what Marx had to say: '...you cannot transcend philosophy without realizing it'. David McLellan (Ed.), *Karl Marx: Selected Writings* (Oxford: Oxford University Press, 1977), p.68.
9 *MESW*, p.430. It was in this same speech that Engels drew the famous parallel between Marx and Darwin: 'Just as Darwin discovered the law of development of organic nature, so Marx discovered the law of development of human history' (p.429). I shall have much to say about this interpretation of Marx. Suffice it to say at this point that even here, Engels'

portrait of Marx as a 'man of science' is tempered by a recognition that 'science was for Marx a historically dynamic, revolutionary force' and that 'his real mission in life was to contribute...to the overthrow of capitalist society...[and] to contribute to the liberation of the modern proletariat' (p.430).

10 In a letter to Joseph Weydemeyer written on 5 March 1852, Marx assesses his own originality thus: '...no credit is due to me for discovering either the existence of classes in modern society or the struggle between them...What I did that was new was to demonstrate: 1) that the *existence of classes* is merely linked to *particular historical phases in the development of production*, 2) that class struggle necessarily leads to the *dictatorship of the proletariat*, 3) that this dictatorship itself only constitutes the transition to the *abolition of all classes* and to a *classless society*'. *MESC* p.64. It is the dictatorship of the proletariat, then, that provides the necessary link between existing conditions and the classless future.

11 *Documents of the First International, 1864–1866* (London: Lawrence & Wishart, 1962) p.288. Norman Geras claims that the 'principle of self-emancipation is central, not incidental, to historical materialism' in his article 'Marxism and Proletarian Self-Emancipation', *Radical Philosophy* (1973) No.6, pp.20–22.

12 'in reality the Young Hegelians gradually turned Hegel's dialectic, to which the concept of mediation was essential, into one which held all mediation to be anathema', David McLellan, *The Young Hegelians and Karl Marx* (London: Macmillan, 1980), p.18. Witness also Lukács' comment that 'bourgeois thinkers...can...critically dissect Hegel's false synthesis, but are forced either to repudiate dialectics virtually altogether (Feuerbach) or to reduce them to a purely subjective one (Bruno Bauer)', *DR*, p.247.

13 McLellan, *The Young Hegelians and Karl Marx*, p.8. Witness also Hegel's remark that 'once the realm of notions is revolutionized, actuality does not hold out', cited by Alex Callinicos, *Marxism and Philosophy* (Oxford: Clarendon Press, 1983) p.27.

14 *MECW* III, p.176.

15 And which had led to the dismissal of Bruno Bauer from his university post and Marx's consequent abandonment of any hope of pursuing an academic career.

16 '*Feuerbach* is the only one who has a *serious, critical* attitude to the Hegelian dialectic and who has made genuine discoveries in this field': *MECW* III, p.328.

17 *MECW* III, p.342.

18 Cited by McLellan, *The Young Hegelians and Karl Marx*, p.99.

19 Lukács notes in his 1926 essay 'Moses Hess and the Problem of Idealist Dialectics' that 'Marx took over directly from Hegel...rejecting the Feuerbachian "improvement" on Hegel at the point where Feuerbach

rejects the Hegelian conception of mediation and thus loses "the methodological possibility of acknowledging and recognizing the social reality of the present in its reality and yet still reacting to it critically – not moralistically-critical, but in the sense of practical-critical activity". George Lukács, *Tactics and Ethics Political Writings, 1919–1929* (London: New Left Books, 1972) pp. 202–3. In his 1967 preface to *History and Class Consciousness* Lukács gives as one of the reasons for the importance of his 1923 work its implicit adherence to this view, held in contradistinction to the overestimation of Feuerbach's role as an intermediary between Hegel and Marx by Plekhanov and others, *HCC*, p.xxi.

20 Marx makes this point in his letter to Ruge in March 1843: 'Feuerbach's aphorisms seem to me incorrect only in one respect, that he refers too much to nature and too little to politics. That, however, is the only alliance by which present-day philosophy can become truth'. *MECW* I, p.400.

21 *MECW* IV, p.93. This passage was written by Engels, and though it reflects his more enthusiastic appreciation of Stirner at the time, there can be little doubt that it was endorsed by Marx – particularly in view of the extensive work put by Marx into what was originally intended as a short pamphlet but which became a lengthy book.

22 *MECW* III, p.354.

23 *MECW* XXXVIII, p.12.

24 Though as Colletti reminds us, use of the transformative critique is a long-standing philosophical device far from unique to Feuerbach. See his introduction to Marx's *Early Writings* (Harmondsworth: Penguin, 1975).

25 *MECW*, III, p.355. In this letter also, Marx seeks Feuerbach's support against Bruno Bauer's advocacy of elitist criticism, and refers to his intention to 'publish a small booklet attacking this aberration of criticism' (p.356), a booklet that was to become *The Holy Family*.

26 'We cannot yet pass from theory to practice because we still lack a complete and fully developed theory' wrote Feuerbach in a letter to Ruge dated 20 June 1843 – cited by Adolfo Sanchez Vazquez, *The Philosophy of Praxis* (London: Merlin, 1977) p.87.

27 R. Tucker, *Philosophy and Myth in Karl Marx* (New York: Cambridge University Press, 1961) pp.113–4.

28 A charge repeated by Heinz Lubasz, 'Marx's Conception of the Revolutionary Proletariat', *Praxis* (1969) Vol.I, No.1–2, 280–90, by Timothy McCarthy, *Marx and the Proletariat: A Study in Social Theory* (Westport: Greenwood Press, 1978) and by Craig Calhoun, *The Question of Class Struggle: Social Foundations of Popular Radicalism During the Industrial Revolution* (Oxford: Basil Blackwell, 1982).

29 According to the 1851 census, out of a total urban population of a little over 9 million, only 1,331,260 were employed in 'grande industrie' – and by no means were all of these situated in Paris. See Roger Price,

The French Second Republic: A Social History (London: Batsford, 1972) and *The Economic Modernisation of France* (London: Croom Helm, 1975). In the latter he notes that 'as late as 1851 the census revealed three million workers employed in workshops compared with 1.5 million in "grande industrie"' (p.94).

30 As Sidney Hook remarks, 'Marx was evidently not born a marxist': his theoretical uniqueness developed over time and in (usually hostile) relationship with other theoretical viewpoints. Sidney Hook, *From Hegel to Marx: Studies in the Intellectual Development of Karl Marx* (University of Michigan Press, 1962), p.11.

31 Allen Oakley discusses the differing claims for the date and place of writing the Introduction, as well as the date of Marx's turn to political economy, in his *The Making of Marx's Critical Theory: A Bibliographical Analysis* (London: Routledge & Kegan Paul, 1983) pp.20–3.

32 *MECW*, III, p.142.

33 *Ibid.*, p.144.

34 *Ibid.*

35 *Ibid.*, p.145.

36 *Ibid.*, p.151.

37 *Ibid.*, p.155.

38 *Ibid.*, p.152.

39 *Ibid.*, p.159.

40 *Ibid.*, p.154.

41 *Ibid.*, p.159.

42 *Ibid.*, p.166.

43 *Ibid.*, p.164.

44 *Ibid.*, pp.169–70.

45 *Ibid.*, p.174.

46 *Ibid.*, p.154.

47 *Ibid.*, p.159.

48 *Ibid.*, p.166.

49 R.Tucker, *Philosophy and Myth in Karl Marx* (New York: Cambridge University Press, 1961), p.115.

50 *Ibid.*, p.113.

51 *Ibid.*, p.114.

52 S.Avineri, *The Social and Political Thought of Karl Marx* (London: Cambridge University Press, 1968), p.56.

53 *Ibid.*, p.57.

54 David McLellan, *Marx Before Marxism*, 2nd Edition (London: Macmillan, 1980), p.157. The impact of Paris upon the evolution of Marx's political thought is also stressed by Hal Draper – see his *Karl Marx's Theory of Revolution*, Vol.1: *State and Bureaucracy* (New York: Monthly Review Press, 1977), chapter 6.

55 Cited by McLellan, *Marx Before Marxism*, p.130.

56 Franz Mehring, *Karl Marx, The Story of His Life* (London: George Allen & Unwin, 1936), p.74. Isaiah Berlin asserts that 'The social, political and artistic ferment of Paris in the middle of the nineteenth century is a phenomenon without parallel in European history', *Karl Marx*, 4th Edition (Oxford: Oxford University Press, 1978) p.61, but limits its impact upon Marx primarily to those revolutionaries he met at this time – principally Engels, Bakunin, Weitling and Proudhon, as well as the influence of the writings of Saint-Simon and Fourier.

57 E.A. Olssen, 'Marx and the Resurrection', *Journal of the History of Ideas* (1968) XXIX, 1, pp.131–40.

58 Heinz Lubasz, 'Marx's Conception of the Revolutionary Proletariat', *Praxis* (1969) I, 1–2, pp.280–90; Timothy McCarthy, *Marx and the Proletariat: A Study in Social Theory* (Westport: Greenwood Press, 1978); David W. Lovell, *Marx's Proletariat: The Making of a Myth* (London: Routledge, 1988); Krishan Kumar, 'Can the Workers be Revolutionary?', *European Journal of Political Research* (1978) 6, pp.357–79.

59 This is the charge levelled by Alvin Gouldner's posthumously published *Against Fragmentation: The Origins of Marxism and the Sociology of Intellectuals* (New York: Oxford University Press, 1985), as well as by Roger Price in his *The French Second Republic* (London: Batsford, 1972), though this latter work is concerned more with Marx's *The Eighteenth Brumaire of Louis Bonaparte* (1851–2). See also Craig Calhoun, *The Question of Class Struggle: Social Foundations of Popular Radicalism during the Industrial Revolution* (Oxford: Basil Blackwell, 1982).

60 David McLellan, *Karl Marx – His Life and Thought* (London: Macmillan, 1973), p.97. McLellan notes that in Germany factory workers constituted less than 4% of the total male adult population (p.98).

61 See Carol Johnson, 'The Problem of Reformism and Marx's Theory of Fetishism', *New Left Review* (1980) No.119, pp.70–96. I will take up this question in the next chapter.

62 *MECW* III, p.183.

63 *Ibid.*, p.181.

64 *Ibid.*, p.182.

65 *Ibid.*, p.185.

66 *Ibid.*

67 Goran Therborn regards this approach to the proletariat as indicative of the 'Volksgeist conception' (p.343), conceived at a time 'when Marx conceived of the proletariat as the solution to the problem of German philosophy' (p.343), a position, needless to say, that Therborn believes Marx later radically altered. See his *Science, Class and Society* (London: New Left Books, 1976) on this point.

68 *MECW* III, p.186.

69 *Ibid.*, p.185.

70 'For Marx in this period the world-historical mission of the proletariat derived not so much from its socio-economic position within borgeois society as from a philosophical conception of the proletariat as the negation and embodiment of what is universally human...', Vazquez, *The Philosophy of Praxis*, p.102.

71 Thus Robert Blauner mentions capitalism only once in his book on the factory worker and his industry, and this only to reject the view that alienation is its consequence. It is, rather, the product of 'factory technology and industrial organization', the different forms of which makes possible a 'recasting' of 'a politically loaded controversy into a manageable scientific question' (p.4); see his *Alienation and Freedom: The Factory Worker and His Industry* (Chicago: The University of Chicago Press, 1964). This reification of technology is criticized by Harry Braverman in his *Labor and Monopoly Capital: The Degradation of Work in the Twentieth Century* (New York: Monthly Review Press, 1974), chapter 9.

72 *MECW* III, p.187.

73 *Ibid.*, p.197.

74 *Ibid.*, p.198.

75 *MECW* IV, p.204.

76 *Ibid.*, pp.204–5.

77 *Ibid.*

78 *Ibid.*, p.281.

79 *Ibid.*, p.282.

80 Mehring, *Karl Marx*, p.85.

81 *Ibid.*, p.85, or Nietzsche's remark on Schopenhauer: 'The errors of great men are venerable because they are more fruitful than the truths of little men', in Walter Kaufmann (Ed.), *The Portable Nietzsche* (New York: Viking Press, 1954) p.30.

82 *MECW* IV, p.37.

83 *Ibid.* There is also Marx's comment, made in a speech to the Central Authority of the Communist League, that 'I have always defied the momentary opinions of the proletariat', *MECW* X, p.628.

84 Cited by Mehring, *Karl Marx*, p.78.

85 Lubasz, 'Marx's Conception of the Revolutionary Proletariat', p.288.

86 McCarthy, *Marx and the Proletariat*, p.70.

87 Lubasz, 'Marx's Conception of the Revolutionary Proletariat', p.290.

88 *MECW*, XXXVIII, p.92.

Chapter 2: Marx and the Proletariat: 1848 and After

1 Karl Korsch gives the following summary of Marx's development: 'First, he criticised religion philosophically. Then he criticised religion and philosophy politically. Finally, he criticised religion, philosophy, politics and all other ideologies economically.' Karl Korsch, *Marxism and Philosophy*

(New York: Monthly Review Press, 1970), p.85, n.66. Incidentally, this latter point Korsch sees achieved in the 1843 introduction.

2 *MECW* III, p.336. This point is discussed by Richard Schacht in chapter 5 of his *Hegel and After: Studies in Continental Philosophy between Kant and Sartre* (University of Pittsburgh, 1975).

3 We should bear in mind, however, that because these are merely tendential descriptions of real historical processes, and because such historical processes may vacillate between both polarities as they themselves alter over time, there consequently arises the danger of over schematization.

4 *Capital* I, pp.351–475, 667–724.

5 'Freedom...can only consist in socialised man, the associated producers, rationally regulating their interchange with Nature, bringing it under their common control, instead of being ruled by it as by the blind forces of Nature...But it nonetheless still remains a realm of necessity. Beyond it begins that development of human energy which is an end in itself, the true realm of freedom, which, however, can blossom forth only with this realm of necessity as its basis. The shortening of the working day is its basic prerequisite'; *Capital* III, p.820.

6 'It [the Paris Commune] was essentially a working class government, the produce of the struggle of the producing against the appropriating class, the political form at last discovered under which to work out the economic emancipation of labour'; *MESW*, p.290.

7 Interestingly, Bernstein regarded the earlier writings of Marx and Engels – primarily *The Communist Manifesto* – as the most determinist and which were modified over time: 'it cannot be denied that Marx and Engels originally assigned to the non-economic factors a much less influence on the evolution of society, a much less power of modifying by their action the conditions of production than in their later writings...Thus we see the materialist conception of history to-day in another form than it was presented at first by its founders. It has gone through a development already, it has suffered limitations in absolutist interpretation', *Evolutionary Socialism*, (New York: Schoken, 1961) pp.15–16.

8 Karl Marx and Frederick Engels, *The Holy Family or Critique of Critical Criticism: Against Bruno Bauer and Company*, written at the end of 1844 and published in 1845. See *MECW* IV.

9 *MECW* IV, p.36.

10 *Ibid.*, p.36.

11 *Ibid.*, pp.36–7.

12 *Ibid.*, pp.52–3.

13 Similarly, in 'The Civil War in France', Marx notes that 'They [the working class] have no ideals to realise, but to set free the elements of the new society with which the old collapsing society itself is pregnant'; *MESW*, p.291.

14 Karl Marx, *The Poverty of Philosophy: Answer to The Philosophy of Poverty by M. Proudhon*, written and published in 1847. See *MECW* VI.

15 This is the same argument Marx develops against the so-called Citizen Weston (and by implication also against Lassalle) and the 'iron law of wages' in his *Wages, Price and Profit* of 1865 (see *MESW*). Most economics text books refer to strikes as merely the ultimate sanction available to trade unions in their attempt to control the labour market. For typical examples see Richard G. Lipsey, *An Introduction to Positive Economics* 4th Edition (London: Weidenfeld & Nicolson, 1975) chapter 28, and Paul A. Samuelson, *Economics* 9th Edition (Tokyo: McGraw-Hill Kogakusha, 1973) pp.588–9.

16 The supposed 'irrationality' of strikes is discussed in Richard Hyman, *Strikes* (London: Fontana/Collins, 1972) chapter 5 where he cites A.M. Ross thus: 'Editorial columns are studded with mathematical demonstrations that the workers would have been much better off if they had accepted the employer's final offer and stayed at work' (p.112). Though less true these days, the point remains.

17 The belief that this was no longer so has been common currency since the end of the last war and, less credibly, before then. It was, however, a central part of the socialist case for many years. For example, in 'Wages, Price and Profit', Marx notes that the 'very necessity *of general political action* affords the proof that in its merely economic action capital is the stronger side'; *MESW*, p.223.

18 This is taken from Karl Marx and Frederick Engels, *The German Ideology*, written between November 1845 and August 1846 and first published in full in 1932; *MECW* V, pp.371–2.

19 All quotes from *MECW* VI, p.211.

20 Karl Marx and Frederick Engels, *Manifesto of the Communist Party*, written in December 1847–January 1848 and published in 1848.

21 *MECW* VI, pp.489–90.

22 *Ibid.*, p.493.

23 *Ibid.*, p.494.

24 *Ibid.*, p.496.

25 Witness Engels' letter to Bloch: 'Marx and I are ourselves partly to blame for the fact that the younger people sometimes lay more stress on the economic side than is due to it. We had to emphasize the main principle *vis-à-vis* our adversaries, who denied it, and we had not always the time, the place or the opportunity to give their due to the other elements involved in the interaction'; Engels to Bloch, 21 September 1890, *MESW*, p.683, *MESC*, p.396. See also Engels' letters to Schmidt of 27 October 1890 and Mehring of 14 July 1890.

26 *Grundrisse*, p.100.

27 See, for example, Marx's remarks on Edmund Burke: 'this sycophant, who in the pay of the English oligarchy, played the romantic laudator

temporis acti against the French revolution, just as, in the pay of the North American Colonies, at the beginning of the American troubles, he had played the liberal against the English oligarchy, was an out and out vulgar bourgeois', *Capital* I, p.711; on Jeremy Bentham: 'that insipid, pedantic, leather-tongued oracle of the ordinary bourgeois intelligence of the 19th century. Bentham is among philosophers what Martin Tupper is among poets', *ibid.*, pp.570–1 (Marx refers to Tupper elsewhere as 'his aversion': see 'Marx's Confession' cited in David McLellan, *Karl Marx: His Life and Thought* [London: Macmillan,1973], p.456); and on Thomas Malthus: 'that master of plagiarism' who 'adored' the ruling class 'like a true priest', *Capital* I, pp. 475, 495. See also Marx's remarks on the relation between Malthus, his theory of population and celibacy in *ibid.*, pp.578–9, n.1. There is no shortage of such unflattering comments in Marx's writings.

28 Cited by Roman Rosdolsky, *The Making of Marx's 'Capital'* (London: Pluto, 1977) p.64.

29 *Capital* I, p.788.

30 *Ibid.*, p.789.

31 Karl Marx, 'Moralising Criticism and Critical Morality', *MECW* VI, p.319.

32 M. Hess, *Briefwechsel* (The Hague, 1959) p.151, cited by David McLellan (Ed.), *Marx: The First Hundred Years* (London: Fontana, 1983) p.152.

33 McLellan notes that 'Virtually from the outset Marx was pessimistic about the success of the Commune' and cites Oberwinder thus: 'two days after the beginning of the insurrection, Marx wrote to Vienna that it had no chance of success', McLellan, *Karl Marx: His Life and Thought*, p.393. And ten years later Marx could write that the Commune 'was merely the rising of a city under exceptional conditions, the majority of the Commune was by no means socialist, nor could it be', Marx to Nieuwenhuis, February 1881, *MESC*, p.318.

34 *MECW* X, p.510.

35 *Ibid.*. p.626.

36 This interpretation is a matter of deep controversy. The view that Marx did in fact alter his political views at this time is argued by Richard N. Hunt, *The Political Ideas of Marx and Engels*, Vol.1: *Marxism and Totalitarian Democracy, 1818–1850* (London: Macmillan, 1975), chapter.7; David McLellan, *Karl Marx: His Life and Thought*, chapter 5, especially pp.246–250. The continuity of Marx's politics is advocated by Hal Draper, *Karl Marx's Theory of Revolution*, Vol.2: *The Politics of Social Classes* (New York: Monthly Review Press, 1978), chapter 10 and Special Note E; Robin Blackburn, 'The Politics of Marx and Engels', *New Left Review* (1976) No.97, pp.3–35; Michael Lowy, *The Politics of Combined and Uneven Development: The Theory of Permanent Revolution* (London: Verso, 1981); Alan Gilbert, *Marx's Politics: Communists and Citizens* (Oxford: Martin Robertson, 1981).

37 *MECW* X, p.626.
38 *MECW* VI, p.211.
39 *MESW*, p.182.
40 Lukács' remarks on Adorno are apt here: 'A considerable part of the leading German intelligentsia, including Adorno, have taken up residence in the "Grand Hotel Abyss" which I described in connection with my critique of Schopenhauer as "a beautiful hotel, equipped with every comfort, on the edge of an abyss, of nothingness, of absurdity. And the daily contemplation of the abyss between excellent meals or artistic entertainments, can only heighten the enjoyment of the subtle comforts offered"', Preface to his *The Theory of the Novel*, p.22. The original reference to Schopenhauer may be found (with a slightly differing translation) in *DR*, pp.242–3. See also the discussion of the pessimism of the Frankfurt School by J.G. Merquior, *Western Marxism* (London: Paladin, 1986), pp.110–117, 130–138.
41 A problem that is intensified by the seizure of power by movements claiming a marxist inspiration, but in conditions where the overwhelming priority has been one of industrialization rather than communalization.
42 Ernest Mandel, *The Formation of the Economic Thought of Karl Marx, 1843 to Capital* (London: New Left Books, 1977).
43 *Ibid.*, pp.73–4.
44 This crisis was predicted by both Marx and Engels, see *MECW* XV, pp.34–5, 74, and gave both men a certain amount of perverse pleasure, see *ibid.*, p.203.
45 McLellan notes that it was the outbreak of the 1857 crisis that moved Marx 'to a frantic attempt to bring his economic studies to some sort of a conclusion'; *Karl Marx – His Life and Thought*, p.290.
46 At one stage Marx did plan to write a separate work on the 1857 crisis, but this plan, like so many others, never materialized; see *MECW* XL, p.224.
47 Engels to Marx, 15 November 1857, *ibid.*, p.203.
48 *Ibid.*
49 Engels to Marx, 17 December 1857, *ibid.*, p.223.
50 This is not to condemn Engels's optimism as somehow at odds with Marx's own views. The letters written by Engels to Marx were never meant to be anything more than fragmentary comments written by someone experiencing at first hand the effect of crisis upon the bourgeoisie, and could in no meaningful way be compared with Marx's own integration of these facts with his theoretical system.
51 I will deal with the interpretation of those who thought that Marx and Engels did provide this in the following chapter.
52 '...these regularly recurring catastrophes lead to their repetition on a higher scale and finally to its violent overthrow', *Grundrisse*, p.750.

53 'This periodical fluctuation between the largest volume of reproduction and its contraction to partial suspension, this cycle of slump, boom, and crisis, as it has been called, is the most striking peculiarity of capitalist reproduction', Rosa Luxemburg, *The Accumulation of Capital* (London: Routledge & Kegan Paul, 1951), p.35.
54 In 'Reform or Revolution?', Mary-Alice Waters (Ed.), *Rosa Luxemburg Speaks* (New York: Pathfinder), p.83. Bernstein's treatment of the 'self-regulation' of capitalism led him to reject not only the 'breakdown' of capitalism, but also the very idea that capitalism was an historical phenomenon. See Lucio Colletti's essay 'Bernstein and the Marxism of the Second International' in his *From Rousseau to Lenin: Studies in Ideology and Society* (London: New Left Books, 1972), especially pp. 48–56.
55 The 'world crisis' is 'the most complicated phenomenon of capitalist production', *Theories of Surplus Value*, II, p.501.
56 *Grundrisse*, p.748.
57 *Ibid.*, p.749.
58 *Ibid.*, pp.749–50.
59 Luxemburg provides as examples of such despotic political actions the building of the Egyptian pyramids, of the Suez canal and the consolidation of the Great Wall of China: these led to the interruption of regular economic life for long periods; see her *The Accumulation of Capital*, p.33.
60 As Howard and King argue, Marx's (or any other) theory of crisis must show 'not only that the profit rate declines, but also that it declines sufficiently to preclude accumulation', *The Political Economy of Marx*, 2nd Edition (Harlow: Longman, 1985), p.222.
61 '...the instrument of labour strikes down the labourer', *Capital* III, p.407.
62 '...the relation between the mass of the means of production employed...and the mass of labour necessary for their employment', *Capital* III, p.612
63 The difference in the rate of increase is due to the fact that the increased productivity of labour lowers not only the exchange-value of labour power but also part of capital itself, since the cost of its reproduction is lowered.
64 This basis of Marx's theory has also been subject to severe criticism. See Geoff Hodgson, 'The Theory of the Falling Rate of Profit', *New Left Review* (1974) No.84, pp.55–82, and his *Trotsky and Fatalistic Marxism* (London: Spokesman Books, 1975). It is interesting to compare such criticisms with those made by Eduard Bernstein in his *Evolutionary Socialism* (New York: Schoken, 1961).
65 *Grundrisse*, p.750.
66 A task that Engels was also to attempt in his account of 'The Peasant War in Germany' published in 1850. In this work he was to note that 'The worst thing that can befall the leader of an extreme party is to be compelled to assume power at a time when the movement is not yet

ripe for the domination of the class he represents and for the measures this domination implies. What he *can* do depends not on his will but on the degree of antagonism between the various classes, and on the level of development of the material means of existence, of the conditions of production and commerce upon which the degree of intensity of the class contradictions always reposes. What he *ought* to do, what his party demands of him, again depends not on him, but also not on the degree of development of the class struggle and its conditions. He is bound to the doctrines and demands hitherto propounded which, again, do not follow from the class relations of the moment, or from the more or less accidental level of production or commerce, but from his more or less penetrating insight into the general result of the social and political movement. Thus, he necessarily finds himself in an unsolvable dilemma. What he *can* do contradicts all his previous actions and principles and the immediate interests of his party, and what he *ought* to do cannot be done. In a word, he is compelled to represent not his party or his class, but the class for whose domination the movement is then ripe. In the interests of the movement he is compelled to advance the interests of an alien class, and to feed his own class with talk and promises, and with the asseveration that the interests of that alien class are their own interests. He who is put in this awkward position is irrevocably lost.' *MECW* X, pp.469–70. What a fine description of the strategy of electoralism this is!

67 Witness the description of the resistance of the Swiss as 'the struggle of stubborn shepherds against the onward march of historical developments, the struggle of obstinate, rooted local interests against the interests of the whole nation, the struggle of crude ignorance against enlightenment, of barbarism against civilization'; *MECW* VI, p.639. See also Marx's comments on the American Civil War and his enthusiastic support of the Union against the Confederacy. A useful collection of Marx's writings may be found in Saul K. Padover (Ed.), *Karl Marx: On America and the Civil War* (New York: McGraw-Hill, 1972).

68 *MECW* VI, pp.528–9.

69 *Ibid.*, p.303.

70 *Ibid.*, p.494.

71 For example, Marx was never tempted by the radicalism of the peasantry, partly because of their support for Louis Bonaparte, but also because 'their mode of production isolates them from one another instead of bringing them together into mutual intercourse', and thus 'homologous magnitudes' are formed 'much as potatoes in a sack form a sack of potatoes'. *MESW* p.170; *MECW* XI, p.187.

72 *MECW* VI, p.494.

73 For example, E.P. Thompson in his critique of Althusserian marxism, *The Poverty of Theory and Other Essays* (London: Merlin, 1978).

74 Russell Jacoby, *Dialectic of Defeat: Contours of Western Marxism* (Cambridge: Cambridge University Press, 1981).
75 *PW*, p.203. This is in direct contradiction with the opinion of Louis Althusser: see his *Politics and History* (London: New Left Books, 1977), pp.176–86 and *For Marx* (London: New Left Books, 1977), pp.44–8.
76 *PW*, p.188.
77 *MECW* XI, p.103.
78 *Concise Oxford English Dictionary*, 5th Edition (1964), p.25. See the discussion in Perry Anderson, *Arguments within English Marxism* (London: Verso, 1980).
79 *Capital* I, p.21.
80 *Ibid*., p.27.
81 See H. Stuart Hughes, *Consciousness and Society: The Reorientation of European Social Thought* (London: Paladin, 1974).
82 Marx to Weydemeyer, 5 March 1852, *MESW*, p.669, *MESC*, pp.62–5, *MECW* XXXIX, pp.60–6.

Chapter 3: Georg Lukács and Orthodoxy

1 I will examine the views expounded by Lukács in this work in the next chapter.
2 On Lenin see David McLellan, *Marxism After Marx* (London: Macmillan, 1979) chapter 7; for Trotsky: John Molyneux, *Leon Trotsky's Theory of Revolution* (Brighton: Harvester, 1981) introduction.
3 Nor do I wish to claim that if only Kautsky, Plekhanov and the rest had adopted a different philosophical or political position then things would have been different. Such a voluntarist position appoaches the problem from the wrong direction, from the standpoint of leadership rather than from what was being led. What we need to explain is why certain views prevailed over others, not to engage in a pointless exercise in accusatory condemnation and a fruitless search for possible alternative scenarios. Different leaders would have made a difference only if they had been followed; the leaders that did exist were followed, and the question of betrayal was of little or no consequence to those supposedly betrayed. See Paul Mattick, 'Karl Kautsky: from Marx to Hitler', in his *Anti-Bolshevik Communism* (London: Merlin, 1978).
4 '[T]he Leninist-Stalinist version of socialism was a possible interpretation, though certainly not the only possible one, of Marx's doctrine' L. Kolakowski, *Main Currents of Marxism*, Vol.I (Oxford :Oxford University Press, 1978) p.418.
5 Golo Mann, *The History of Germany Since 1789*, (Harmondsworth: Penguin, 1974), Part VII and VIII.
6 The standard works on the Second International are: Julius Braunthal, *History of the International 1864 – 1914* (London: Thomas Nelson, 1966),

G. D. H. Cole, *The Second International 1889 – 1914* (1963), W. L. Guttsman, *The German Social Democractic Party 1875 – 1933: From Ghetto to Government* (London: Allen & Unwin, 1981), James Joll, *The Second International 1889 – 1914* (London: Weidesfield & Nicolson, 1955), Bertrand Russell, *German Social Democracy* (London: Allen & Unwin, 1965), Carl E. Schorske, *German Social Democracy 1905 – 1917: The Development of the Great Schism* (Cambridge Mass.: Harvard University Press, 1983). See also Peter Gay, *The Dilemma of Democratic Socialism: Eduard Bernstein's Challenge to Marx* (New York: Collier Books, 1952), Leszek Kolakowski, *Main Currents of Marxism* Vol.II (1978), Werner Thonnessen, *The Emancipation of Women: The Rise and Decline of the Women's Movement in German Social Democracy, 1863–1933* (London: Pluto Press, 1973).

7 See Maurice Dobb, *Studies in the Development of Capitalism* (London: Routledge & Kegan Paul, 1963) chapter 7, and Wolfgang Abendroth, *A Short History of the European Working Class* (London: New Left Books, 1972).

8 For an account of the consequences of these developments upon British politics see Perry Anderson, 'The Figures of Descent', *New Left Review* (1987) No.161.

9 F. Engels, 'Socialism in Germany, 1891–1892', included in W.O. Henderson, *The Life of Friedrich Engels* Vol.II (1976), pp.796–809.

10 H. Stuart Hughes, *Consciousness and Society, The Reorientation of Euroopean Social Thought 1890–1930*, (St. Albans: Paladin, 1974), pp.41–2.

11 *Ibid.*, p.41.

12 See Marcel Liebman, '1914: The Great Schism', *Socialist Register* (London: Merlin, 1964).

13 M. Salvadori, *Karl Kautsky and the Socialist Revolution 1880–1938*, (1979) p.19.

14 This is not to imply that the masses exercised political power, either directly or via their elected representatives – as is suggested, for example, by Ortega Y Gasset in his book *The Revolt of the Masses* (London: Unwin, 1961). The role of the masses was one merely of a recipient of political ideology and organization controlled by the various political elites.

15 W. L. Guttsman notes that German social democracy 'was one of the models of the modern mass party which arose during the second half of the nineteenth century', *The German Social Democratic Party*, p.3. This organizational strength was also the subject of Robert Michels, *Political Parties: A Sociological Study of the Oligarchical Tendencies of Modern Democracy* (London: Collier Macmillan, 1968).

16 In Britain a similar situation had developed at an earlier stage, and in circumstances where its own 'great workers' party' – Chartism – had already been defeated. See Theodore Rothstein, *From Chartism to Labourism*, (London: Lawrence & Wishart, 1983). When the imperialist epoch once again brought the working class onto the political stage,

in Britain this was entirely under the compass of the liberal–conservative duopoly, and when independent labour politics did emerge it was from the start dominated by an alliance between liberal reformers and the representatives of labour, i.e. it was not independent of the bourgeoisie. On the origins of the Labour Party see: Ralph Miliband, *Parliamentary Socialism: A Study in the Politics of Labour* (London: Merlin, 1972), David Coates, *The Labour Party and the Struggle for Socialism* (Cambridge: Cambridge University Press, 1975), James Hinton, *Labour and Socialism: A History of the British Labour Movement 1867–1974* (Brighton: Wheatsheaf, 1983), Geoffrey Foote, *The Labour Party's Political Thought: A History* (Beckenham: Croom Helm, 1986).

17 James W. Gerard, *My Four Years in Germany* (London: Hodder & Stoughton, 1917) pp.284, 288.

18 Harry J. Marks, 'The Sources of Reformism in the Social Democratic Party of Germany 1890–1914', *The Journal of Modern History*, Vol.XI pp.334–56 (1939) provides us with the following account of the party's sympathizers from Zinoviev: they were 'the strata of the electorate recruited mainly from the petty bourgeoisie who do not belong to the Social Democratic Party, are not convinced socialists, but who, under the influence of this or that accidental circumstance, adhere for the time being to the Social Democracy and in the elections give it their vote' (p.346). How like the electoral support of the British Labour Party, with the exception that the SPD made at least some effort to convert its sympathizers to socialism. The role of the trade unions, and especially the trade union bureaucracy in the rightward drift of German social democracy, is discussed in Carl E. Schorske, *German Social Democracy, 1905–1917*.

19 'Did We Not Begin the Propaganda of Marxism Too Early in Backward Russia?', cited by S. Baron, Between Marx and Lenin: George Plekhanov, in L. Labedz (Ed.), *Revisionism* (London: Allen & Unwin, 1962). See also Samuel H. Baron, *Plekhanov – The Father of Russian Marxism* (London: Routledge & Kegan Paul, 1963).

20 Kautsky's work *The Class Struggle* (*Erfurt Program*) (New York: W. W. Norton, 1971) is his elaboration of this programme.

21 It was the thrust of Bernstein's case that the tradition of this revolutionary phraseology could be profitably cast aside to leave a political practice more in tune with the demands of the moment: 'The practice of the German party has frequently, indeed almost always, been opportunist in character...its policy has in every case proved more correct than its phraseology. Hence I have no wish to reform the actual policy of the party...; what I am striving for, and as a theoretician must strive for, is a unity between theory and reality, between phraseology and action', correspondence with Bebel, cited by Lucio Colletti, 'Bernstein and the Marxism of the Second International', in his *From Rousseau to Lenin: Studies in Ideology and Society* (London: New Left Books, 1972) p.49. See also the concluding chapter of Bernstein's *Evolutionary Socialism: A Criticism and Affirmation* (New York: Schocken, 1961).

22 Karl Kautsky *The Class Struggle*, p.173.

23 Cited by Baron 'Between Marx and Lenin' p.52.

24 Interestingly enough this is the very point made against orthodoxy itself by Paul Mattick, who argues that while orthodoxy could achieve gains while capitalism was in an expansionary stage, this was at the cost of diluting its revolutionary politics and would leave the working class impotent when expansion gives way to contraction. Paul Mattick, *Anti-Bolshevik Communism* (London: Merlin, 1978).

25 Jukka Paastella argues that there is a contradiction between the determinism of Marx's critique of political economy and his political voluntarism. As I have demonstrated in the previous two chapters however, there is in fact only a contradiction in so far as Marx's philosophical account is misread so as to be directly applicable to any given political situation. The point is that his philosophy refers to the essential characteristics of historical development, whereas the political refers to a given conjuncture: to this extent the philosophical and the political refer to different entities. But the contradiction does not exist within Marx but within the contingency of history. See Jukka Paastella, *Marx's and Engels' Concepts of the Parties and Political Organizations of the Working Class* (Tampere: University of Tampere, 1985).

26 Kautsky, *The Class Struggle*, p.200.

27 Bernstein *Evolutionary Socialism*, p.xxix. Compare this with Engels' comment that 'We have no final aim. We are evolutionists. We have no intention of dictating final laws to mankind' ('Conversation avec Frederick Engels', *Le Figaro*, 13 May 1893, cited by Paastella, *Marx's and Engle's Concepts*. The apparent similarity between these positions disguises, however, a more fundamental difference. While Engels distinguished between the imposition of a dogmatic end upon the evolution of history, he did not perceive that process of evolution as limited to the expression of the exigencies or contingency of the present – as it was with Bernstein and as it is typically with reformists. For Engels, revolution, the transfer of political power, was *immanent* to historical evolution, while for Bernstein it was entirely absent.

28 As Sidney Hook notes in his introduction to Bernstein's book, 'If one examines the heritage of Bernstein, it seems fair to say that it is his ideas rather than those of his orthodox critics, Karl Kautsky and George Plekhanov, which have won the day, in the sense that they are reflected in the working beliefs of democratic socialist movements in the Western world', Bernstein, *Evolutionary Socialism*, p.xvi.

29 See Lucien Goldmann, 'Is There a Marxist Sociology?', *International Socialism* (1968) No.34, and on the so- called inevitability of socialism: Hal Draper, 'The "Inevitability" of Socialism', *International Socialism* (1963) No.15, and Alasdair MacIntyre, 'Prediction and Politics', *International Socialism* (1963) No.13.

30 Rudolf Hilferding, *Finance Capital* (London: Routledge & Kegan Paul, 1978) p.23. The Finance Minister of the Austrian Republic certainly meant what he said in this respect.
31 For example by Lucio Colletti, *From Rousseau to Lenin* and Sebastiano Timpanaro, *On Materialism* (London: New Left Books, 1975).
32 Cited by Salvadori, *Karl Kautsky*, p.21.
33 'It is by no means necessary that it be accompanied with violence and bloodshed. There are instances in history where the ruling classes were either so exceptionally clear-sighted or so particularly weak and cowardly that they submitted to the inevitable and voluntarily abdicated'; Kautsky, *The Class Struggle*, p.91.
34 Kautsky, cited by Salvadori, *Karl Kautsky*, p.37.
35 Karl Kautsky, *The Class Struggle*, p.90.
36 *Ibid*., p.117.
37 E. Bernstein, cited by Nigel Harris, *Beliefs in Society: The Problem of Ideology* (1968) p.135.
38 Notes scribbled by Bernstein accurately sum up his views thus: 'Peasants do not sink; middle class does not disappear; crises do not grow ever larger; misery and serfdom do not increase. There *is* increase in insecurity, dependence, social distance, social character of production, functional superfluity of property owners', cited by Peter Gay *The Dilemma of Democratic Socialism*, p.250.
39 Kautsky, *The Class Struggle.*, pp.94–5.
40 Cited by Salvadori, *Karl Kautsky*, p.185.
41 *HCC*, p.xvii.
42 *Ibid*., p.xiii.
43 *Ibid*., p.1. The passage reads: 'Let us assume for the sake of argument that recent research had disproved once and for all every one of Marx's individual theses. Even if this were to be proved, every serious "orthodox" Marxist would still be able to accept all such modern findings without reservation and hence dismiss all of Marx's theses *in toto* – without having to renounce his orthodoxy for a single moment. Orthodox Marxism, therefore, does not imply the uncritical acceptance of the results of Marx's investigations. It is not the "belief" in this or that thesis, nor the exegesis of a "sacred" book. On the contrary, orthodoxy refers exclusively to *method*.'
44 *HCC*, p.24.
45 Bernstein, *Evolutionary Socialism*, p.xxix. See note 27 above.
46 *HCC*, p.38.

Chapter 4: Lukács and German Sociology

1 Lee Congdon's book *The Young Lukács* (Chapel Hill, N.C.: University of North Carolina Press, 1983) has demonstrated the complementary character of these processes.

2 *DR*. See also his 'Max Weber and German Sociology' in *Economy and Society* (1972) Vol.I, pp.386–98 for an equally trenchant critique of German sociology. Lukács repeats in this article the story about Max Weber's 'democratic Caesarism' cited below.

3 The reaction of Lukács' friends of this time is discussed by Lee Congdon, 'The Unexpected Revolutionary: Lukács' Road to Marx', *Survey* (1974) Vol.XX, 2/3, pp.196–7.

4 See Arpad Kadarkay, 'Georg Lukács' Road to Art and Marx', *Polity* (1980) Vol.XIII, pp.236–242.

5 Lukács' conversion to communism is also discussed by Edward Timms, 'Mr Lukács Changes Trains', *London Review of Books* (1987) Vol.IX.

6 Georg Lukács, *The Theory of the Novel* (London: Merlin, 1978) p.12.

7 *HCC*, p.ix. The best discussion of Lukács' relation to Simmel is to be found in David Frisby's introduction to Georg Simmel, *The Philosophy of Money* (1978), especially pp.22–9 (henceforth *Money*), and in chapter 3 of Frisby's own *The Alienated Mind* (London: Heinemann, 1983).

8 See Max Weber, 'Politics as a Vocation', included in Gerth and Mills (Eds), *From Max Weber: Essays in Sociology* (1970). The passage in full reads: 'One can say that three pre-eminent qualities are decisive for the politician: passion, a feeling of responsibility, and a sense of proportion. This means passion in the sense of *matter-of-factness*, of passionate devotion to a "cause", to the god or demon who is its overlord. It is not passion in the sense of that inner bearing which my late friend, Georg Simmel, used to designate as "sterile excitation", and which was peculiar to a certain type of Russian intellectual (by no means all of them!). It is an excitation that plays so great a part with our intellectuals in this carnival we decorate with the proud name of "revolution". It is a "romanticism of the intellectually interesting" running into emptiness devoid of all feeling of objective responsibility' (p.115).

9 Cited by Arpad Kadarkay, 'Georg Lukács' Road to Art and Marx', p.231.

10 See Marx's afterword to the 2nd German edition of *Capital* I, pp.23–7.

11 On the emergence of (modern) neo-classical economics and its relationship to social thought see Talcott Parsons, *The Structure of Social Action* (New York: Free Press, 1949). The classical marxist critique of utility theory is Nikolai Bukharin, *Economic Theory of the Leisure Class* (New York: Monthly Review Press, 1972). Goran Therborn has stressed the relation between these two schools of thought in his *Science, Class and Society* (London: New Left Books, 1976), chapter 5, arguing in particular for the importance of such an approach in understanding the significance of Weber's *verstehende* sociology. See p.271 *passim*.

12 In his afterword to the 2nd German Edition of *Capital* I. See also the comments by Engels in his review of Marx's *A Contribution to the Critique of Political Economy* in *MECW* XVI, pp.465–6.

13 '[A]cademic sociology, as it developed particularly in Germany and France, could be seen in part at least as a response by bourgeois society to the danger represented by the Marxist theory of society as an intellectual arm of the socialist movement', Tom Bottomore, 'Sociology', in David McLellan (Ed.), *Marx: The First Hundred Years* (London: Fontana, 1983) p.107.

14 'It was doubtless his book *The Destruction of Reason* which revealed most clearly the destruction of Lukács' own. In a highly undialectical manner, the officially licensed dialectician sweeps all the irrationalist strands of modern philosophy into the camp of reaction and Fascism', in Ernst Bloch *et al., Aesthetics and Politics* (London: Verso, 1980).

15 Michael Lowy, *Georg Lukács – From Romanticism to Bolshevism* (London: New Left Books, 1979).

16 See G.L.Kline, 'Impression of the Man and His Ideas', *Encounter* (pp.62–3), and G. Lichtheim, *Lukács* (London: Fontana/Collins, 1970) p.116, and T. Aczel and T. Meray, *The Revolt of the Mind* (New York: Frederick A. Praeger, 1960) pp.63,83.

17 Conan Fischer discusses the extent of competition and collaboration between the KPD (German Communist Party) and the nazis in his 'Class Enemies or Class Brothers? Communist-Nazi Relations in Germany, 1929–33', *European History Quarterly* (1985) Vol.XV, pp.259–79. See also Leon Trotsky, 'The German Catastrophe: The Responsibility of the Leadership', included in his *The Struggle against Fascism in Germany* (Harmondsworth: Penguin, 1975) for a critique of the theory of social fascism.

18 'I was indeed firmly convinced that I was in the right but I knew also – e.g. from the fate that had befallen Karl Korsch – that to be expelled from the Party meant that it would no longer be possible to participate actively in the struggle against fascism...I wrote my self-criticism as an "entry ticket" to such activity', *HCC*, p.xxx. Lukács goes on: 'My internal, private self-criticism came to the conclusion that if I was so clearly in the right, as I believed, and could still not avoid such a sensational defeat, then there must be grave defects in my practical political activities. Therefore, I felt able to withdraw from my political career with a good conscience and concentrate once more on theoretical matters', *HCC*, p.xxxi. Witness also the following explanation from an interview with *New Left Review*: 'I had no regrets about the ending of my political career [in 1930]. You see, I was convinced I was utterly right in the inner-party disputes in 1928–29 – nothing ever led me to change my mind on this; yet I had completely failed to convince the party of my views. So I thought: if I was so right, and yet so wholly defeated, this could only mean that I had no political abilities as such. So I gave up political work without any difficulty', Georg Lukács, *Record of a Life*, p.180. (This

interview was originally published in *New Left Review* (1971) No.68, pp.49–58.

19 'My expulsion from the Central Committee of the Hungarian Party in no way altered my belief that even with the disastrously sectarian policies of the Third Period, one could only fight effectively against fascism within the ranks of the Communist movement', Georg Lukács, *Record of a Life* pp.180–1. This justification is questioned by Michael Lowy in his *Georg Lukács – From Romanticism to Bolshevism* (London: New Left Books, 1979), where he argues, following Trotsky, that staying loyal to stalinism made any effective struggle against fascism impossible; see pp.199–201.

20 Heidegger 'saw the Nazis as a new hope for decadent Germany; a spiritual force which would halt the decline of Western civilization by opposing equally the "materialism" of America and the marxism of Russia', Roger Waterhouse, 'Heidegger: an Assessment', *Radical Philosophy* (1981) No.27, p.22. Waterhouse cites the following extract from Heidegger's lecture 'On the Fundamental Question of Metaphysics': 'From a metaphysical point of view, Russia and America are the same; the same dreary technological frenzy, the same unrestricted organization of the average man' – Martin Heidegger, *Introduction to Metaphysics* (1961), p.31. On the complex relationship between Werner Sombart and National Socialism see Herman Lebovics, *Social Conservatism and the Middle Classes in Germany 1914–33* (Princeton, NJ: Princeton University Press, 1969) Ch.2. See also Richard Wolin, 'Recent Revelations Concerning Martin Heidegger and National Socialism', *Theory, Culture & Society* (1990) No.7, 73–96.

21 Cited by Roland N. Stromberg, 'The Intellectuals and the Coming of War in 1914', *Journal of European Studies* (1973) Vol.III, No.2, p.115.

22 *Ibid.*, p.113.

23 *Ibid.*, p.110.

24 *Ibid.*, p.111.

25 Gareth Stedman Jones comes close to doing this in his article 'The Marxism of the Early Lukács', *New Left Review* (Ed.), *Western Marxism: A Critical Reader* (1977) pp.11–60 where he writes: 'A simple equation between romanticism and progressive attitudes, however, can only be sustained by ignoring the rabidly racist and elitist character of many of the writings of the later exponents of the tradition (Carlyle, Ruskin, D. H. Lawrence, T. S. Eliot'; pp.22–3. He makes this as a critical point against Raymond Williams' *Culture and Society, 1780–1950* (Harmondsworth: Penguin, 1963), but this supposed 'simple equation' is not at issue: what is is the belief that the romantic critique of science must degenerate into an anti-scientific, irrationalist nihilism. This latter position is of course shared by the later Lukács.

26 Max Weber referred to those 'proto fascist conservatives' who 'sought to re-create Gemeinschaft through a corporate state' as 'ink bottle

Romantics'; cited by Arthur Mitzman, *The Iron Cage: An Historical Interpretation of Max Weber* (New York: Alfred A. Knopf, 1970) p.185.

27 See Richard M. Watt, *The Kings Depart: The Tragedy of Germany, Versailles and the German Revolution* (London: Literary Guild, 1968).

28 Marianne Weber, *Max Weber. A Biography* (New York: John Wiley, 1975).

29 '[T]he ethics of a great military leader should not be measured by yardsticks other than those appropriate to them', *ibid.*, p.651.

30 *Ibid.*, p.653.

31 cited by Ferenc Feher, 'The Last Phase of Romantic Anti-Capitalism: Lukács' Response to the War', *New German Critique* (1977) No.10, p.145.

32 For an interesting example of anti-German propaganda utilizing many of these themes see the war-time anthology edited by W. W. Coole and M. F. Potter, *Thus Spake Germany* (London: George Routledge, 1942).

33 See especially Fritz K. Ringer, *The Decline of the German Mandarins* (Cambridge, Mass.: Harvard University Press, 1969). Also Fritz Stern, *The Failure of Illiberalism* (London: Allen & Unwin, 1972) and *The Politics of Cultural Despair* (Berkeley and Los Angeles: University of California Press, 1961).

34 Georg Lukács, *The Theory of the Novel* (London: Merlin, 1978), p.11. See also Istvan Eorsi (Ed.), *Georg Lukács – Record of a Life*, pp.44–5.

35 Feher, 'The Last Phase of Romantic Anti-Capitalism', p.148.

36 Lukács, *Theory of the Novel*, p.20.

37 It is worth noting here that this was the same point Lukács expressed in his essay 'The Changing Function of Historical Materialism' (1919), where he notes that bourgeois ideology is at two points brought openly to express the idea of class struggle: in its heroic period (prior 1848), and in the imperialist epoch. In this latter period the bourgeoisie make use of those 'renegades from the camp of the proletariat' to provide itself with a 'consciousness of society' that is ultimately based upon 'the scientific method of the proletariat, admittedly in a distorted form'; *HCC*, pp.226–8.

38 *DR*, p.239.

39 Lowy, *Georg Lukács – From Romanticism to Bolshevism*. See also Michael Lowy, 'Marxism and Revolutionary Romanticism', *Telos* (1981) No.49; Michael Lowy and Robert Sayre, 'Figures of Romantic Anti-Capitalism', *New German Critique* (1984) No.32; Michael Lowy, 'The Romantic and the Marxist Critique', unpublished paper presented at the International Conference *Has Socialism a Future?* Glasgow, 1985; Michael Lowy, 'Marcuse and Benjamin: the Romantic Dimension', *Telos* (1980) No.44.

40 Ferdinand Tönnies, *Community and Association [Gemeinschaft und Gesellschaft]* (London: Routledge & Kegan Paul, 1955). Henceforth: *Gemein.*

41 The importance of the book to marxism in general is discussed by Fritz Pappenheim in his *The Alienation of Modern Man: An Interpretation Based on Marx and Tönnies* (New York: Monthly Review, 1959).

42 *Gemein*, p.ix.

43 Raymond Aron, *German Sociology* (Glencoe: Free Press of Glencoe, 1964).
44 Indeed, there was no chair in sociology in any German university before 1918 – see David Frisby, *Georg Simmel* (Chichester and London: Ellis Harwood and Tavistock, 1984).
45 *Gemein*, p.57.
46 *Ibid.*, p.53.
47 *Ibid.*, p.55.
48 *Ibid.*, p.64.
49 *Ibid.*, p.58.
50 *Ibid.*, p.74.
51 *Ibid.*
52 Tönnies was throughout his life to edit and publish works by and about Thomas Hobbes; see W.J.Cahnman, *Ferdinand Tönnies: A New Evaluation* (Leiden: E. J. Brill, 1973) p.40 on this point.
53 *Gemein*, p.87.
54 At the same time, incidentally, Tönnies relates these concepts to masculine and feminine attributes and locates as particularly befitting to women the realm of life and work performed in the home, or its homely society, *Gemeinschaft*. Even here, though, Tönnies raises an important point, arguing that the home is itself transformed by the transition from *Gemeinschaft* to *Gesellschaft*: in this latter, home becomes 'nothing but shelter for those on a journey through the world', p.187.
55 *Gemein*, p.189.
56 *Ibid.*, p.193.
57 *Ibid.*, p.39.
58 *DR*, p.594.
59 Made in the third part of *The Communist Manifesto*, see *MECW* VI, p.507.
60 *MECW* VI, p.508.
61 *Gemein*, p.194.
62 *Ibid.*
63 *Ibid.*, p.270.
64 Theo Pinkus (Ed.), *Conversations with Lukács* (London: Merlin, 1974) p.100. Lukács then adds 'I don't know whether one cannot even say today that this was a fortunate circumstance for my own development.'
65 *HCC*, p.ix.
66 See Frisby's introduction to *Money*, p.15.
67 '[I]t was Simmel who made an issue of the social character of art and this gave me a point of view, a basis for the discussion of literature that went well beyond Simmel's own. It is his philosophy that underpins my book on drama', *Georg Lukács – Record of a Life* (1983) p.37. See also Lowy, *Georg Lukács – From Romanticism to Bolshevism*, pp.97–9; Arato and Breines, *The Young Lukács* (London: Pluto, 1979), pp.13–32.
68 *DR*, p.443.

69 *Ibid*., p.446.
70 *Ibid*., p.455.
71 'Nietzsche stated this aristocratic bias in an overt, reactionary-militant manner whereas Simmel, in accordance with the pre-war social situation, contented himself with a haughty aloofness from the "crowd"', *DR*, p.456.
72 *Ibid*., p.458.
73 Lukács' originality in reconstructing these ideas of Marx is questioned by Henry B. Shue in 'Lukács: Notes on his Originality', *Journal of the History of Ideas* (1973) Vol.XXXIV, No.4, pp.645–50, who points out that Lukács had access to significant sections of the *Grundrisse* and works written by Marx at the same time and which expressed similar ideas to those contained in the 'Paris Manuscripts'. As George Lichtheim indicates in his 'Reply to Professor Shue', *ibid*., pp.651–2, however, what is really significant is that Lukács was able to draw conclusions from his reading of such works that escaped the notice of Kautsky, and indeed anyone else.
74 *Money*, p.56.
75 *DR*, p.452.
76 'History and Class Consciousness follows Hegel in that it too equates alienation with objectification', *HCC*, p.xxiv.
77 *Ibid*.
78 *Ibid*.
79 *Ibid*..
80 *Ibid*., p.94.
81 *Ibid*., pp.94–5.
82 *Money*, p.278.
83 Robert Michels in his book *Political Parties* (London: Collier Macmillan, 1968) does a similar thing: his study of German social democracy shows how that party, far from representing a structural/institutional break with the bureaucratization of modern life, is actually further evidence of its universality.
84 I will return to this point when I look in more detail at Lukács' theory of reification in the next chapter.
85 Cited by Frisby in his introduction to *Money*, p.20.
86 *Money*, p.456.
87 *Ibid*., p.448.
88 *Ibid*., p.449.
89 In Christopher Lasch, *The Culture of Narcissism: American Life in an Age of Diminishing Expectations* (London: Sphere, 1980), expecially chapter 10. See also his (earlier) *Haven in a Heartless World: The Family Besieged* (1977) and, more recently, *The Minimal Self: Psychic Survival in Troubled Times* (London: Pan, 1985).

Chapter 5: Alienation, Reification and Commodity Fetishism

1 *MECW* III. The work was first published in full in 1932.
2 Note however that this is challenged by Henry G. Shue in his article 'Lukács: Notes on his Originality', *Journal of the History of Ideas* (1973) Vol.XXXIV, No.4, pp.645–50.
3 The same concept is also discussed in the latter chapters of the third volume of *Capital*: in particular chapter 48 ('The Trinity Formula') and chapter 51 ('Distribution Relations and Production Relations').
4 Fetish: 'inanimate object worshipped by savages [sic] for its magical powers or as being inhabited by a spirit; principle etc. irrationally reverenced', *The Concise Oxford Dictionary of Current English* (1964), p.447.
5 Cf. the section on estranged labour in the *Economic and Philosophical Manuscripts* where Marx gives the following as his aim: 'Now, therefore, we have to grasp the intrinsic connection between private property, avarice, the separation of labour, capital and landed property; the connection of exchange and competition, of value and the devaluation of men, of monopoly and competition, etc. – we have to grasp this whole estrangement connected with the money system', *MECW* III, p.271.
6 I. I. Rubin, *Essays in Marx's Labour Theory of Value* (Montreal: Black Rose Books, 1973) – a book first published in the same year as Lukács' own seminal work.
7 *Ibid.*, p.5.
8 *Ibid.*, p.57.
9 Lesek Kolakowski, *Main Currents of Marxism*, Vol.1: *The Founders* (Oxford: Oxford University Press, 1978).
10 *Ibid.*, p.262 *passim*. Kolakowski states that he is in agreement 'with those who hold that there is no discontinuity in Marx's thought, and that it was from first to last inspired by basically Hegelian philosophy', p.263.
11 *HCC*, p.157.
12 Adam Schaff, 'Alienation as a Social and Philosophical Problem', *Social Praxis* (1975) Vol.III, pp.7–26. Schaff defines alienation as 'such a relation between a human agent and the product of his activity in which that product, having acquired a socially objective existence and being situated in a given social system, functions not only autonomously (i.e., independently of the intentions of his maker) but, under specified conditions, even against the wishes and intentions of his maker, and sometimes endangers his interests or his very existence', p.11.
13 Schaff criticizes those empirical studies of alienation which 'come to the groundless and erroneous conclusion that the problems of alienation are identical with those of autoalienation', *ibid.*, p.12.
14 Robert Blauner, *Alienation and Freedom: The Factory Worker and his Industry* (Chicago and London: University of Chicago Press, 1964).

Blauner sees his task as 'recasting a politically loaded controversy into a manageable scientific question', (p.4).

15 The Goldthorpe and Lockwood 'affluent worker' studies have shown, moreover, that there is no necessary relation between 'immediate, shop floor work experience and employee attitudes that are of wider reference' because the effects of conditions of work are 'always *mediated* through the meanings which men take to their work and through their own definitions of their work situation, and because these meanings and definitions in turn vary with the particular sets of wants and expectations that men bring to their employment', John H. Goldthorpe *et al.*, *The Affluent Worker in the Class Structure* (Cambridge: Cambridge University Press, 1969). In other words, what is of primary importance is not specific everyday experience but generalized social experience.

16 Schaff, 'Alienation as a Social and Philosophical Problem', p.14. Schaff later admits that Marx himself (in the *Economic and Philosophical Manuscripts*) did base his theory of alienation on precisely such an approach (see p.17).

17 John Horton, 'The Dehumanization of Anomie and Alienation: A Problem in the Ideology of Sociology', *British Journal of Sociology*, Vol.XV (1964): 'Anomie concentrates on barriers to the orderly functioning of society; alienation on barriers to the productive growth of individuals' (p.286).

18 See Norman Geras, *Marx and Human Nature: Refutation of a Legend* (London: Verso, 1983).

19 Marx's criticism of those followers of critical-utopian socialism and communism who 'still dream of experimental realisation of their social Utopias, of founding isolated "philansteres", of establishing "Home Colonies", of setting up a "little Icaria" – duodecimo editions of the New Jerusalem' was based upon their holding onto these views 'in opposition to the progressive historical development of the proletariat', *MECW* VI, p.516; *MESW* p.61 – that is, because they stand apart from the class struggle.

20 As Gajo Petrovic remarks in his essay on alienation in the *Dictionary of Marxist Thought* (Oxford: Basil Blackwell, 1983) (Tom Bottomore, Ed.), alienation from oneself should be regarded not so much as alienation from a factual or normative sense of human nature but as 'alienation from historically created human possibilities, especially from the human capacity for freedom and creativity', (p.13).

21 See David McLellan, *Ideology* (Milton Keynes: Open University Press, 1986) chapter 3 and Perry Anderson, *Considerations on Western Marxism* (London: New Left Books, 1976).

22 Jorge Larrain, *Marxism and Ideology*, (London: Macmillan, 1983).

23 As McLellan notes, 'while for Lenin the power of ideology was due largely to its control of institutions for disseminating its views, for Lukács the

ideological subordination of the proletariat was more embedded in the very economic and social organization of capitalist society' (*Ideology*, p.27).

24 'Whereas in Lukács the analysis of ideology remains at an undifferentiated level of high intellectual complexity, Gramsci considers ideology at different levels', Larrain, *Marxism and Ideology*, p.82. See also McLellan, *Ideology*, p.28.

25 Joseph McCarney, *The Real World of Ideology*, (Brighton: Harvester, 1980), pp.46–55. McCarney refers to Poulantzas' and Stedman Jones' 'empiricist perspective' (p.53) and their 'sociologism' (p.54) as contrasted with the theoretical orientation of Marx, Lenin and Lukács.

26 McLellan, *Ideology*, refers to Lukács' account as 'excessively abstract' and lacking in 'almost any empirical reference' (p.27).

27 See for example Lukács' article 'Freud's Psychology of the Masses' included in his *Reviews and Articles* (London: Merlin, 1983).

28 *Capital* I, p.77.

29 *HCC*, p.86.

30 Gareth Stedman Jones, 'The Marxism of the Early Lukács' in *New Left Review* (Ed.), *Western Marxism: A Critical Reader* (London: New Left Books, 1977), pp.43–5. See also Alex Callinicos (1983), p.78, and David McLellan *Ideology*, p.28.

31 *HCC*, p.80.

32 *Ibid.*, p.169.

33 *Ibid.*, p.178.

34 *Ibid.*, p.181.

35 *Ibid.*, p.86.

36 *Ibid.*, p.87.

37 This point has been forcefully made by François George, 'Forgetting Lenin', *Telos* (1973–74) No.18: 'Lenin not only accepts but vindicates the structure of the capitalist enterprise' (p.54). David Selbourne refers to the way in which use of terms like 'the working class' imprison the individual, 'confine him to it [his role within the division of labour] in a hated thraldom supervised both by capital and by the socialist intellectual', and how 'the human-as-worker is trapped by socialist, and especially Marxist theory within categories and structures of argument which have always referred only to a part, and a shrinking part, of individual function', *Against Socialist Illusions* (1984), pp.70–1.

38 Jose Ortega y Gasset, however, regards these developments as synonomous; for him the one fact of utmost importance in the public life of Europe 'is the accession of the masses to complete social power', *The Revolt of the Masses* (London: Unwin, 1961), p.9 – a work first published in 1930.

39 It might be said that the experience of religion yields an example of alienation that does not require such a *thingification*. However, while this may be true in so far as religion is restricted to its spiritual aspects, religion has invariably been followed by the icons and symbols of the

church, which itself claims to be the essential mediator between individual experience and that to which that experience is directed, namely God.

40 As becomes clear (below) I do not mean by this that the system of exploitation peculiar to capitalism is based upon an unequal change in the economic or juridical sense, but that the formal equality in which the wage contract is formulated disguises the underlying social and political inequality between the respective classes.

41 *HCC*, p.83.

42 *Ibid.*, p.85.

43 *Ibid.*, p.86.

44 There is, for example, the case of the bread riots discussed by E.P. Thompson in his book *The Making of the English Working Class* (London: Victor Gollancz, 1963) Ch. 3, where notions of natural economy and natural right led rioters to seize what they regarded as unfairly priced bread and proceed to offer it for sale at what they regarded as its "natural" price. See also the remarks on this matter in chapter 2 above.

45 For a taste of the vast literature on this topic specifically related to the example of the United States see: Werner Sombart, *Why is There No Socialism in the United States?* (White Plains, NY: M.E. Sharpe, 1976); David M. Potter, *People of Plenty: Economic Abundance and the American Character* (1954); Christopher Lasch, *The Agony of the American Left: One Hundred Years of Radicalism* (1973); James Weinstein, *Ambiguous Legacy: The Left in American Politics* (1975); Daniel Bell, *Marxian Socialism in the United States* (Princeton, NJ: Princeton University Press, 1967); David Watson, *Why is There No Socialism in the United States?* (Winchester: King Alfred's College, 1981); Eric Foner, 'Why is There No Socialism in the United States?', *History Workshop Journal* (1984); Mike Davis, *Prisoners of the American Dream* (London: Verso, 1986); J Karabel, 'The Failure of American Socialism Reconsidered', *Socialist Register* (1979).

46 *HCC*, p.87.

47 See Tony Cliff, *Lenin*, Vol.4: *The Bolsheviks and World Revolution* (1979) Ch.9.

48 Fernando Claudin, *The Communist Movement: From Comintern to Cominform* (1975).

49 In this respect, mention has to be made of Lenin's notion of stick-bending which, while it has the undoubted benefit of allowing tactical considerations to be tailored to particular political conjunctures, does carry with it the danger of opportunism, or of adaptation to circumstances unacceptable to the revolutionary. At what point tactical considerations degenerate into opportunism is difficult to determine; much of Lenin's attraction to Lukács concerns his ability to avoid this – see the reference to Lenin's *realpolitik* in Lukács' short book, *Lenin: A Study in the Unity of His Thought* (London: New Left Books, 1977).

50 On this see Andrew Arato and Paul Breines, *The Young Lukács and the Origins of Western Marxism* (London: Pluto, 1979) Ch. 10.

51 Frank Eckelt, 'The Internal Policies of the Hungarian Soviet Republic', in Ivan Volgyes (Ed.), *Hungary in Revolution, 1918–1919* (Lincoln, Neb.: University of Nebraska Press, 1971); Rudolf Tokes, *Bela Kun and the Hungarian Soviet Republic* (New York: Praeger, 1967); Andrew C. Janos, *The Politics of Backwardness in Hungary 1825–1945* (Princeton, NJ: Princeton University Press, 1982), Ch.IV; Oscar Jaszi, *Revolution and Counter-Revolution in Hungary* (London: P.S. King, 1924), Chs.IX–X; Andrew C. Janos and William B. Slottman (Eds), *Revolution in Perspective: Essays on the Hungarian Soviet Republic of 1919* (Berkeley: University of California Press, 1971).

52 Victor Serge retails the story of Lenin's analysis of the March Action to the Executive Committee of the Communist International in which he 'ten or more times' used the phrase 'les bêtises de Bela Kun', in his *Memoirs of a Revolutionary, 1901–1941* (Oxford: Oxford University Press, 1967) p.140. See also Leon Trotsky, *The Third International after Lenin* (London: New Park, 1974) p.240.

53 *HCC*, p.94.

54 *Ibid.*, p.102.

55 Cited in *ibid.*, p.107.

56 *Ibid.*, p.109.

57 *Ibid.*, pp.109–10.

58 *Ibid.*, p.128.

59 *Ibid.*, p.110.

60 *Ibid.*, p.112.

61 It is this construction – and the conclusion drawn from it (which I discuss below) – that causes Callinicos to criticize the continued influence of the bourgeois notion of subjectivity upon Lukács' epistemology. However, Lukács' point is surely correct, that objectivistic epistemologies are by their very nature impossible to justify, are self-defeating. The case of Karl Popper is instructive, in that his attempt to construct on objectivistic epistemology, the notion of verification, actually imposes standards of scientificity upon science that it is unable to meet, with the consequence that he is open to the criticisms levelled by Thomas Kuhn in his *The Structure of Scientific Revolutions* (Chicago: University of Chicago Press, 1970) 2nd Edition.

62 *HCC*, p.120.

63 *Ibid.*, p.121.

64 *Ibid.*

65 *Ibid.*

66 *Ibid.*, p.122.

67 See H. Stuart Hughes, *Conciousness and Society* (St Albans: Paladin, 1974) for an account of this process.

68 *HCC*, p.10.
69 Richard G. Lipsey, *An Introduction to Positive Economics* (London: Weidenfeld & Nicolson, 1975) is a typical and widely influential example.
70 Cf. Marx's comment that 'all science would be superfluous if the outward appearance and the essence of things directly coincided', *Capital* III, p.817.
71 For as Thomas Kuhn has indicated in his *Structure of Scientific Revolutions*, the actual practice of scientists is not quite the same as their methodology would suggest.
72 *Lenin* (1977) p.84. Interestingly, this phrase was taken by Lukács from Lenin's own attack on the journal *Kommunismus* (of which Lukács was co-editor), and in particular on articles by Bela Kun 'On the Question of the Parliamentary Boycott', which, according to Lenin, 'absolutely evades what is most important, that which constitutes the very gist, the living soul, of Marxism – a concrete analysis of a concrete situation', and Lukács' 'On the Question of Parliamentarism'. See V. I. Lenin, *Collected Works* XXXI (London: Lawrence & Wishart, 1976), pp.165–7.
73 *HCC*, p.8.
74 *Ibid.*, p.9.
75 See Lucio Colletti's introduction to Karl Marx, *Early Writings* (Harmondsworth: Penguin, 1975) pp.35–6.
76 In his book *Ludwig Feuerbach and the End of Classical German Philosophy of 1888*, included in *MESW* pp.584–622.
77 *MESW*, p.595.
78 *HCC*, p.133.
79 Frederick Engels, *Anti-Dühring* (London: Lawrence & Wishart, 1975), p.3.
80 Antonio Gramsci, *Selections from the Prison Notebooks* (London: Lawrence & Wishart, 1971), p.448.

Chapter 6: Lukács, Revolution and the Party

1 'It is evident that the whole structure of capitalist production rests on the interaction between a necessity subject to strict laws in all isolated phenomena and the relative irrationality of the total process'; *HCC*, p.102.
2 'Whatever the subject of debate, the dialectical method is concerned with the same problem: knowledge of the historical process in its entirety'; *ibid.*, p.34
3 'The primacy of the category of totality is the bearer of the principle of revolution in science'; *ibid.*, p.27.
4 *Ibid.*, p.13.
5 *Ibid.*, p.20.
6 The essay commences thus: 'It is not the primacy of economic motives in historical explanation that constitutes the decisive difference between marxism and bourgeois thought, but the point of view of totality' and

continues 'The primacy of the category of totality is the bearer of the principle of revolution in science'; *ibid.*, p.27.

7 The identity of thought and existence 'is that they are aspects of one and the same real historical and dialectical process'; *ibid.*, p.204. Alex Callinicos seems to think that Althusser's philosophical separation of being and thought is something to be commended as deriving from Marx, whereas in truth it owes more to Feuerbach. See his *Althusser's Marxism* (London: Pluto, 1976), p.25.

8 'The proletariat as the subject of thought in society destroys at one blow the dilemma of impotence'; *HCC*, p.39.

9 *Ibid.*, p.28

10 *Ibid.*. p.31.

11 *Ibid.*, p.29.

12 Karl Kautsky, 'Ultra Imperialism', *New Left Review* (1979) No.59, pp.41–6 developed the notion, immediately prior to the outbreak of the First World War, that the development of imperialism had made the threatening war less, rather than more likely because the general course of capitalism could not permit an interruption in its process of accumulation.

13 G.A. Cohen, 'The Structure of Proletarian Unfreedom', *Philosophy and Public Affairs* (1983) Vol.XII, No.1, pp.70–83; A.J. Skillen, 'Workers' Interests and the Proletarian Ethic: Conflicting Strains in Marxian Anti-Moralism', *Canadian Journal of Philosophy* (1981) Vol.VII, pp.155–70.

14 Even for the epitome of the enlightened bourgeois individual – the artist – there was no escaping the vulgarizing and corrupting influence of capitalist society. Lukács' book *The Soul and Form* and his essay 'The Poverty of Spirit' were evidence of that, from a writer who at the time aspired to the noble and virtuous escapist role and function of the artist.

15 'The objective economic evolution could do no more than create the position of the proletariat in the production process...But the objective evolution could only give the proletariat the opportunity and the necessity to change society. Any transformation can only come about as the product of the – free – action of the proletariat itself', *HCC*, pp.208–9.

16 *Ibid.*, pp.249,250.

17 *Ibid.*, p.252.

18 *Ibid.*, p.251.

19 *MECW* III, p.183.

20 *HCC*, p.2.

21 'Among the factors that determine the direction to be taken, the proletariat's correct understanding of its own historical position is of the very first importance'; *ibid.*, p.311.

22 *Ibid.*, p.3.

23 This 'crisis of marxism' was first noted by Karl Korsch in 1927: 'Marxism today is in the midst of an historical and theoretical crisis. It is not simply

a crisis within the *marxist movement*, but a crisis of *Marxism itself*, cited by Erica Sherover-Marcuse, *Emancipation and Consciousness* (Oxford: Basil Blackwell, 1986) p.12.

24 'The Russian Revolution was not made against a capitalist state at all. The Tsarism which fell in 1917 was a feudal apparatus: the Provisional Government never had time to replace it with a new or stable bourgeois apparatus. The Bolsheviks made a *socialist revolution*, but from beginning to end they never confronted the *central enemy* of the workers movement in the West', Perry Anderson, *Lineages of the Absolutist State* (London: Verso, 1979) p.359.

25 *HCC*, p.xvii.

26 *Ibid.*, p.xxiii.

27 Lucien Goldmann, *Human Sciences and Philosophy* (London: Jonathan Cape, 1969), p.51.

28 Victor Zitta, *Georg Lukács. Marxism, Alienation, Dialectics, Revolution. A Study in Utopia and Ideology* (The Hague: Martinus Nijhoff, 1964). See on this book Ben Brewster, 'A Very Bad Biography of Lukács', *New Left Review* (1965) No.33. Zitta's book provides a wealth of sometimes fascinating biographical detail, but is compromised by its uncompromising cold war ideology and its psychological invective against the personality of Lukács – not to mention its inaccuracies uncovered by Brewster.

29 *HCC*, p.40.

30 This criticism is made most forcibly by Andrew Arato and Paul Breines in *The Young Lukács and the Origins of Western Marxism* (London: Pluto, 1979), who refer to his 'utopian mythologizing' (p.159), and by Lee Congdon, *The Young Lukács* (Chapel Hill, N.C.: University of North Carolina Press, 1983), who asserts that the work 'is a dogmatics invulnerable to external criticism or argument...a blueprint for tyranny' (p.186).

31 *HCC*, p.239.

32 See Carol Johnson, 'The Problem of Reformism and Marx's Theory of Fetishism', *New Left Review* (1980) No.119.

33 Leszek Kolakowski, *Main Currents of Marxism: Its Origins, Growth and Dissolution* (Oxford: Oxford University Press, 1978), Vol.III: *The Breakdown*: 'Lukács' chief work was devoted, in fact, to providing leninism with a better philosophical basis than Lenin himself had offered' (p.284).

34 As do Ernesto Laclau and Chantal Mouffe in their *Hegemony and Socialist Strategy: Towards a Radical Democratic Politics* (London: Verso, 1985).

35 'The advance of industry, whose involuntary promoter is the bourgeoisie, replaces the isolation of the labourers due to competition, by their revolutionary combination due to association', 'Manifesto of the Communist Party', *The Revolutions of 1848*, p.79; *MECW* VI, p.496.

36 'The class consciousness of the proletariat does not develop uniformly throughout the whole proletariat, parallel with the objective economic crisis. Large sections of the proletariat remain intellectually under the tutelage of the bourgeoisie; even the severest economic crisis fails to shake them in their attitude. With the result that the standpoint of the proletariat and its reaction to the crisis is much less violent and intense than is the crisis itself', *HCC*, p.304.

37 See W. F. Haug, *Critique of Commodity Aesthetics* (Cambridge: Polity Press, 1986).

38 See further on this Bertell Ollman, *Social and Sexual Revolution: Essays on Marx and Reich* (London: Pluto, 1979).

39 It is thus necessary to distinguish between those elements that are historically contingent and those that are of more general application – and this devalues significant sections of the book, a fact recognized by Lenin himself: 'the basic mistake of those who polemicize against "What Is To Be Done?" today, is that they tear this work out of the context of a definite historical milieu, a definite, now already long past period of development of our party... "What Is To Be Done?" polemically corrected Economism, and it is false to consider the contents of the pamphlet outside of its connection with this task'; Lenin cited by Tony Cliff, *Rosa Luxemburg* (London: Socialist Review Publishers, 1968) p.48.

40 This was retrospectively titled the 1st Congress of the RSDLP at the 2nd Congress. This 1st Congress was a very small affair, and most of the delegates were arrested immediately afterwards. The 2nd Congress witnessed the split between Mensheviks and Bolsheviks.

41 See Tony Cliff, *Lenin, Vol.I: Building the Party* (London: Pluto, 1976) and V. I. Lenin, 'The Heritage We Renounce' in his *Selected Works* I, pp.57–91.

42 Lenin, *Selected Works* I, p.109.

43 *Ibid.*, p.110.

44 *Ibid.*, p.120.

45 *Ibid.*, pp.120–1.

46 *Ibid.*, p.123.

47 *Ibid.*

48 This is an example of a 'genetic fallacy', judging a phenomenon on the grounds of its historical origin and disregarding its subsequent historical evolution and current structured content.

49 'This, *taken by itself* is in essence still not Social-Democratic work, but merely trade union work'; Lenin, *Selected Works* I, p.69.

50 'Social Democracy leads the struggle of the working class not only for better terms for the sale of labour power, but also for the abolition of the social system which compels the propertyless to sell themselves to the rich'; *ibid.*, p.70.

51 'In order to become a Social-Democrat, the worker must have a clear picture in his mind of the economic nature and the social and political

features of the landlord and the priest, the high state official and the peasant, the student and the tramp; he must know their strong and weak points; he must see the meaning of all the catchwords and sophisms by which each class and each stratum camouflages its selfish strivings and its real "inside workings"; he must understand what interests certain institutions and certain laws reflect and how they reflect them'; *ibid.*, pp.86–7.

52 'The idea of the Communist Party...has yet often been seen purely in *technical* terms rather than as one of the most important *intellectual* questions of the revolution'; *HCC*, p.295.

53 *Ibid.*, p.301.

54 *Ibid.*, p.304.

55 Following Luxemburg, Lukács notes that they might equally lead to 'the mutual destruction of the opposing classes and to a new barbarism'; *HCC*, p.306. See also on this point Norman Geras, *The Legacy of Rosa Luxemburg* (London: New Left Books, 1976) Ch.1.

56 *HCC*, p.316.

57 *Ibid.*, p.318.

58 *Ibid.*, p.319.

59 'The criterion for and the guide to the current relationship between class and the party can be found nowhere but in the class consciousness of the proletariat'; *ibid.*, p.322.

60 *Ibid.*, p.327.

61 Lukács, Lenin: A Study on the Unity of his Thought (London: New Left Books, 1977) p.35.

62 *Ibid.*, p.31.

63 *Ibid.*, p.36.

64 *Ibid.*, p.38.

65 *Ibid.*, p.86.

66 Victor Serge's expression for the mid-century setbacks of stalinism and fascism.

Conclusion

1 Christopher Hitchens, *Prepared For The Worst* (London: Chatto & Windus, 1989) p.240.

2 Maurice Merleau-Ponty, *Signs* (Evanston, Ill.: Northwestern University Press, 1964) p.10.

3 Maurice Merleau-Ponty, *Adventures of the Dialectic* (Evanston, Ill.: Northwestern University Press, 1973) p.207.

4 Russell Jacoby, *Dialectic of Defeat* (Cambridge: Cambridge University Press, 1981).

5 For an example of this approach see Chris Harman, *The Lost Revolution: Germany 1918 to 1923* (London: Bookmarks, 1982).

6 *MECW* V, p.214.

Bibliography

ABENDROTH, Wolfgang, *A Short History of the European Working Class* (London: New Left Books, 1972).

ABERCROMBIE, Nicholas & Bryan S. TURNER, 'The Dominant Ideology Thesis', *British Journal of Sociology* (1978) XXIX, 2, 149–70.

ABRAMS, M.H., *Natural Supernaturalism* (New York: Norton, 1973).

ACZEL, Tamas & Tibor Meray, *The Revolt of the Mind: A Case History of Intellectual Resistance behind the Iron Curtain* (New York: Frederick A. Praeger, 1960).

ADORNO, T.W., Else FRENKEL-BRUNSWICK, David J. LEVINSON & R. Nevitt SANFORD, *The Authoritarian Personality* (New York: Harper & Row, 1950).

AGGER, Ben (Ed.), *Western Marxism: An Introduction. Classical and Contemporary Sources* (Santa Monica: Goodyear Publishing, 1979).

ADLER, Alan (Ed.), *Theses, Resolutions and Manifestos of the First Four Congresses of the Third International* (London: Ink Links, 1980).

ALEXANDER, Edward, 'Memories of a Brief Encounter', *Problems of Communism* (1972) XXI, 6, 67–71.

ALI, Tariq (Ed.), *The Stalinist Legacy: Its Impact on Twentieth-Century World Politics* (Harmondsworth: Penguin, 1984).

ALTHUSSER, Louis, *For Marx* (London: New Left Books, 1977).

ALTHUSSER, Louis, *Politics and History: Montesquieu, Rousseau, Hegel and Marx* (London: New Left Books, 1977).

ALTHUSSER, Louis, *Lenin and Philosophy and Other Essays* (London: New Left Books, 1977).

ALTHUSSER, Louis, & Etienne BALIBAR, *Reading Capital* (London: New Left Books, 1970).

ANCHOR, Robert, 'Lukács as Interpreter of German Culture', *History and Theory* (1980) XIX, 277–93

ANCHOR, Robert, 'Review of Lowy & Arato/Breines', *Telos* (1981) No.48, 197–205.

ANDERSON, John, *Studies in Empirical Philosophy* (Sydney: Angus & Robertson, 1962).

ANDERSON, Perry, *Considerations on Western Marxism* (London: New Left Books, 1976).

ANDERSON, Perry, *Lineages of the Absolutist State* (London: Verso, 1979).

ANDERSON, Perry, *Arguments within English Marxism* (London: Verso, 1980).

ANDERSON, Perry, 'Class Struggle in the Ancient World', *History Workshop Journal* (1983) No.16, 57–73.

ANDERSON, Perry, *In the Tracks of Historical Materialism* (London: Verso, 1983).

ANDERSON, Perry, 'The Figures of Descent', *New Left Review* (1987) No.161.

ANDERSON, Perry, 'A Culture in Contraflow – I', *New Left Review* (1990) No.180, 41–78.

ANDERSON, Perry & Robin BLACKBURN (Eds), *Towards Socialism* (London: Fontana, 1965).

ARATO, Andrew, 'Georg Lukács: The Search for a Revolutionary Subject', in Dick Howard & Karl E. Klare (Eds), *The Unknown Dimension: European Marxism since Lenin* (New York: Basic Books, 1972).

ARATO, Andrew, 'Lukács' Theory of Reification', *Telos* (1972) No.11, 25–66.

ARATO, Andrew, 'Notes on History and Class Consciousness', *Philosophical Forum* (1972) Vol.III, Nos3–4, 386–400.

ARATO, Andrew, 'The Second International: A Reexamination', *Telos* (1973/4), No.18, 2–52.

ARATO, Andrew & Paul BREINES, The Young Lukács and the Origins of Western Marxism (London: Pluto, 1979).

ARBLASTER, Anthony, *The Rise and Decline of Western Liberalism* (Oxford: Basil Blackwell, 1984).

ARCHIBALD, W. Peter, 'Using Marx's Theory of Alienation Empirically', *Theory and Society* (1978) No.6, 119–132.

ARINOWITZ, Stanley, *False Consciousness: The Shaping of American Working Class Consciousness* (New York: McGraw Hill, 1973).

ARINOWITZ, Stanley, *The Crisis in Historical Materialism: Class, Politics and Culture in Marxist Theory* (New York: Praeger, 1981).

ARINOWITZ, Stanley, Russell JACOBY, Paul PICCONE & Trent SCHROYER, 'Symposium on Class', *Telos* (1976) No.28, 145–166.

ARON, Raymond, *The Opium of the Intellectuals* (London: Secker & Warburg, 1957).

ARON, Raymond, *German Sociology* (Glencoe: Free Press of Glencoe, 1964).

ARTHUR, Chris, 'The Revolution Betrayed', *Radical Philosophy* (1972) No.3, 2–9.

AVINERI, Shlomo, 'The Hegelian Origins of Marx's Political Thought', *The Review of Metaphysics* (1967) Vol.XXI, No.1, 33– 50.

AVINERI, Shlomo, *The Social and Political Thought of Karl Marx* (London: Cambridge University Press, 1968).

BACHRACH, Peter, *The Theory of Democratic Elitism – A Critique* (New York: University Press of America, 1980).

BACHRACH, Peter & Morton S. BARATZ, 'Two Faces of Power', *The American Political Science Review* (1962) Vol.LVI, 947–52.

BAILEY, Sydney D., 'The Revision of Marxism', *The Review of Politics* (1954) Vol. XVI, 452–62.

BALL, Terence, 'Marx and Darwin – A Reconsideration', *Political Theory* (1979) Vol.VII, No.4, 469–83.

BANNAN, John F., *The Philosophy of Merleau–Ponty* (New York: Harcourt, Brace & World, 1967).

BARANSKI, Zygmunt & John R. SHORT, *Developing Contemporary Marxism* (London: Macmillan, 1985).

BARBALET, J.M., *Marx's Construction of Social Theory* (London: Routledge & Kegan Paul, 1983).

BARITZ, Loren, *The Servants of Power: A History of the Use of Social Science in American Industry* (Middletown: Westleyan University Press, 1960).

BARON, Samuel H., *Plekhanov – The Father of Russian Marxism* (London: Routledge & Kegan Paul, 1963).

BARZUN, Jacques, *Darwin, Marx, Wagner. Critique of a Heritage* (New York: Doubleday Anchor, 1958).

BATES, Thomas R., 'Antonio Gramsci and the Bolshevization of the PCI', *Journal of Contemporary History* (1976) Vol.XI, Nos2–3, 115–31.

BAXANDALL, Lee, 'Georg Lukács and the Dangling Man', *Philosophical Forum* (1972) Vol. III, Nos3–4, 498–510.

BEBEL, August, *Woman under Socialism* [*Die Frau und der Socialismus*] (New York: Schocken, 1971).

BEER, Max, *Fifty Years of International Socialism* (London: George Allen & Unwin, 1935).

BEKERMAN, Gerard, *Marx and Engels. A Conceptual Concordance* (Oxford: Basil Blackwell, 1981).

BELL, Daniel, 'The Debate on Alienation', in Leopold Labedz (Ed.), *Revisionism. Essays on the History of Marxist Ideas* (London: George Allen & Unwin, 1962).

BELL, Daniel, *Marxian Socialism in the United States* (Princeton, NJ: Princeton University Press, 1967).

BENDIX, Reinhard & Seymour Martin LIPSET, *Class, Status, and Power: Social Stratification in Comparative Perspective* (London: Routledge & Kegan Paul, 1967, 2nd Edition).

BERGER, Peter & Stanley PULLBERG, 'Reification and the Sociological Critique of Consciousness', *History and Theory* (1965) Vol.IV, No.2, 196–211.

BERKI, R.N., 'Evolution of a Marxist Thinker', *Problems of Communism* (1972) Vol.XXI, No.6, 52–61.

BERLIN, Isaiah, *Karl Marx*, 4th Edition (Oxford: Oxford University Press, 1978).

BERNSTEIN, Eduard, *Evolutionary Socialism: A Criticism and Affirmation* [*Die Voraussetzungen des Sozialismus und die Aufgaben der Sozialdemokratie*] (New York: Schocken, 1961).

BERNSTEIN, Richard J., *Praxis and Action* (London: Duckworth, 1972).
BILLINGTON, James H., *Mikhailovsky and Russian Populism* (Oxford: Oxford University Press, 1958).
BINNS, Peter, 'The Marxist Theory of Truth', *Radical Philosophy* (1973) No.4, 3–9.
BINNS, Peter, 'The Triviality of Althusser', *Radical Philosophy* (1974) No.7, 30–3.
BLACKBURN, Robin (Ed.), *Ideology in Social Science. Readings in Critical Social Theory* (London: Fontana, 1972).
BLACKBURN, Robin, 'Marxism: Theory of Proletarian Revolution', *New Left Review* (1976) No.97, 3–35.
BLACKBURN, Robin, & Alexander COCKBURN (Eds) *The Incompatibles: Trade Union Militancy and the Consensus* (Harmondsworth: Penguin, 1967).
BLAUNER, Robert, *Alienation and Freedom: The Factory Worker and his Industry* (Chicago and London: University of Chicago Press, 1964).
BLOCH, Ernst, Georg LUKÁCS, Bertholt BRECHT, Walter BENJAMIN & Theodor ADORNO, *Aesthetics and Politics* (London: Verso, 1980).
BLOOMFIELD, John (Ed.), *Class, Hegemony and Party* (London: Lawrence & Wishart, 1977).
BOBER, M.M., *Karl Marx's Interpretation of History*, 2nd Edition (Cambridge Mass.: Harvard University Press, 1962).
BOHM-BAWERK, Eugen von, *Karl Marx and the Close of his System* (Paul M. Sweezy, Ed.), (London: Merlin, 1975).
BOTTOMORE, Tom, *Marxist Sociology* (London: Macmillan, 1975).
BOTTOMORE, Tom, *Sociology as Social Criticism* (London: George Allen & Unwin, 1975).
BOTTOMORE, Tom, *Political Sociology* (London: Hutchinson, 1979).
BOTTOMORE, Tom (Ed.), *A Dictionary of Marxist Thought* (Oxford: Basil Blackwell, 1983)
BOTTOMORE, Tom, & Patrick GOODE (Eds), *Austro-Marxism* (Oxford: Clarendon Press, 1978).
BOTTOMORE, Tom, & Patrick GOODE, *Readings in Marxist Sociology* (Oxford: Clarendon Press, 1983).
BOTTOMORE, Tom, & Robert NISBET (Eds), *A History of Sociological Analysis* (London: Heinemann, 1979).
BOUDIN, Louis B., *The Theoretical System of Karl Marx: In the Light of Recent Criticism* (Chicago: Charles H. Kerr, 1920).
BRACHER, Karl Dietrich, *The Age of Ideologies: A History of Political Thought in the Twentieth Century* (London: Weidenfeld & Nicolson, 1984).
BRAUNTHAL, Julius, *In Search of the Millenium* (London: Victor Gollancz, 1945).
BRAUNTHAL, Julius, *History of the International 1864–1914* (London: Thomas Nelson, 1966).

BRAVERMAN, Harry, *Labor and Monopoly Capital: The Degradation of Work in the Twentieth Century* (New York: Monthly Review Press, 1974).

BRAYBROOKE, David, 'Diagnosis and Remedy in Marx's Doctrine of Alienation', *Social Research* (1958) Vol.XXV, No.4, 325–45.

BREINES, Paul, 'Review of Parkinson & Lichtheim', *Telos* (1970) No.6, 318–24.

BREINES, Paul (Ed.) *Critical Interruptions: New Left Perspectives on Herbert Marcuse* (New York: Herder & Herder, 1972).

BREINES, Paul, 'Lukács, Revolution and Marxism, 1885–1918: Notes on Lukács' "Road to Marx"', *Philosophical Forum* (1972) Vol.III, Nos3–4, 401–21.

BREINES, Paul, 'Praxis and its Theorists; the Impact of Lukács and Korsch in the 1920's', *Telos* (1972) No.11, 67–103.

BREINES, Paul, 'Marxism, Romanticism, and the Case of Georg Lukács', *Studies in Romanticism* (1977) Vol.XVI, No.4, 473–89.

BREINES, Paul, 'Young Lukács, Old Lukács, New Lukács', *Journal of Modern History* (1979) Vol.LI, 533–46.

BREINES, Paul, 'The Two Marxisms: Vintage Gouldner', *Theory and Society* (1981) No.10, 249–64.

BREWSTER, Ben, 'A Very Bad Biography of Lukács', *New Left Review* (1965) No.33, 94–6.

BRIEFS, Goetz A., *The Proletariat: A Challenge to Western Civilization* (New York: Arno, 1975).

BROWNE, Paul, 'An Unclaimed Legacy: Caudwell's Marxist Dialectics', *Science and Society* (1984) Vol.XLVIII, No.2, 192–210.

BUICK, Adam, 'Leninism versus Proletarian Self-Emancipation', *Radical Philosophy* (1974) No.7, 28–9.

BUKHARIN, Nikolai, *Imperialism and the Accumulation of Capital* (New York: Monthly Review Press, 1972).

BUKHARIN, Nikolai, *The Economic Theory of the Leisure Class* (New York: Monthly Review Press, 1972).

BUKHARIN, Nikolai, *Historical Materialism.* A System of Sociology (Ann Arbor: University of Michigan, 1978).

BUKHARIN, Nikolai *et al.*, *Marxism and Modern Thought* (London: George Routledge, 1935).

BULLIVANT, Keith (Ed.), *Culture and Society in the Weimar Republic* (Manchester: Manchester University Press, 1977).

CAHNMAN, Werner J., *Ferdinand Tönnies: A New Evaluation, Essays and Documents* (Leiden: E.J. Brill, 1973).

CALHOUN, Craig, *The Question of Class Struggle: Social Foundations of Popular Radicalism during the Industrial Revolution* (Oxford: Basil Blackwell, 1982).

CALLINICOS, Alex, *Althusser's Marxism* (London: Pluto, 1976).

CALLINICOS, Alex, *Is There a Future for Marxism?* (London: Macmillan, 1982).

CALLINICOS, Alex, *Marxism and Philosophy* (Oxford: Clarendon Press, 1983).

CALLINICOS, Alex, *The Revolutionary Ideas of Karl Marx* (London: Bookmarks, 1983).

CALLINICOS, Alex, 'Anthony Giddens. A Contemporary Critique', *Theory and Society* (1985) No.14, 135–74.

CALLINICOS, Alex, *Making History: Agency, Structure and Change in Social Theory* (Oxford: Polity, 1989).

CALLINICOS, Alex (Ed.), *Marxist Theory* (Oxford: Oxford University Press, 1989).

CALLINICOS, Alex, 'Exploitation, Justice, and Socialism: A Critique of John Roemer's Game-Theoretical Marxism', mimeo, n.d..

CARCHEDI, G., *Problems in Class Analysis: Production, Knowledge, and the Function of Capital* (London: Routledge & Kegan Paul, 1983).

CARLO, Antonio, 'Lenin on the Party', *Telos* (1970) No.17, 2–40.

CARR, E.H., *What is History?* (Harmondsworth: Penguin, 1964).

CARVER, Terrell, 'Marx, Engels and Dialectics', *Political Studies* (1980) No.28, 353–63.

CARVER, Terrell, 'Marx – and Engels's "Outlines of a Critique of Political Economy"', *History of Political Thought* (1983) Vol.IV, No.2, 357–65.

CARVER, Terrell, 'Marx, Engels and Scholarship', *Political Studies* (1984) Vol.XXXII, 249–56.

CHISOLM, Roger & Marilu McCARTY, *Principles of Economics* (Glenview: Scott, Foresman & Co., 1978).

CHOMSKY, Noam, *American Power and the New Mandarins* (Harmondsworth: Penguin, 1969).

CLAUDIN, Fernando, *The Communist Movement: From Comintern to Cominform* (Harmondsworth: Penguin, 1975).

CLIFF, Tony, *Rosa Luxemburg* (London: Socialist Review Publishers, 1968).

CLIFF, Tony, *Russia, a Marxist Analysis* (London: International Socialism, 1970).

CLIFF, Tony, *Lenin*, Vol.I: *Building the Party* (London: Pluto, 1976).

CLIFF, Tony, *Lenin*, Vol.4: The Bolsheviks and World Revolution (London: Pluto, 1979).

COATES, David, *The Labour Party and the Struggle for Socialism* (Cambridge: Cambridge University Press, 1975).

COCKBURN, Alexander, & Robin BLACKBURN (Eds.), *Student Power: Problems, Diagnosis, Action* (Harmondsworth: Penguin, 1969).

COHEN, Gerald A., 'Bourgeois and Proletarians', *Journal of the History of Ideas* (1968) Vol.XXIX, No.2, 211–30.

COHEN, G.A., 'The Workers and the Word: Why Marx had the Right to Think he was Right', *Praxis* (1968) Vol.IV, Nos3–4, 376–90.

COHEN, G.A., 'Karl Marx and the Withering Away of Social Science', *Philosophy and Public Affairs* (1972) Vol.I, No.2, 182–203.

COHEN, G.A., 'Marx's Dialectic of Labour', *Philosophy and Public Affairs* (1974) Vol.III, No.3, 235–61.

COHEN, G.A., *Karl Marx's Theory of History: A Defence* (Oxford: Oxford University Press, 1978).

COHEN, G.A., 'The Structure of Proletarian Unfreedom', *Philosophy and Public Affairs* (1983) Vol.XII, No.1, 70–83.

COHEN, Jean L., *Class and Civil Society: The Limits of Marxian Critical Theory* (Oxford: Martin Robertson, 1983).

COHEN, Jean Louise, 'System and Class: the Subversion of Emancipation', *Social Research* (1978) Vol.XLV, No.4, 789–843.

COHEN, Marshall, Thomas NAGEL & Thomas SCANLON (Eds), *Marx, Justice, and History:A Philosophy and Public Affairs Reader* (Princeton: Princeton University Press, 1980).

COHEN, Stephen F., 'Bolshevism and Stalinism', in Ernest A. Munze (Ed.), *Totalitarianism Reconsidered* (New York: Port Washington, 1981).

COLE, G.D.H., *The Second International 1889–1914*, Part One (London: Macmillan, 1963).

COLLETTI, Lucio, 'The Question of Stalin', *New Left Review* (1970), No.61, 61–81.

COLLETTI, Lucio, 'Antonio Gramsci and the Italian Revolution', *New Left Review* (1971) No.65, 87–99.

COLLETTI, Lucio, *From Rousseau to Lenin: Studies in Ideology and Society* (London: New Left Books, 1972).

COLLETTI, Lucio, *Marxism and Hegel* (London: New Left Books, 1973).

COLLIER, Andrew, 'Truth and Practice', *Radical Philosophy* (1973) No.5, 9–16.

CONGDON, Lee, 'The Making of a Hungarian Revolutionary: the Unpublished Diary of Bela Balazs', *Journal of Contemporary History* (1973) Vol.VIII, No.3, 57–74.

CONGDON, Lee, 'The Unexpected Revolutionary: Lukács's Road to Marx', *Survey* (1974) Vol.XX, Nos2–3, 176–205.

CONGDON, Lee, *The Young Lukács* (Chapel Hill N.C.: University of North Carolina Press, 1983).

COOLE, W.W. & M.F. POTTER (Eds), *Thus Spake Germany* (London: George Routledge, 1942).

COTTRELL, Allin, *Social Classes in Marxist Theory* (London: Routledge & Kegan Paul, 1984).

COULTER, Jeff, 'Marxism and the Engels Paraodox', *Socialist Register 1971* (London: Merlin, 1971).

CROSLAND, C.A.R., *The Future of Socialism* (London: Jonathan Cape, 1956).

CURRAN, James (Ed.), *The Future of the Left* (Cambridge: Polity Press, 1984).

CUTLER, Antony, Barry HINDESS, Paul HIRST & Athar HUSSAIN, *Marx's Capital and Capitalism Today*, Vol.1 (London: Routledge & Kegan Paul, 1977).

DAGHIRI, Giairo, 'Lukács' Theory of the Offensive', *Telos* (1971) No.10, 147–54.

DAHL, R.A., 'A Critique of the Ruling Elite Model', *The American Political Science Review* (1958) Vol.LII, 463–9.

DAHRENDORF, Ralf, *Class and Class Conflict in Industrial Society* (London: Routledge & Kegan Paul, 1959).

DALLMAYR, Fred R., 'History and Class Consciousness: Georg Lukács' Theory of Social Change', *Politics and Society* (1970) No.1, 113–31.

DAVIS, Mike, 'Why the Working Class is Different', *New Left Review* (1980) No.123, 3–44.

DAVIS, Mike, *Prisoners of the American Dream* (London: Verso, 1986).

DEBENJAK, Bozidar, 'Engels and the Problem of Alienation', *Social Praxis* (1975) Vol.III, 45–62.

DELLA VOLPE, Galvano, 'The Marxist Critique of Rousseau', *New Left Review* (1970) No.59, 97–109.

DEUTSCHER, Isaac, 'Georg Lukács and "critical realism"', in his *Marxism in our Time* (Tamara Deutscher, Ed.), (London: Jonathan Cape, 1972).

DOBB, Maurice, *Studies in the Development of Capitalism* (London: Routledge & Kegan Paul, 1963).

DOMBROSKI, Robert S., 'Timpanaro's Materialism: An Introduction', *Journal of the History of Ideas* (1983) Vol.XLIV, No.2, 311–26.

DRAPER, Hal, 'The "Inevitability of Socialism"', *International Socialism* (1963) No.15, 21–8.

DRAPER, Hal, 'Marx and Engels on Women's Liberation', *International Socialism* (1970) No.44, 20–9.

DRAPER, Hal, 'The Principle of Self-Emancipation in Marx and Engels', *Socialist Register 1971* (London: Merlin, 1971).

DRAPER, Hal, *Karl Marx's Theory of Revolution*, Vol.1: *State and Bureaucracy* (New York: Monthly Review Press, 1977).

DRAPER, Hal, *Karl Marx's Theory of Revolution*, Vol.2: *The Politics of Social Classes* (New York: Monthly Review Press, 1978).

DUNAYEVSKAYA, Raya, *Marxism and Freedom From 1776 until Today* (London: Pluto, 1971).

DUNAYEVSKAYA, Raya, *Rosa Luxemburg, Women's Liberation, and Marx's Philosophy of Revolution* (Brighton: Harvester, 1981).

DUNCAN, Graeme & Steven LUKES, 'The New Democracy', *Political Studies* (1963) Vol.XI, No.2, 156–77.

DURKHEIM, Emile, *The Division of Labour in Society* (New York: The Free Press, 1964).

EAGLETON, Terry, *The Western Marxists* (London: Workers' Socialist League, n.d.).

ECCLESHALL, Robert, Vincent GEOGHEGAN, Richard JAY & Rick WILFORD, *Political Ideologies: An Introduction* (London: Hutchinson, 1984).

EGYED, Bela, 'Marxism, Science and Ideology', *Social Praxis* (1980) Vol.VII, 91–127.

ELLIOTT, Charles F., 'Quis Custodiet Sacra? Problems of Marxist Revisionism', *Journal of the History of Ideas* (1967) Vol.XXVII, No.1, 71–86.

ELSTER, Jon, *Making Sense of Marx* (Cambridge: Cambridge University Press, 1985).

ENGELS, Frederick, *Dialectics of Nature* (Moscow: Progress Publishers, 1954).

ENGELS, Frederick, *Anti-Dühring: Herr Eugen Duhring's Revolution in Science* (London: Lawrence & Wishart, 1975).

ENGELS, Frederick, 'Socialism in Germany 1891–1892', in William Otto Henderson, *The Life of Friedrich Engels* Vol.2, (London: Cass, 1976).

ENSOR, R.C.K., *Modern Socialism as Set Forth by Socialists in their Speeches, Writings and Programmes* (London & New York: Harper and Brothers, 1907).

EORSI, Istvan, 'Georg Lukács and Gelebtes Denken: The right to the last word', *New German Critique* (1981) No.23, 115–29.

FEDERICI, Silvia, 'Notes on Lukács' Aesthetics', *Telos* (1972), No.11, 141–51.

FEENBURG, Andrew, 'Reification and the Antinomies of Socialist Thought', *Telos* (1971) No.10, 93–118.

FEENBURG, Andrew, 'Lukács and the Critique of "Orthodox" Marxism', *The Philosophical Forum* (1972) Vol.III, Nos3–4, 422–67.

FEENBURG, Andrew, 'Culture and Practice in the Early Marxist Works of Lukács', *Berkeley Journal of Sociology* (1981) No.26, 27–40.

FEENBURG, Andrew, *Lukács, Marx and the Sources of Critical Theory* (Oxford: Martin Robertson, 1981).

FEHER, Ferenc, 'Arato-Breines & Lowy on Lukács: Review Essay', *New German Critique* (1981) No.23, 131–9.

FEHER, Ferenc, 'Grandeur and Decline of a Holistic Philosophy: a Discussion of Martin Jay's *Marxism and Totality*. The Adventures of a Concept from Lukács to Habermas', *Theory and Society* (1973) Vol.XIV, No.6, 863–76.

FEHER, Ferenc, 'Is the Novel Problematic? A Contribution to the Theory of the Novel', *Telos* (1973) No.15, 41–74.

FEHER, Ferenc, 'The Last Phase of Romantic Anti-Capitalism: Lukács' Response to the War', *New German Critique* (1977) No.10, 139–54.

FEHER, Ferenc, 'Lukács and Benjamin: Parallels and Contrasts', *New German Critique* (1985) No.34, 125–38.

FEHER, Feher, 'Lukács in Weimar', *Telos* (1979) No.39, 113–36.

FERNBACH, David, 'Avineri's View of Marx', *New Left Review* (1969) No.56, 62–8.

FERRI, Enrico, *Socialism and Positive Science: Darwin-Spencer-Marx* (London: ILP, 1905).

FETSCHER, Iring, *Marx and Marxism* (New York: Herder & Herder, 1971).

FEUER, Lewis, 'What is Alienation? The Career of a Concept', *New Politics* (1962), Vol.II, 116–34.

FEUERBACH, Ludwig, *The Essence of Christianity* (New York: Harper & Row, 1957).

FEUERBACH, Ludwig, *Principles of the Philosophy of the Future* (*Grundsätze der Philosophie der Zukunft*) (Indianapolis: Bobbs-Merrill, 1966).

FISCHER, Conan, 'Class Enemies of Class Brothers? Communist-Nazi Relations in Germany, 1929–33', *European History Quarterly* (1985) Vol.XV, 259–79.

FISCHER, Ernst, 'Georg Lukács and the Theory of Reflection', *The Philosophical Forum* (1972) Vol.III, Nos3–4, 326–39.

FLETCHER, Roger, 'British Radicalism and German Revisionism: The Case of Eduard Bernstein', *The International History Review* (1982) Vol.IV, No.3, 339–70.

FONER, Eric, 'Why is There no Socialism in the United States?', *History Workshop Journal* (1984) No.17, 57–80.

FOOTE, Geoffrey, *The Labour Party's Political Thought: A History* (Beckenham: Croom Helm, 1986).

FOSTER, John, *Class Struggle and the Industrial Revolution: Early Industrial Capitalism in Three English Towns* (London: Methuen, 1977).

FRANKEL, Boris, *Marxian Theories of the State: A Critique of Orthodoxy* (Melbourne: Arena Publications Association, 1978).

FREUND, Julien, 'German Sociology in the Time of Max Weber', in Tom Bottomore and Robert Nisbet (Eds), *A History of Sociological Analysis* (London: Heinemann, 1979).

FRIED, Albert & Ronald Sanders (Eds), *Socialist Thought – a Documentary History* (Edinburgh: Edinburgh University Press, 1964).

FRISBY, David, *The Alienated Mind: The Sociology of Knowledge in Germany 1918–1933* (London: Heinemann, 1983).

FRISBY, David, *Georg Simmel* (Chichester and London: Ellis Harwood and Tavistock, 1984).

FRISBY, David, *Fragments of Modernity: Theories of Modernity in the Work of Simmel, Kraucauer, and Benjamin* (Cambridge: Polity Press, 1985).

FURET, François, *Marx and the French Revolution* (Chicago: The University of Chicago Press, 1988).

GABEL, Joseph, *False Consciousness: An Essay on Reification* (Oxford: Basil Blackwell, 1975).

GALLIE, Duncan, *In Search of the New Working Class Automation and Social Integration within the Capitalist Enterprise* (Cambridge: Cambridge University Press, 1978).

GAY, Peter, *The Dilemma of Democratic Socialism: Eduard Bernstein's Challenge to Marx* (New York: Collier Books, 1962).

GAY, Peter, *Weimar Culture: The Outsider as Insider* (Westport, Conn.: Greenwood Press, 1968).

GEARY, Dick, *Karl Kautsky* (Manchester: Manchester University Press, 1987).

GELLNER, Ernest, *Thought and Change* (London: Weidenfeld & Nicolson, 1964).

GEORGE, Francois, 'Forgetting Lenin', *Telos* (1973) No.18, 53–88.

GERARD, James W., *My Four Years in Germany* (London: Hodder & Stoughton, 1917).

GERAS, Norman, 'Essence and Appearance: Aspects of Fetishism in Marx's Capital', *New Left Review* (1971) No.65, 69–85.

GERAS, Norman, 'Marxism and Proletarian Self-Emancipation', *Radical Philosophy* (1973) No.6, 20–2.

GERAS, Norman, *The Legacy of Rosa Luxemburg* (London: New Left Books, 1976).

GERAS, Norman, 'Lenin, Trotsky and the Party', *International* (1977), Vol.IV, No.2, 3–8.

GERAS, Norman, 'Classical Marxism and Proletarian Representation', *New Left Review* (1981) No.125, 75– 89.

GERAS, Norman, *Marx and Human Nature: Refutation of a Legend* (London: Verso, 1983).

GIDDENS, Anthony, *Central Problems in Social Theory: Action, Structure and Contradiction in Social Analysis* (London: Macmillan, 1979).

GIDDENS, Anthony, 'Classes, Capitalism, and the State: a Discussion of Frank Parkin, "Marxism and Class Theory: A Bourgeois Critique"', *Theory and Society* (1980) No.9, 877–94.

GIDDENS, Anthony, *Classes, Power, and Conflict: Classical and Contemporary Debates* (London: Macmillan, 1982).

GIDDENS, Anthony, *Profiles and Critiques in Social Theory* (London: Macmillan, 1982).

GIDDENS, Anthony, *Social Theory and Modern Sociology* (Cambridge: Polity Press, 1987).

GIDDENS, Anthony & Jonathan H. TURNER (Eds), *Social Theory Today* (Stanford: Stanford University Press, 1987).

GILBERT, Alan, *Marx's Politics: Communists and Citizens* (Oxford: Martin Robertson, 1981).

GINER, Salvador, *Mass Society* (London: Martin Robertson, 1976).

GLUCKSMANN, Miriam, 'Lucien Goldmann: Humanist or Marxist?', *New Left Review* (1969) No.56, 49–68.

GNEUSS, Christian, 'The Precursor: Eduard Bernstein', in Leopold Labedz (Ed.), *Revisionism* (London: George Allen & Unwin, 1962).

GODELIER, Maurice, *Rationality and Irrationality in Economics* (London: New Left Books, 1972).

GOLDMANN, Lucien, 'The Early Writings of Georg Lukács', *Tri-Quarterly* (1967) No.9, 165–81.

GOLDMANN, Lucien, 'Is There a Marxist Sociology?', *International Socialism* (1968) No.34, 13–21.
GOLDMANN, Lucien, *Human Sciences and Philosophy* (London: Jonathan Cape, 1969)
GOLDMANN, Lucien, 'Introduction to the Problems of a Sociology of the Novel', *Telos* (1973) No.18, 122–35.
GOLDMANN, Lucien, *Lukács and Heidegger: Towards a New Philosophy* (London: Routledge & Kegan Paul, 1977).
GOLDSTEIN, Philip, 'Romanticism and Modernity in Lukácsian and Althusserian Marxism', in Norman Fischer, Philip Goldstein, N. Georgopoulos & Louis Paksourasi (Eds), *Continuity and Change in Marxism* (Atlantic Highlands, N.J.: Humanities Press, 1982).
GOLDTHORPE, John H.,David LOCKWOOD, Frank BECHOFER & Jennifer PLATT, *The Affluent Worker: Industrial Attitudes and Behaviour* (Cambridge: Cambridge University Press, 1968).
GOLDTHORPE, John H., *et al*, *The Affluent Worker: Political Attitudes and Behaviour* (Cambridge: Cambridge University Press, 1968).
GOLDTHORPE, John H., *et al*, *The Affluent Worker in the Class Structure* (Cambridge: Cambridge University Press, 1969).
GORMAN, Robert A., *Neo-Marxism: The Meanings of Modern Radicalism* (Westport Conn.: Greenwood Press, 1982).
GORZ, André, *Farewell to the Working Class: An Essay on Post-Industrial Socialism* [*Adieux au Proletariat*]. (London: Pluto Press, 1982).
GOUGH, Ian, 'Marx's Theory of Productive and Unproductive Labour', *New Left Review* (1972) No.76, 47–72.
GOULDNER, Alvin W., 'Comments on History and Class Consciousness', in his *For Sociology: Renewal and Critique in Sociology Today* (Harmondsworth: Allen Lane, 1973).
GOULDNER, Alvin W., *For Sociology: Renewal and Critique in Sociology Today* (Harmondsworth: Allen Lane, 1973).
GOULDNER, Alvin W., 'Stalinism: A Study of Internal Colonialism', *Telos* (1978) No.34, 5–48.
GOULDNER, Alvin W., *The Two Marxisms: Contradictions and Anomalies in the Development of Theory* (London: Macmillan, 1980).
GOULDNER, Alvin W., *Against Fragmentation: The Origins of Marxism and the Sociology of Intellectuals* (New York: Oxford University Press, 1985).
GRAHL, Bert & Paul PICCONE (Eds), *Towards a New Marxism* (St.Louis, Missouri: Telos Press, 1973).
GRAMSCI, Antonio, *Selections from the Prison Notebooks* (London: Lawrence & Wishart, 1971).
GRAMSCI, Antonio, *Selections from Political Writings 1910–1920* (London: Lawrence & Wishart, 1977).
GRAMSCI, Antonio, *Selections from Political Writings, 1921–1926* (London: Lawrence & Wishart, 1978).

GRAMSCI, Antonio, *Soviets in Italy* (Nottingham: The Institute for Workers' Control, n.d.).

GREGORY, Frederick, *Scientific Materialiam in Nineteenth Century Germany* (Dordrecht: D.Reidel Publishing Co., 1977).

GRYTTINGS, Wayne, 'Midwives, Vanguards, and Class Consciousness', in Norman Fischer, Philip Goldstein, N. Georgopoulos & Louis Patsourasi (Eds), *Continuity and Change in Marxism* (Atlantic Highlands, N.J.: Humanities Press, 1982).

GUNN, Richard, 'Is Nature Dialectical?', *Marxism Today* (1977), February, 45–52.

GUSTAFFSON, Bo, 'Friedrich Engels and the Historical Role of Ideologies', *Science and Society* (1966) No.30, 257–74.

GUTTSMAN, W.L., *The German Social Democratic Party, 1875–1933: From Ghetto to Government* (London: Allen & Unwin, 1981).

HABERMAS, Jurgen, *Theory and Practice* [*Theorie und Praxis*] (London: Heinemann, 1974).

HABERMAS, Jurgen, 'The Place of Philosophy in Marxism', *The Insurgent Sociologist* (1975) Vol.V, No.2, 41–8.

HALL, Alex, 'The War of Words: Anti-Socialist Offensives and Counter-Propaganda in Wilhelmine Germany 1890–1914', *Journal of Contemporary History* (1976) Vol.XI, Nos2–3, 11–42.

HALSEY, A.H., *Change in British Society*, 2nd Edition (Oxford: Oxford University Press, 1981).

HAMPSHIRE, Stuart, *Spinoza* (Harmondsworth: Penguin, 1951).

HARMAN, Chris, *How the Revolution was Lost* (London: Socialist Worker, 1969).

HARMAN, Chris, *The Lost Revolution: Germany 1918 to 1923* (London: Bookmarks, 1982).

HARRIS, Nigel, *Beliefs in Society: The Problem of Ideology* (Harmondsworth: Penguin, 1968).

HARRIS, Nigel, 'The Anarchist Argument', *International Socialism* (1973) No.54, 22–4.

HARRIS, Nigel, *Of Bread and Guns: The World Economy in Crisis* (Harmondsworth: Penguin, 1983).

HAUG, W.F., *Critique of Commodity Aesthetics: Appearance, Sexuality and Advertising in Capitalist Society* (Cambridge: Polity Press, 1986).

HAUPT, Georges, *Aspects of International Socialism 1871–1914: Essays by Georges Haupt* (Cambridge: Cambridge University Press, 1986).

HAYEK, Friedrich August, *The Fatal Conceit: The Errors of Socialism* (London: Routledge, 1988).

HEARN, Francis, 'The Dialectical Uses of Ideal Types', *Theory and Society* (1975) Vol.II, 531–61.

HECKMAN, John, 'Hyppolite and the Hegel Revival in France', *Telos* (1973) No.16, 128–45.

HEGEL, G. W. F., *The Philosophy of History* (New York: Power Publications, 1956).

HEGEL, G. W. F., *Hegel's Logic: Part 1 of the Encyclopaedia of the Philosophical Sciences* [1830] (Oxford: Clarendon Press, 1975).

HELLER, Agnes, '"Von der Armut am Geiste". A Dialogue by the Young Lukács', *The Philosophical Forum* (1972) Vol.III, Nos3–4, 360–70.

HELLER, Agnes, 'Group Interest, Collective Consciousness, and the Role of the Intellectual in Lukács and Goldmann', *Social Praxis* (1979) Vol.VI, Nos3–4, 177–91.

HELLER, Agnes & Ferenc FEHER, *The Postmodern Political Condition* (Cambridge: Polity Press, 1988).

HELLER, Erich, *The Disinherited Mind: Essays in Modern German Literature and Thought* (Harmondsworth: Penguin, 1961).

HENDERSON, William Otto, *The Life of Friedrich Engels*, 2 Vols. (London: Frank Cass, 1976).

HERF, Jeffrey, 'Review of Lowy', *Telos* (1978) No.37, 226–35.

HILFERDING, Rudolf, *Finance Capital* [*Das Finanzkapital*] (London: Routledge & Kegan Paul, 1981).

HINDESS, Barry, *Politics and Class Analysis* (Oxford: Basil Blackwell, 1987).

HINTON, James, *Labour and Socialism: A History of the British Labour Movement 1867–1974* (Brighton: Wheatsheaf, 1983).

HITCHENS, Christopher, *Prepared For The Worst: Selected Essays and Minority Reports* (London: Chatto & Windus, 1989).

HOBSBAWM, Eric J., *Labouring Men: Studies in the History of Labour* (London: Weidenfeld & Nicolson, 1968).

HOBSBAWM, Eric J., 'Confronting Defeat: the German Communist Party', *New Left Review* (1970) No.61, 83–92.

HOBSBAWM, Eric J., *The Forward March of Labour Halted*? (London: Verso, 1981).

HOBSBAWM, Eric J., (Ed.), *The History of Marxism*, Vol.1: *Marxism in Marx's Day* (Brighton: Harvester, 1982).

HODGSON, Geoff, 'The Theory of the Falling Rate of Profit', *New Left Review* (1974), No.84, 55–82.

HODGSON, Geoff, *Trotsky and Fatalistic Marxism* (London: Spokesman Books, 1975).

HOFFMAN, John, *Marxism and the Theory of Praxis: A Critique of Some New Versions of Old Fallacies* (London: Lawrence & Wishart, 1975).

HOFFMAN, John, 'The Dialectics of Nature: "The Natural-Historical Foundation of our Outlook"', *Marxism Today* (1977) January, 11–18.

HOOK, Sidney, *Marx and the Marxists: The Ambiguous Legacy* (Princeton: D. Van Nostrand, 1955).

HOOK, Sidney, *From Hegel to Marx: Studies in the Intellectual Development of Karl Marx* (Ann Arbor: University of Michigan, 1962).

HOOK, Sidney, 'The Enlightenment and Marxism', *Journal of the History of Ideas* (1968) Vol.XXIX, 93–108.

HOROWITZ, Irving Louis, *Radicalism and the Revolt against Reason: The Social Theories of Georges Sorel with a Translation of his Essay on the Decomposition of Marxism* (London: Routledge & Kegan Paul, 1961).

HOROWITZ, Irving Louis, & B. Hayes, 'For Marx/Against Engels', *Social Praxis* (1980) Vol.VII, 59–75.

HORTON, John, 'The Dehumanization of Anomie and Alienation: A Problem in the Ideology of Sociology', *British Journal of Sociology* (1964) Vol.XV, No.4, 283–300.

HORTON, John, & Fari Filsoufi, 'Left-Wing Communism: An Infantile Disorder in Theory and Method', *The Insurgent Sociologist* (1977) Vol.VII, No.1, 5–17.

HOWARD, Dick, *The Development of the Marxian Dialectic* (Carbondale & Edwardsville: Southern Illinois University Press, 1972).

HOWARD, Dick, 'Review of Istvan Meszaros, *Aspects of History and Class Consciousness*', *Telos* (1972) No.11, 152–60.

HOWARD, Dick, *The Marxian Legacy* (London: Macmillan, 1977).

HOWARD, Dick, & Karl E. Klare (Eds), *The Unknown Dimension – European Marxism since Lenin* (New York: Basic Books, 1972).

HOWARD, M.C. & J.E. KING, *The Political Economy of Marx*, 2nd Edition (Harlow: Longman, 1985).

HOWE, Irving (Ed.), *A Handbook of Socialist Thought* (London: Victor Gollancz, 1972).

HUBERMAN, Leo, *Man's Worldly Goods: The Story of the Wealth of Nations* (London: Victor Gollancz, 1937).

HUGHES, H. Stuart, *The Obstructed Path: French Social Thought in the Years of Desperation, 1930–1960* (New York: Harper & Row, 1968).

HUGHES, H. Stuart, *Consciousness and Society: The Reorientation of European Social Thought, 1890–1930* (St. Albans: Paladin, 1974).

HUGHES, H. Stuart, *The Sea Change: The Migration of Social Thought, 1930–1965* (New York: Harper & Row, 1975).

HUNT, Alice Riggs, *Facts about Communist Hungary* (London: Workers' Socialist Federation, n.d.).

HUNT, Richard N., *The Political Ideas of Marx and Engels*, Vol.1: *Marxism and Totalitarian Democracy, 1818–1850* (London: Macmillan, 1975).

HUNT, Richard N., *The Political Ideas of Marx and Engels*, Vol.2: *Classical Marxism, 1850–1895* (London: Macmillan, 1984).

HYAMS, Edward, *The Millenium Postponed* (London: Secker & Warburg, 1974).

HYMAN, Richard, *Strikes* (London: Fontana/Collins, 1972).

HYMAN, Richard, 'Andre Gorz and his Disappearing Proletariat', *Socialist Register 1983* (London: Merlin, 1983).

HYPPOLITE, Jean, *Studies on Marx and Hegel* (New York: Basic Books, 1969).

ISRAEL, Joachim, *Alienation. From Marx to Modern Sociology: A Macrosociological Analysis* (Boston: Allyn & Bacon, 1971).

ISRAEL, Joachim, 'Alienation and Reification', *Social Praxis* (1975) Vol.III, Nos 1–2, 27–43.

JACOBY, Russell, 'The Politics of Subjectivity: Notes on Marxism, the Movement, and Bourgeois Society', *Telos* (1971) No.9, 116–26.

JACOBY, Russell, 'Towards a Critique of Automatic Marxism: the Politics of Philosophy from Lukács to the Frankfurt School', *Telos* (1971) No.10, 119–46.

JACOBY, Russell, 'The Politics of the Crisis Theory: Toward the Critique of Automatic Marxism II', *Telos* (1975) No.23, 3–52.

JACOBY, Russell, *Social Amnesia: A Critique of Conformist Psychology from Adler to Laing* (Boston: Beacon Press, 1975).

JACOBY, Russell, 'A Falling Rate of Intelligence', *Telos* (1976) No.27, 141–6.

JACOBY, Russell, 'The Politics of Objectivity: Notes on the U.S. Left', *Telos* (1977) No.34, 74–88.

JACOBY, Russell, 'Political Economy and Class Unconsciousness', *Theory and Society* (1978) Vol.V, 11–18.

JACOBY, Russell, 'What is Conformist Marxism?', *Telos* (1980) No.45, 19–43.

JACOBY, Russell, *Dialectic of Defeat: Contours of Western Marxism* (Cambridge: Cambridge University Press, 1981).

JAKUBOWSKI, Franz, *Ideology and Superstructure in Historical Materialism* (London: Allison & Busby, 1976).

JALEE, Pierre, *How Capitalism Works* (New York: Monthly Review Press, 1977).

JAMESON, Frederic, *Marxism and Form: Twentieth Century Dialectical Theories of Literature* (Princeton, N.J.: Princeton University Press, 1971).

JANOS, Andrew C., *The Politics of Backwardness in Hungary 1825–1945* (Princeton, N.J.: Princeton University Press, 1982).

JANOS, Andrew C., & William B. SLOTTMAN, *Revolution in Perspective: Essays on the Hungarian Soviet Republic of 1919* (Berkeley: University of California Press, 1971).

JASZI, Oscar, *Revolution and Counter-Revolution in Hungary* (London: P. S. King, 1924).

JAY, Martin, 'The Concept of Totality in Lukács and Adorno', in Shlomo Avineri (Ed.), *Varieties of Marxism* (The Hague: Martinus Nijhoff, 1977).

JAY, Martin, *Marxism and Totality: The Adventures of a Concept from Lukács to Habermas* (Cambridge: Polity Press, 1984).

JOHNSON, Carol, 'The Problem of Reformism and Marx's Theory of Fetishism', *New Left Review* (1980) No.119, 70–96.

JOHNSON, Carol, 'Philosophy and Revolution in the Young Marx', *Science and Society* (1983) Vol.XLVII, No.1, 66–83.

JOHNSON, Richard, Gregor McLENNAN, Bill SCHWARTZ & David SUTTON, (Eds), *Making Histories: Studies in History-Writing and Politics* (London: Hutchinson, 1982).

JOLL, James, *The Second International 1889–1914* (London: Weidenfeld & Nicolson, 1955).

KADARKAY, Arpad, 'Georg Lukács's Road to Art and Marxism', *Polity* (1980) Vol.XIII, No.2, 230–60.

KAMENKA, Eugene, *The Philosophy of Ludwig Feuerbach* (London: Routledge & Kegan Paul, 1970).

KAPP, Yvonne, 'Karl Marx's Children: Family Life 1844–1855', in Betty Matthews (Ed.), *Marx: A Hundred Years On* (London: Lawrence & Wishart, 1983).

KARABEL, Jerome, 'The Failure of American Socialism Reconsidered', *Socialist Register 1979* (London: Merlin, 1979).

KATZNELSON, Ira & Aristide R. ZOLBERG, *Working Class Formation: Nineteenth-Century Patterns in Western Europe and the United States* (Princeton N.J.: Princeton University Press, 1986).

KAUFMANN, Walter (Ed.), *The Portable Nietzsche* (New York: Viking Press, 1954).

KAUTSKY, Karl, *Frederick Engels: His Life, his Work and his Writings* (Chicago: Charles H. Kerr, 1899).

KAUTSKY, Karl, *Terrorism and Communism: A Contribution to the Natural History of Revolution* (London: The National Labour Press, 1920).

KAUTSKY, Karl, *The Dictatorship of the Proletariat* (Ann Arbor: University of Michigan Press, 1964).

KAUTSKY, Karl, *The Class Struggle: Erfurt Program* (New York: W.W. Norton, 1971).

KAUTSKY, Karl, 'Ultra-Imperialism', *New Left Review* (1979) No.59, 41–6.

KAY, Geoffrey, *The Economic Theory of the Working Class* (London: Macmillan, 1979).

KEAT, Russell, & John Urry, *Social Theory as Science* (London: Routledge & Kegan Paul, 1975).

KELLNER, Douglas, 'Introduction to Marcuse's "On the Philosophical Foundation of the Concept of Labour"', *Telos* (1973) No.16, 2–8.

KELLNER, Douglas, 'Ideology, Marxism and Advanced Capitalism', *Socialist Review* (1978) Vol.VIII, 6, No.42, 37–65.

KELLNER, Douglas, 'Remarks on Alvin Gouldner's, *The Two Marxisms*', *Theory and Society* (1981) No.10, 265–77.

KELLNER, Douglas, 'Karl Korsch and Marxism', in Norman Fischer, Philip Goldstein, N. Georgopoulos & Louis Patsourasi (Eds), *Continuity and Change in Marxism* (Atlantic Highlands, N.J.: Humanities Press, 1982).

KETTLER, David, 'Culture and Revolution: Lukács in the Hungarian Revolution of 1918', *Telos* (1971) No.10, 35– 92.

KINDERSLEY, Richard, *The First Russian Revisionists: A Study of 'Legal Marxism' in Russia* (Oxford: Oxford University Press, 1962).

KLINE, George L., 'Impressions of the Man and his Ideas', *Problems of Communism* (1972) Vol.XXI, No.6, 62–6.

KNEI-PAZ, Baruch, *The Social and Political Thought of Leon Trotsky* (Oxford: Clarendon Press, 1978).

KOLAKOWSKI, Leszek, 'Intellectuals, Hope and Heresy', *Encounter* (1971) Vol.XXXVI, No.4, 42–8.

KOLAKOWSKI, Leszek, *Marxism and Beyond: On Historical Understanding and Individual Responsibility* (London: Granada, 1971).

KOLAKOWSKI, Leszek, *Positivist Philosophy from Hume to the Vienna Circle* (Harmondsworth: Penguin, 1972).

KOLAKOWSKI, Leszek, *Main Currents of Marxism: Its Origins, Growth, and Dissolution*, Vol.1: *The Founders*; Vol. 2: *The Golden Age*; Vol.3: *The Breakdown* (Oxford: Oxford University Press, 1978).

KOLAKOWSKI, Leszek, 'The Devil in History: A Conversation with George Urban', *Encounter* (1981) Vol.LVI, No.1, 9–26.

KOLAKOWSKI, Leszek, 'Miliband's Anti-Kolakowski', *Political Studies* (1981) Vol.XXIX, No.1, 123–5.

KOLAKOWSKI, Leszek, & Stuart HAMPSHIRE (Eds), *The Socialist Idea: A Reappraisal* (London: Quartet, 1977).

KORNHAUSER, William, *The Politics of Mass Society* (London: Routledge & Kegan Paul, 1960).

KORSCH, Hedda, 'Memories of Karl Korsch', *New Left Review* (1972) No.76, 35–45.

KORSCH, Karl, *Marxism and Philosophy* (New York: Monthly Review Press, 1970).

KORSCH, Karl, *Three Essays on Marxism* (London: Pluto Press, 1971).

KRIEGER, Leonard, *The German Idea of Freedom: History of a Political Tradition (1650–1870)* (Chicago: University of Chicago Press, 1957).

KRUKS, Sonia, 'The Philosophy of Merleau-Ponty', *Radical Philosophy* (1975) No.11, 17–24.

KUHN, Thomas S., *The Structure of Scientific Revolutions*, 2nd Edition (Chicago: University of Chicago Press, 1970).

KUMAR, Krishan, 'Can the Workers be Revolutionary?', *European Journal of Political Research* (1978) No.6, 357–79.

KUPER, Adam & Jessica KUPER (Eds), *The Social Science Encyclopedia* (London: Routledge & Kegan Paul, 1985).

LABEDZ, Leopold (Ed.), *Revisionism: Essays on the History of Marxist Ideas* (London: Allen & Unwin, 1962).

LACLAU, Ernesto & Chantal MOUFFE, *Hegemony and Socialist Strategy: Towards a Radical Democratic Politics* (London: Verso, 1985).

LAKATOS, Imre & Alan MUSGRAVE, *Criticism and the Growth of Knowledge* (Cambridge: Cambridge University Press, 1970).

LARRAIN, Jorge, *Marxism and Ideology* (London: Macmillan, 1983).
LASCH, Christopher, *The Agony of the American Left: One Hundred Years of Radicalism* (Harmondsworth: Penguin, 1973).
LASCH, Christopher, *Haven in a Heartless World: The Family Besieged* (New York: Basic Books, 1977).
LASCH, Christopher, *The Culture of Narcissism:American Life in an Age of Diminishing Expectations* (London: Sphere, 1980).
LASCH, Christopher, *The Minimal Self: Psychic Survival in Troubled Times* (London: Pan, 1985).
LASLETT, Peter & W.G. RUNCIMAN (Eds), *Philosophy, Politics and Society*, 3rd Series (Oxford: Basil Blackwell, 1967).
LASZLO, Ervin, *The Communist Ideology in Hungary: Handbook for Basic Research* (Dordrecht: D. Reidel, 1966).
LEBOVICS, Herman, *Social Conservatism and the Middle Classes in Germany, 1914–1933* (Princeton, N.J.: Princeton University Press, 1969).
LEFEBVRE, Henri, *Dialectical Materialism* (London: Jonathan Cape, 1968).
LEFEBVRE, Henri, *The Sociology of Marx* (Harmondsworth: Penguin, 1972).
LEFEBVRE, Henri, *The Survival of Capitalism: Reproduction of the Relations of Production* (London: Allison & Busby, 1976).
LEFTWICH, Adrian (Ed.), *What is Politics? The Activity and its Study* (Oxford: Basil Blackwell, 1984).
LENIN, V.I., *Collected Works in 45 Volumes* (London: Lawrence & Wishart, 1960–9).
LENIN, V.I., *Selected Works in Three Volumes* (Moscow: Progress Publishers, 1975).
LENIN, V.I., *Materialism and Empirio-Criticism: Critical Comments on a Reactionary Philosophy* (Peking: Foreign Languages Press, 1972).
LEONHARD, Wolfgang, *Child of the Revolution* (London: Ink Links, 1979).
LESER, Norbert, 'Austro-Marxism: A Reappraisal', *Journal of Contemporary History* (1976) Vol.11, Nos2–3, 133–48.
LICHTHEIM, George, 'An Intellectual Disaster', *Encounter* (1963) Vol.XV, No.5, 74–80.
LICHTHEIM, George, *Marxism: An Historical and Critical Study* (London: Routledge & Kegan Paul, 1964).
LICHTHEIM, George, *The Concept of Ideology and Other Essays* (New York: Vintage Books, 1967).
LICHTHEIM, George, *Lukács* (London: Fontana/Collins, 1970).
LICHTHEIM, George, *From Marx to Hegel and Other Essays* (London: Orbach & Chambers, 1971).
LICHTHEIM, George, 'Reply to Professor Shue', *Journal of the History of Ideas* (1973) Vol.XXXIV, No.4, 651–2.
LICHTHEIM, George, *A Short History of Socialism* (London: Fontana/Collins, 1975).

LICHTMAN, Richard, 'Marx's Theory of Ideology', *Socialist Revolution* (1975) No.23, 45–77.

LIEBMAN, Marcel, '1914: The Great Schism', *Socialist Register 1964* (London: Merlin, 1964).

LINDSAY, Jack, *The Crisis in Marxism* (Bradford-on-Avon: Moonraker Press, 1981).

LIPSET, Seymour Martin, 'Whatever Happened to the Proletariat? An Historic Mission Unfulfilled', *Encounter* (1981) Vol.LVI, No.6, 18–34.

LIPSEY, Richard G., *An Introduction to Positive Economics*, 4th Edition (London: Weidenfeld & Nicolson, 1975).

LIVERGOOD, Norman D., *Activity in Marx's Philosophy* (The Hague: Martinus Nijhoff, 1967).

LOBKOWICZ, Nicholas (Ed.), *Marx and the Western World* (Notre Dame, Ind.: University of Notre Dame Press, 1967).

LOBKOWICZ, Nicholas, *Theory and Practice: History of a Concept from Aristotle to Marx* (Notre Dame, Ind.: University of Notre Dame Press, 1967).

LOCKWOOD, David, 'Sources of Variation in Working-Class Images of Society', *Sociological Review* (1966) Vol.14, No.2, 249–67.

LOVELL, David W., *Marx's Proletariat: The Making of a Myth* (London: Routledge, 1988).

LOWITH, Karl, *From Hegel to Nietzsche: The Revolution in Nineteenth Century Thought* (London: Constable, 1965).

LOWITH, Karl, *Max Weber and Karl Marx* (London: George Allen & Unwin, 1982).

LOWY, Michael, *Georg Lukács – From Romanticism to Bolshevism* (London: New Left Books, 1979).

LOWY, Michael, 'Marcuse and Benjamin: The Romantic Dimension', *Telos* (1980) No.44, 25–33.

LOWY, Michael, 'Marxism and Revolutionary Romanticism', *Telos* (1981) No.49, 83–95.

LOWY, Michael, *The Politics of Combined and Uneven Development: The Theory of Permanent Revolution* (London: Verso, 1981).

LOWY, Michael & SAYRE, 'Figures of Romantic Anti-Capitalism', *New German Critique* (1984) No.32, 42–92.

LOWY, Michael, 'The Romantic and the Marxist Utopia', unpublished mimeo, 1985.

LOWY, Michael & Ernst BLOCH, 'Interview with Ernst Bloch', *New German Critique* (1976) No.9, 35–45.

LOZOVSKY, A., *Marx and the Trade Unions* (London: Martin Lawrence, 1935).

LUBASZ, Heinz, 'Marx's Conception of the Revolutionary Proletariat', *Praxis* (1969) Vol.V, Nos1–2, 280–90.

LUBASZ, Heinz, 'Marx's Initial Problematic: The Problem of Poverty', unpublished mimeo, n.d.

LUCKMANN, Thomas (Ed.), *Phenomenology and Sociology* (Harmondsworth: Penguin, 1978).
LUDZ, Peter C., 'Hauser and Lukács', *Telos* (1979) No.41, 175–84.
LUKÁCS, Georg, *The Meaning of Contemporary Realism* (London: Merlin, 1963).
LUKÁCS, Georg, *Essays on Thomas Mann* (London: Merlin, 1964).
LUKÁCS, Georg, *Goethe and his Age* (London: Merlin, 1968).
LUKÁCS, Georg, 'The Twin Crises (Interview), *New Left Review* (1970) No.60, 36–47.
LUKÁCS, Georg, 'A Conversation with Lukács', *Encounter* (1971) Vol.XXXVII, No.4, 30–6.
LUKÁCS, George, 'The Development of the Budapest School', *Times Literary Supplement* (11 June 1971), No.3615, p.3.
LUKÁCS, Georg, 'Lukács on his Life and Work' (interview), *New Left Review* (1971) No.68, 49–58.
LUKÁCS, Georg, *History and Class Consciousness: Studies in Marxist Dialectics* (London: Merlin, 1971).
LUKÁCS, Georg, 'Max Weber and German Sociology', *Economy and Society* (1972) Vol.I, 386–98.
LUKÁCS, Georg, 'On the Phenomenology of the Creative Process', *The Philosophical Forum* (1972) Vol.III, Nos3–4, 314–25.
LUKÁCS, Georg, 'On Poverty and Spirit. A Conversation and a Letter', *The Philosophical Forum* (1972) Vol.III, Nos3–4, 371–85.
LUKÁCS, Georg, *Tactics and Ethics: Political Writings, 1919–1929* (London: New Left Books, 1972).
LUKÁCS, Georg, *Marxism and Human Liberation*, ed. E. San JUAN Jr. (New York: Delta, 1973).
LUKÁCS, Georg, 'The Old Culture and the New Culture', in Bert Grahl & Paul Piccone (Eds), *Towards a New Marxism* (St.Louis, Missouri: Telos Press, 1973).
LUKÁCS, Georg, *Soul and Form* (London: Merlin, 1974).
LUKÁCS, Georg, *The Young Hegel: Studies in the Relations between Dialectics and Economics* (London: Merlin, 1975).
LUKÁCS, Georg, Ernst BLOCH, Bertholt BRECHT, Walter BENJAMIN & Theodor ADORNO, *Aesthetics and Politics* (London: New Left Books, 1977).
LUKÁCS, Georg, 'Bolshevism as a Moral Problem', *Social Research* (1977) Vol.XLIV, No.3, 416–24.
LUKÁCS, Georg, *Lenin: A Study in the Unity of his Thought* (London: New Left Books, 1977).
LUKÁCS, Georg, *Hegel's False and his Genuine Ontology* (London: Merlin, 1978).
LUKÁCS, Georg, *Labour* (London: Merlin, 1978).
LUKÁCS, Georg, *Marx's Basic Ontological Principles* (London: Merlin, 1978).

LUKÁCS, Georg, *The Theory of the Novel: A Historico-Philosophical Essay on the Forms of Great Epic Literature* (London: Merlin, 1978).
LUKÁCS, Georg, *Writer and Critic and Other Essays* (London: Merlin, 1978).
LUKÁCS, Georg, *The Destruction of Reason* (London: Merlin, 1980).
LUKÁCS, Georg, *Essays on Realism* (London: Lawrence & Wishart, 1980).
LUKÁCS, Georg, *Georg Lukács Record of a Life: An Autobiographical Sketch*, ed. Istvan Eorsi (London: Verso, 1983).
LUKÁCS, Georg, *Reviews and Articles from* Die rote Fahne (London: Merlin, 1983).
LUKES, Steven, 'Alienation and Anomie', in Peter LASLETT & W.G. RUNCIMAN (Eds), *Philosophy, Politics and Society*, 3rd Series (Oxford: Basil Blackwell, 1967).
LUXEMBURG, Rosa, *The Accumulation of Capital* (London: Routledge & Kegan Paul, 1951).
LUXEMBURG, Rosa, *The Accumulation of Capital – An Anti-Critique* (New York: Monthly Review Press, 1972).
LYND, Staughton, *Intellectual Origins of American Radicalism* (London: Wildwood House, 1973).
McBRIDE, William Leon, *The Philosophy of Marx* (London: Hutchinson, 1977).
MACCIO, Marco, 'One the Late Lukács', *Telos* (1972) No.11,135–51.
McCARNEY, Joe, *The Real World of Ideology* (Brighton: Harvester, 1980).
McCARNEY, Joseph, *Social Theory and the Crisis of Marxism* (London: Verso, 1990).
McCARTHY, Timothy, *Marx and the Proletariat: A Study in Social Theory* (Westport Conn.: Greenwood Press, 1978).
McCOY, Charles A., & John PLAYFORD (Eds), *Apolitical Politics: A Critique of Behaviouralism* (New York: Thomas Y. Crowell, 1967).
McINNES, Neil, *The Western Marxists* (London: Alcove Press, 1972).
MacINTYRE, Alasdair, 'Prediction and Politics', *International Socialism* (1963) No.13, 15–19.
MacINTYRE, Alasdair, 'Marxist Mask and Romantic Face. Lukács on Thomas Mann', *Encounter* (1965) Vol.XXIV, No.4, 64–72.
McLELLAN, David, 'Marx's view of the Unalienated Society', *The Review of Politics* (1969) Vol.XXXI, No.4, 459–65.
McLELLAN, David, *Karl Marx: His Life and Thought* (St.Albans: Granada, 1976).
McLELLAN, David (Ed.), *Karl Marx: Selected Writings* (Oxford: Oxford University Press, 1977).
McLELLAN, David, *Marxism After Marx: An Introduction*, 2nd Edition (London: Macmillan, 1979).
McLELLAN, David, *Marx before Marxism* (London: Macmillan, 1980).
McLELLAN, David, *The Young Hegelians and Karl Marx* (London: Macmillan, 1980).

McLELLAN, David (Ed.), *Karl Marx: Interviews and Recollections* (London: Macmillan, 1981).

McLELLAN, David, 'The Materialist Conception of History', in Eric J. Hobsbawm (Ed.), *The History of Marxism*, Vol.1: *Marxism in Marx's Day* (Brighton: Harvester, 1982).

McLELLAN, David, *Karl Marx: The Legacy* (London: BBC, 1983).

McLELLAN, David, *Marx: The First Hundred Years* (London: Fontana, 1983).

McLELLAN, David, 'Theoretical Roots of Liberal, Democratic National Communism', in Howard Machin (Ed.), *National Communism in Western Europe: A 3rd Way for Socialism* (London: Methuen, 1983).

McLELLAN, David, *Ideology* (Milton Keynes: Open University Press, 1986).

MacPHERSON, Crawford B., 'Market concepts in Political Theory', *Canadian Journal of Economics and Political Science* (1961) Vol.XXVII, 490–7.

MacPHERSON, Crawford B., *The Political Theory of Possessive Individualism: Hobbes to Locke* (Oxford: Oxford University Press, 1962).

MacPHERSON, Crawford B., 'The Maximization of Democracy' in Peter Laslett & W. G. Runciman, *Philosophy, Politics and Society*, 3rd series (Oxford: Blackwell, 1967).

MacPHERSON, Crawford B., 'The False Roots of Western Democracy', in Fred R. Dallmayr (Ed.), *From Contract to Community: Political Theory at the Crossroads* (New York: Marcel Dekker, 1978).

McQUARIE, Donald (ed.), *Marx: Sociology / Social Change / Capitalism* (London: Quartet, 1978).

MAGRI, Lucio, 'Problems of the Marxist Theory of the Revolutionary Party', *New Left Review (*1970), No.60, 97–128.

MAHAIRA-ODONI, Eleni, 'Review of Laura Boella, *Il Giovane Lukács* La Formazione Intellectuate e la Filosofia Politica, 1907–1929', *Telos* (1979) No.41, 214–41.

MANDEL, Ernest, *Marxist Economic Theory* (London: Merlin, 1968).

MANDEL, Ernest, *An Introduction to Marxist Economic Theory* (New York: Pathfinder, 1970).

MANDEL, Ernest, *The Leninist Theory of Organization* (London: IMG, 1971).

MANDEL, Ernest, *The Formation of the Economic Thought of Karl Marx: 1843 to Capital* (London: New Left Books, 1977).

MANN, Golo, *The History of Germany since 1789* (Harmondsworth: Penguin, 1974).

MANN, Michael, 'The Social Cohesion of Liberal Democracy', *American Sociological Review* (1970) Vol.XXXV, 423–39.

MANN, Michael, *Consciousness and Action among the Western Working Class* (London: Macmillan, 1973).

MANN, Thomas, *Reflections of a Non-Political Man* (Lorrimar, 1986).

MANSER, A.R., *The End of Philosophy: Marx and Wittgenstein* (Southampton: Camelot Press, 1973).

MARCUSE, Herbert, 'The Obsolescence of Marxism', in N. Lobkowicz (Ed.), *Marx and the Western World* (Notre Dame, Ind.: Notre Dame University Press, 1967).

MARCUSE, Herbert, *Negations: Essays in Critical Theory* (London: Allen Lane, 1968).

MARCUSE, Herbert, 'Contributions to a Phenomenology of Historical Materialism', *Telos* (1969) No.4, 3–34.

MARCUSE, Herbert, *One Dimensional Man* (London: Sphere, 1972).

MARCUSE, Herbert, 'On the Philosophical Foundation of the Concept of Labor in Economics', *Telos* (1973) No.16.

MARCUSE, Herbert, 'The Relevance of Reality', in Charles J. Bontempo & S. Jack Odell (Eds), *The Owl of Minerva – Philosophers on Philosophy* (New York: McGraw Hill, 1975).

MARCUSE, Herbert, *The Aesthetic Dimension: Towards a Critique of Marxist Aesthetics* (London: Macmillan, 1979).

MAREK, Franz, *Philosophy of World Revolution* (London: Lawrence & Wishart, 1969).

MARKOVICS, Mihailo, 'The concept of revolution', *Praxis* (1969) Vol.V, Nos1–2, 41–54.

MARKOVIC, Mihailo, *The Contemporary Marx: Essays on Humanist Communism* (Nottingham: Spokesman Books, 1974).

MARKS, Harry J., 'The Sources of Reformism in the Social Democratic Party of Germany, 1890–1914', *The Journal of Modern History* (1939) Vol.XI, 334–56.

MARKUS, George, *Marxism and Anthropology: The Concept of 'Human Essence' in the Philosophy of Marx* (Assen: Van Goroum, 1978).

MARKUS, Gyorgy, 'Marxist Humanism', *Science and Society* (1966) Vol.XXX, 275–87.

MARKUS, Gyorgy, 'On Georg Lukács' Unpublished Aesthetics', *The Philosophical Forum* (1972) Vol.III, Nos3–4, 309–13.

MARKUS, Gyorgy, 'The Soul and Life: The Young Lukács and the Problem of Culture', *Telos* (1977) No.32, 95–115.

MARSHALL, Gordon, David ROSE, Howard NEWBY & Carolyn VOGLER, *Social Class in Modern Britain* (London: Unwin Hyman, 1989).

MARX, Karl, *Capital: A Critique of Political Economy*,Vol.1: *The Process of Production of Capital* (London: Lawrence & Wishart, 1954).

MARX, Karl, Capital: A Critique of Political Economy, Vol.II: *The Process of Circulation of Capital* (London: Lawrence & Wishart, 1974).

MARX, Karl, *Capital: A Critique of Political Economy*, Vol.III: *The Process of Capitalist Production as a Whole* (London: Lawrence & Wishart, 1974).

MARX, Karl, *Theories of Surplus Value Part 1, Part 2, Part 3* (3 Vols) (London: Lawrence & Wishart, 1969, 1969, 1972).

MARX, Karl, *On America and the Civil War*, ed. Saul K. Padover (New York: McGraw-Hill, 1972).

MARX, Karl, *Grundrisse: Foundations of the Critique of Political Economy* (rough draft) (Harmondsworth: Penguin, 1973).

MARX, Karl, *The Revolutions of 1848: Political Writings* Vol.1 (Harmondsworth: Penguin, 1973).

MARX, Karl, *Surveys From Exile: Political Writings* Vol.2 (Harmondsworth: Penguin, 1973).

MARX, Karl, *The First International and After: Political Writings* Vol.3 (Harmondsworth: Penguin, 1974).

MARX, Karl, *Early Writings* (Harmondsworth: Penguin, 1975).

MARX, Karl, *Selected Writings*, ed. David McLellan (Oxford: Oxford University Press, 1977).

MARX, Karl, 'An Interview with Karl Marx from 1879', *Intercontinental Press* (1980) 21 April 1980, Vol.XVIII, 15.

MARX, Karl, and Frederick ENGELS, *Selected Correspondence* (Moscow: Progress Publishers, 1965).

MARX, Karl, and Frederick ENGELS, *Selected Works in One Volume* (London: Lawrence & Wishart, 1968).

MARX, Karl and Frederick ENGELS, *Collected Works* (London: Lawrence & Wishart, 1975–)

MATTICK, Paul, *Anti-Bolshevik Communism* (London: Merlin, 1978).

MATTICK, Paul, *Economics, Politics, and the Age of Inflation* (London: Merlin, 1978).

MATTICK, Paul, *Economic Crisis and Crisis Theory* (London: Merlin, 1981).

MEHRING, Franz, *Karl Marx: The Story of His Life* (London: George Allen & Unwin, 1936).

MEIKLE, Scott, *Essentialism in the Thought of Karl Marx* (London: Duckworth, 1985).

MELLOS, Koula, 'The Concept of Ideology in Marx', *Social Praxis* (1980) Vol.VII, 5–19.

MEPHAM, John, 'The Theory of Ideology in Capital', *Radical Philosophy* (1972) No.2, 12–19.

MEPHAM, John, 'Who Makes History? Althusser's Anti-Humanism', *Radical Philosophy* (1973) No.6, 23–30.

MERLEAU-PONTY, Maurice, *In Praise of Philosophy* (Evanston, Ill.: Northwestern University Press, 1963).

MERLEAU-PONTY, Maurice, *Sense and Non-Sense* (Evanston, Ill.: Northwestern University Press, 1964).

MERLEAU-PONTY, Maurice, *Signs* (Evanston, Ill.: Northwestern University Press, 1964).

MERLEAU-PONTY, Maurice, *Humanism and Terror: An Essay on the Communist Problem* (Boston: Beacon Press, 1969).

MERLEAU-PONTY, Maurice, *Adventures of the Dialectic* (Evanston, Ill.: Northwestern University Press, 1973).

MERQUIOR, J.G., *Western Marxism* (London: Paladin, 1986).

MESZAROS, Istvan, *Aspects of History and Class Consciousness* (London: Routledge & Kegan Paul, 1971).

MESZAROS, Istvan, 'Ideology and Social Science', *Socialist Register 1972* (London: Merlin, 1972).

MESZAROS, Istvan, *Lukács' Concept of Dialectic* (London: Merlin, 1972).

MESZAROS, Istvan, *Marx's Theory of Alienation* (London: Merlin, 1972).

MESZAROS, Istvan, 'Jean-Paul Sartre: a Critical Tribute', *Socialist Register 1975* (London: Merlin, 1975).

MESZAROS, Istvan, 'Marx "Philosopher"', in Eric J. Hobsbawm (Ed.), *The History of Marxism*, Vol.1: *Marxism in Marx's Day* (Brighton: Harvester, 1982).

MESZAROS, Istvan, 'Marx's "Social Revolution" and the Division of Labour', *Radical Philosophy* (1986) No.44, 14–23.

MEWES, Horst, 'On the Concept of Politics in the Early Works of Karl Marx', *Social Research* (1976) Vol.XLIII, No.2, 276–94.

MEYER, Alfred G., *Marxism: The Unity of Theory and Practice* (Ann Arbor: University of Michigan Press, 1963).

MEYER, Henry Cord (Ed.), *The Long Generation: Germany from Empire to Ruin, 1913–1945* (New York: Harper & Row, 1973).

MEYERHOFF, Hans (Ed.), *The Philosophy of History in our Time: An Anthology* (New York: Doubleday/Anchor, 1959).

MICHELS, Robert, *Political Parties:: A Sociological Study of the Oligarchical Tendencies of Modern Democracy* (London: Collier Macmillan, 1968).

MILIBAND, Ralph, *Parliamentary Socialism: A Study in the Politics of Labour* (London: Merlin, 1972).

MILIBAND, Ralph, *Marxism and Politics* (Oxford: Clarendon Press, 1977).

MILIBAND, Ralph, 'Kolakowski's Anti-Marx', *Political Studies* (1981) Vol.XXIX, No.1, 115–25.

MILIBAND, Ralph, *Capitalist Democracy in Britain* (Oxford: Oxford University Press, 1982).

MILIBAND, Ralph, 'Class Analysis', in Anthony Giddens & Jonathan H. Turner (Eds), *Social Theory Today* (Stanford: Stanford University Press, 1987).

MILLER, James, 'Marxism and Subjectivity. Remarks on Georg Lukács and Existential Phenomenology', *Telos* (1970) No.6, 175–83.

MILLER, James, *History and Human Existence from Marx to Merleau-Ponty* (Berkeley: University of California Press, 1979).

MILLER, Susan, & Heinrich POTTHOFF, *A History of German Social Democracy from 1848 to the Present* (Leamington Spa: Berg, 1986).

MILLS, C. Wright, *The Marxists* (Harmondsworth: Penguin, 1963).

MITZMAN, Arthur, *The Iron Cage: An Historical Interpretation of Max Weber* (New York: Alfred A. Knopf, 1970).

MITZMAN, Arthur, *Sociology and Estrangement: Three Sociologists of Imperial Germany* (New York: Alfred A. Knopf, 1973).

MOLYNEUX, John, *Marxism and the Party* (London: Pluto Press, 1978).

MOLYNEUX, John, *Leon Trotsky's Theory of Revolution* (Brighton: Harvester, 1981).
MOORE, Stanley, 'Utopian Themes in Marx and Mao: A Critique for Modern Revisionists', *Monthly Review* (1969) Vol.XXI, No.2,.33–44.
MORAWSKI, Stefan, 'Mimesis – Lukács' Universal Principle', *Science and Society* (1968) Vol.XXXII, 26–38.
MORGAN, Roger, *The German Social Democrats and the First International, 1864–1872* (Cambridge: Cambridge University Press, 1965).
MOSCA, Gaetano, *The Ruling Class [Elementi di Scienza Politici]* (Westport Conn.: Greenwood Press, 1980).
MOSSE, George L., *The Crisis of German Ideology: Intellectual Origins of the Third Reich* (London: Weidenfeld & Nicolson, 1966).
MYERS, Frank E., 'Social Class and Political Change in Western Industrial Systems', *Comparative Politics* (1970).
NAIR, Sami, 'Goldmann's Legacy', *Telos* (1981) No.48, 142–8.
NAMIER, Lewis, *1848: The Revolution of the Intellectuals* (London: Oxford University Press, 1946).
NELSON, Cary & Lawrence GROSSBERG (Eds), *Marxism and the Interpretation of Culture* (Houndmills: Macmillan, 1988).
NEW LEFT REVIEW (Eds), *Western Marxism: A Critical Reader* (London: New Left Books, 1977).
NICOLAUS, Martin, in Donald McQuarrie (Ed.), *Marx: Sociology, Social Change, Capitalism* (London: Quartet, 1978).
NISBET, Robert A., 'The Decline and Fall of Social Class', *Pacific Sociological Review* (1959) Vol.II, No.1, 11–17.
NOBLE, David F., *America By Design: Science, Technology, and the Rise of Corporate Capitalism* (Oxford: Oxford University Press, 1977).
NOVACK, George, *Humanism and Socialism* (New York: Pathfinder, 1973).
NOVACK, George, *Polemics in Marxist Philosophy* (New York: Monad, 1978).
NOVE, Alec, *Was Stalin Really Necessary? Some Problems of Soviet Political Economy* (London: George Allen & Unwin, 1964).
NOVE, Alec, *The Economics of Feasible Socialism* (London: George Allen & Unwin, 1983).
NOYES, P.H., *Organization and Revolution: Working Class Associations in the German Revolutions of 1848–1849* (Princeton, N.J.: Princeton University Press, 1966).
OAKLEY, Allen, *The Making of Marx's Critical Theory* (London: Routledge & Kegan Paul, 1983).
O'CONNOR, James, 'Capital Accumulation, Economic Crisis and the Mass Worker', *Social Praxis* (1979) Vol.VI, 5–18.
OLLMAN, Bertell, *Alienation: Marx's Conception of Man in Capitalist Society* (London: Cambridge University Press, 1971).

OLLMAN, Bertell, *Social and Sexual Revolution: Essays on Marx and Reich* (London: Pluto, 1979).

OLLMAN, Bertell, *What is Marxism? A Bird's Eye View* (New York: Red Hot Publications, 1982).

OLLMAN, Bertell, 'How to Study Class Consciousness…and Why We Should', unpublished mimeo presented at the International Conference 'Has Socialism a Future?', Glasgow, 1985.

OLSSEN, E.A., 'Marx and the Resurrection', *Journal of the History of Ideas* (1968) Vol.XXIX, No.1, 131–40.

O'NEILL, John, 'The Concept of Estrangement in the Early and Later Writings of Karl Marx', *Philosophy and Phenomenological Research* (1964–5) Vol.XXV, 64–84.

O'NEILL, John, *Sociology as a Skin Trade: Essays towards a Reflexive Sociology* (London: Heinemann, 1972).

O'NEILL, John, *For Marx Against Althusser* (Washington: University Press of America, 1982).

ORTEGA Y GASSET, José, *The Revolt of the Masses* (London: Unwin, 1961).

PAASTELA, Jukka, *Marx's and Engels' Concepts of the Parties and Political Organizations of the Working Class* (Tampere: University of Tampere, 1985).

PANNEKOEK, Anton, 'The Theory of the Collapse of Capitalism', *Capital and Class* (1977) No.1, 62–81.

PAPPENHEIM, Fritz, *The Alienation of Modern Man: An Interpretation Based on Marx and Tönnies* (New York: Monthly Review, 1959).

PAREKH, Bhikhu (Ed.), *The Concept of Socialism* (London: Croom Helm, 1975).

PAREKH, Bhikhu, *Marx's Theory of Ideology* (London: Croom Helm, 1982).

PARENTI, Michael, *Power and the Powerless* (New York: St. Martin's Press, 1978).

PARENTI, Michael, *Democracy for the Few*, 4th Edition (New York: St. Martin's Press, 1983).

PARINETTO, Luciano, 'The Legend of Marx's Atheism', *Telos* (1983–4) No.58, 7–19.

PARKIN, Frank, *Marxism and Class Theory: A Bourgeois Critique* (London: Tavistock, 1979).

PARKIN, Frank, *Max Weber* (Chichester & London: Ellis Harwood & Tavistock, 1982).

PARKINSON, G.H.R. (Ed.), *Georg Lukács, the Man, his Work and his Ideas* (London: Weidenfeld & Nicolson, 1970).

PARKINSON, G.H.R., *Georg Lukács* (London: Routledge & Kegan Paul, 1977).

PARKINSON, G.H.R. (Ed.), *Marx and Marxisms* (Cambridge: Cambridge Uuiversity Press, 1982).

PARRY, Geraint, *Political Elites* (London: George Allen & Unwin, 1969).

PARSONS, Talcot, *The Structure of Social Action*, 2nd Edition. *A Study in Social Theory with Special Reference to a Group of Recent European Writers* (New York: Free Press, 1949).

PARSONS, Talcot, *Politics and Social Structure* (New York: Free Press, 1969).

PASCAL, Roy, *From Naturalism to Expressionism: German Literature and Society, 1880–1918* (London: Weidenfeld & Nicolson, 1973).

PASTOR, Peter, 'The Vix Mission in Hungary, 1918–19', *Slavic Review* (1970) Vol.XXIX, No.3, 481–98.

PATERSON, R.W.K., *The Nihilistic Egoist Max Stirner* (London: Oxford University Press for University of Hull, 1971).

PICCONE, Paul, 'Lukács' History and Class Consciousness Half a Century Later', *Telos* (1969) No.4, 95–112.

PICCONE, Paul, 'Dialectic and Materialism in Lukács', *Telos* (1972) No.11, 105–33.

PICCONE, Paul, 'Reading the Grundrisse: Beyond "Orthodox" Marxism', *Theory and Society* (1975) 2, 235–55.

PINKUS, Theo (Ed.), *Conversations with Lukács* (London: Merlin, 1974).

PIZZORNO, Alessandro (Ed.), *Political Sociology* (Harmondsworth: Penguin, 1971).

PLAMENATZ, John, *Man and Society: A Critical Examination of Some Important Social and Political Theories from Machiavelli to Marx* (London: Longman, 1963).

PLEKHANOV, G.V., *Materialismus Militans: Reply to Mr. Bogdanov* (Moscow: Progress Publisher, 1973).

PLEKHANOV, G.V., *The Materialist Conception of History* (London: Lawrence & Wishart, 1976).

PLEKHANOV, G.V., *The Role of the Individual in History* (London: Lawrence & Wishart, 1976).

PLEKHANOV, G.V., *Selected Philosophical Works*, 5 Vols (Moscow: Progress Publishers, 1977).

PLEKHANOV, G.V., *Fundamental Problems of Marxism* (London: Lawrence & Wishart, n.d.).

PLOTKE, David, 'Marxism, Sociology and Crisis: Lukács' Critique of Weber', *Berkeley Journal of Sociology* (1975) 20, 181–230.

POPPER, Karl R., *Conjectures and Refutations: The Growth of Scientific Knowledge* (London: Routledge & Kegan Paul, 1963).

POPPER, Karl R., *The Open Society and its Enemies*, Vol.2: *The High Tide of Prophecy: Hegel, Marx and the Aftermath* (London: Routledge & Kegan Paul, 1966).

POTTER, David M., *People of Plenty: Economic Abundance and the American Character* (Chicago: University of Chicago Press, 1954).

PRAWER, S.S., *Karl Marx and World Literature* (Oxford: Oxford University Press, 1978).

PRICE, Roger, *The French Second Republic: A Social History* (London: B.T. Batsford, 1972).

PRICE, Roger, *The Economic Modernisation of France* (London: Croom Helm, 1975).

PRZEWORSKI, Adam, 'Proletariat into a Class: The Process of Class Formation from Karl Kautsky's the Class Struggle to Recent Controversies', *Politics and Society* (1977), Vol.VII, No.4, 343–401.

PRZEWORSKI, Adam, 'Social Democracy as a Historical Phenomenon', *New Left Review* (1980) No.122, 27–88.

PRZEWORSKI, Adam, *Capitalism and Social Democracy* (Cambridge: Cambridge University Press, 1985).

RADER, Melvin, *Marx's Interpretation of History* (New York: Oxford University Press, 1979).

RADNOTI, Sandor, 'Bloch and Lukács: Two Radical Critics in a "God-Forsaken World"', *Telos* (1975) No.25, 155–64.

RAPOPORT, Anatol, 'A view of the Intellectual Legacy of Karl Marx', *Social Sciences Information* (1968) Vol.VII, No.4, 7–25.

REVAI, Jozsef, 'A Review of Georg Lukács' "History and Class Consciousness"', *Theoretical Practice* (1971) I, Part 1, 22–30.

RINGER, Fritz K., *The Decline of the German Mandarins: The German Academic Community, 1890–1933* (Cambridge, Mass.: Harvard University Press, 1969).

ROSDOLSKY, Roman, *The Making of Marx's Capital* (London: Pluto Press, 1980).

ROSE, David (Ed.), *Social Stratification and Economic Change* (London: Hutchinson, 1988).

ROSENBURG, Morris, 'Perceptual Obstacles to Class Consciousness', *Social Forces* (1953) Vol. XXXII, 22–7.

ROSSANDA, Rossana, 'Class and Party', *Socialist Register 1970* (London: Merlin, 1970).

ROTENSTREICH, Nathan, 'Practice and Theory – Kant, Marx, Lukács', in Shlomo Avineri (Ed.), *Varieties of Marxism* (The Hague: Martinus Nijhoff, 1977).

ROTHSTEIN, Theodore, *From Chartism to Labourism: Historical Sketches of the English Working Class Movement* (London: Lawrence & Wishart, 1983).

RUBEL, Maximilien, & Margaret MANALE, *Marx without Myth: A Chronological Study of his Life and Work* (Oxford: Basil Blackwell, 1975).

RUBIN, David-Hillel, *Marxism and Materialism: A Study in Marxist Theory of Knowledge* (Brighton: Harvester, 1977).

RUBIN, Isaak Illich, *Essays on Marx's Theory of Value* (Montreal: Black Rose Books, 1973).

RUBINSTEIN, Annette T., 'Three Red Letter Days: Interviews with Gyorgy Lukács', *Science and Society* (1984) Vol.XLVIII, No.3, 344–9.

RUNCIMAN, W.G., *Social Science and Political Theory*, 2nd Edition (Cambridge: Cambridge University Press, 1969).

RUNCIMAN, W.G., *A Treatise on Social Theory*, Vol.I: *The Methodology of Social Theory* (Cambridge: Cambridge University Press, 1983).

RUNCIMAN, W.G., *A treatise on social theory* Vol. II: Substantive Social Theory (Cambridge: Cambridge University Press, 1989).

RUSSELL, Bertrand, *German Social Democracy* (London: Allen & Unwin, 1965).

RYAN, Alan, *The Philosophy of the Social Sciences* (London: Macmillan, 1970).

RYAN, Alan, (Ed.), *The Philosophy of Social Explanation* (Oxford: Oxford University Press, 1973).

SALVADORI, Massimo (Ed.), *Modern Socialism* (New York: Harper & Row, 1968).

SALVADORI, Massimo, *Karl Kautsky and the Socialist Revolution, 1880–1938* (London: New Left Books, 1979).

SAMUEL, Raphael (Ed.), *People's History and Socialist Theory* (London: Routledge & Kegan Paul, 1981).

SAMUEL, Raphael, & Gareth STEDMAN JONES, *Culture, Ideology and Politics: Essays for Eric Hobsbawm* (London: Routledge & Kegan Paul, 1982).

SAMUELSON, Paul A., *Economics*, 9th Edition (Tokyo: McGraw-Hill Kogakusha, 1973).

SARTRE, Jean-Paul, 'Merleau-Ponty', in his *Situations* (London: Hamish Hamilton, 1965).

SARTRE, Jean-Paul, *The Communists and Peace* (London: Hamish Hamilton, 1969).

SARTRE, Jean-Paul, 'Masses, Spontaneity, Party', *Socialist Register 1970* (London: Merlin, 1970).

SARTRE, Jean-Paul, 'An Interview with Jean-Paul Sartre: Replies to Structuralism', *Telos* (1971) No.9, 110–15.

SARTRE, Jean-Paul, 'Elections: A Trap for Fools', in *Sartre in the Seventies* (London: Andre Deutsch, 1978).

SARTRE, Jean-Paul, 'Today's Hope: Conversations with Sartre', *Telos* (1980) No.44, 155–81.

SARUP, Madan, 'Merleau-Ponty's Politics', *Radical Philosophy* (1975) No.12, 29–30.

SCHACHT, Richard, *Hegel and After: Studies in Continental Philosophy between Kant and Sartre* (Pittsburgh: University of Pittsburgh, 1975).

SCHAEFFER, Robert K., 'A Critique of the "New Class" Theorists: Towards a Theory of Working Class in America', *Social Praxis* (1976/77), Vol. IV, Nos1–2, 75–99.

SCHAFF, Adam, 'The Consciousness of a Class and Class Consciousness. Comments on G. Lukács' Essay Geschichte und Klassenbewusstsein', *Philosophical Forum* (1972) Vol.III, Nos3–4, 340–59.

SCHAFF, Adam. 'Marxist Theory on Revolution and Violence', *Journal of the History of Ideas* (1973) Vol.XXXIV, No.2, 263–70.

SCHAFF, Adam, 'Alienation as a Social and Philosophical Problem', *Social Praxis* (1975) Vol.III, 7–26.

SCHMIDT, Alfred, *The Concept of Nature in Marx* (London: New Left Books, 1971).

SCHMIDT, Alfred, *History and Structure: An Essay on Hegelian-Marxist and Structuralist Theories of History* (Cambridge: MIT Press, 1981).

SCHMIDT, James, 'The Concrete Totality and Lukács' Concept of Proletarian Bildung', *Telos* (1975) No.24, 2–40.

SCHORSKE, Carl E., *German Social Democracy, 1905–1917: The Development of the Great Schism* (Cambridge Mass.: Harvard University Press, 1983).

SCHWARZBACH, F.S., 'Review of Feenburg, Lukács, Marx, and the Sources of Critical Theory', *Theory and Society* (1984) Vol.XIII, No.1, 142–8.

SCRUTON, Roger, 'Thinkers of the Left: Gyorgy Lukács', *The Salisbury Review* (1985) Vol.III, No.3, 35–42.

SCRUTON, Roger, *Thinkers of the New Left* (Harlow: Longman, 1985).

SEABROOK, Jeremy, *What Went Wrong? Working People and the Ideals of the Labour Movement* (London: Victor Gollancz, 1978).

SEDGWICK, Peter, 'Natural Science and Human Theory: A Critique of Herbert Marcuse', *Socialist Register 1966* (London: Merlin, 1966).

SEERY, John E., 'Marxism as Artwork: Weber and Lukács in Heidelburg', *Berkeley Journal of Sociology* (1982) 27, 129–65.

SELBOURNE, David, *Against Socialist Illusion: A Radical Argument* (London, 1984).

SELIGER, Martin, *The Marxist Conception of Ideology* (Cambridge: Cambridge University Press, 1972).

SERGE, Victor, *Memoirs of a Revolutionary 1901–1941* (Oxford: Oxford University Press, 1967).

SERGE, Victor, *Year One of the Russian Revolution* (Harmondsworth: Allen Lane/Penguin Press, 1972).

SEWELL, William H. Jr., *Work and Revolution in France: The Language of Labor from the Old Regime to 1848* (New York: Cambridge University Press, 1980).

SHANIN, Teodor (Ed.), *Late Marx and the Russian Road: Marx and 'the Peripheries of Capitalism'* (London: Routledge & Kegan Paul, 1984).

SHEROVER-MARCUSE, Erica, *Emancipation and Consciousness: Dogmatic and Dialectical Perspectives in the Early Marx* (Oxford: Basil Blackwell, 1986).

SHUE, Henry G., 'Lukács: Notes on his Originality', *Journal of the History of Ideas* (1973) Vol.XXXIV, No.4, 645–50.

SIMMEL, Georg, *The Philosophy of Money* (London: Routledge & Kegan Paul, 1978).

SKILLEN, Anthony, 'Workers Interests and the Proletarian Ethic; Conflicting Strains in Marxian Anti-Moralism', *Canadian Journal of Philosophy* (1981) Vol.VII, 155–170.

SLAUGHTER, Cliff, *Marxism and the Class Struggle* (London: New Park, 1975).
SNEDEKER, George, 'The Politics of Epistemology: Georg Lukács and the Critique of Epistemology', *Science and Society* (1985) Vol.XLIX, No.4, 437–50.
SOMBART, Werner, *Socialism and the Social Movement* (London: J.M.Dent, 1909).
SOMBART, Werner, *The Quintessence of Capitalism: A Study of the History and Psychology of the Modern Business Man* (London: T.Fisher Unwin, 1915).
SOMBART, Werner, *Why is There No Socialism in the United States?* (White Plains, NY: M.E.Sharpe, 1976).
SOREL, Georges, *Reflections on Violence* (New York: AMS Press, 1975).
SOREL, Georges, *From Georges Sorel: Essays in Socialism and Philosophy* (New York: Oxford University Press, 1976).
SPENGLER, Oswald, *The Decline of the West* (London: George Allen & Unwin).
SPRINZAK, Ehud, 'Marx's Historical Conception of Ideology and Science', *Politics and Society* Vol.V, No.4, 395–416.
STANLEY, J.L., & E. ZIMMERMAN, 'On the Alleged Differences between Marx and Engels', *Political Studies* (1984) Vol.XXXIII, 226–48.
de STE CROIX, G.E.M., 'Karl Marx and the History of Classical Antiquity', *Arethusa* (1975) Vol.VIII, No.1, 7–41.
de STE CROIX, G.E.M., *The Class Struggle in the Ancient Greek World from the Archaic Age to the Arab Conquests* (London: Duckworth, 1981).
STEIGERWALD, Robert, *Marxism and Late Bourgeois Ideology* (Amsterdam: B.R.Gruner, 1981).
STEINER, George, 'Georg Lukács and his Devil's Pact', *Kenyon Review* (1960) Vol.XXII, No.1, 1–18.
STEINER, George, 'In Respect of Georg Lukács', *Encounter* (1963) Vol.XV, No.6, 92–3.
STERN, Fritz, *The Failure of Illiberalism* (London: Allen & Unwin: 1972).
STERN, Fritz, *The Politics of Cultural Despair: A Study in the Rise of the German Ideology* (Berkeley and Los Angeles: University of California Press, 1961).
STIRNER, Max, *The Ego and Its Own* (London: Rebel Press, 1982).
STROMBERG, Roland, N., 'The Intellectuals and the Coming of War in 1914', *Journal of European Studies* (1973) Vol.III, No.2, 109–22.
SUCHTING, W.A., *Marx. An Introduction* (Brighton: Wheatsheaf, 1983).
SWEEZY, Paul M., *The Theory of Capitalist Development: Principles of Marxian Political Economy* (New York: Monthly Review Press, 1968).
SWINGEWOOD, Alan, *Marx and Modern Social Theory* (London: Macmillan, 1975).
SZYMANSKI, Albert, *Class Structure: A Critical Perspective* (New York: Praeger, 1983).

SZYMANSKI, Al, 'Crisis and Vitalization in Marxist Theory', *Science and Society* (1984) Vol.XLIX, No.3, 315–31.

TAYLOR, Charles, 'Marxism and Empiricism' in B. WILLIAMS & A. MONTEFIORE (Eds), *British Analytical Philosophy* (London: Routledge & Kegan Paul, 1966).

TAYLOR, Charles, 'What is Human Agency?', in Theodore Mischel (Ed.), *The Self: Psychological and Philosophical Issues* (Oxford: Basil Blackwell, 1977).

TAYLOR, Simon, *Germany, 1918–1933: Revolution, Counter-Revolution and the Rise of Hitler* (London: Duckworth, 1983).

TERTULIAN, Nicolas, 'On the Later Lukács', *Telos* (1979) No.40, 136–44.

THERBORN, Goran, *Science, Class and Society: On the Formation of Sociology and Historical Materialism* (London: New Left Books, 1976).

THOMPSON, E.P., *The Making of the English Working Class* (London: Victor Gollancz, 1963).

THOMPSON, E.P., *The Poverty of Theory & Other Essays* (London: Merlin, 1978).

THONNESSEN, Werner, *The Emancipation of Women: The Rise and Decline of the Women's Movement in German Social Democracy, 1863–1933* (London: Pluto Press, 1973).

TIMMS, Edward, 'Mr Lukács Changes Trains', *London Review of Books* (1987) Vol.IX,4, 8–9.

TIMOFEEV, Timur, 'Marx and Working Class Development', *Social Sciences Information* (1968) Vol.VII, No.5, 37–49.

TIMPANARO, Sebastiano, *On Materialism* (London: New Left Books, 1975).

TOKEI, Ferenc, 'Democracy and Socialism in Georg Lukács' Political Philosophy', *Science and Society* (1990) Vol.54, No.1, 29–41.

TOKES, Rudolf, *Bela Kun and the Hungarian Soviet Republic* (New York: Praeger, 1967).

TOKES, Rudolf L., 'Georg Lukács – His Class and Consciousness', *Studies in Comparative Communism* (1972) Vol.V, No.4, 451–61.

TÖNNIES, Ferdinand, *Community and Association [Gemeinschaft und Gesellschaft]* (London: Routledge & Kegan Paul, 1955).

TORRANCE, John, *Estrangement, Alienation and Exploitation: A Sociological Approach to Historical Materialism* (London: Macmillan, 1977).

TREITSCHKE, Heinrich von, *Selections from Treitschke's Lectures on Politics* (London: Gowans & Gray, 1914).

TROTSKY, Leon, *The Third International after Lenin* (London: New Park, 1974).

TROTSKY, Leon, *In Defence of Marxism: Against the Petty Bourgeois Opposition* (London: New Park, 1975).

TROTSKY, Leon, *The Struggle against Fascism in Germany* (Harmondsworth: Penguin, 1975).

TUCKER, Robert C., *Philosophy and Myth in Karl Marx* (London: Cambridge University Press, 1961).
VAJDA, Mihaly, 'Law, Ethics and Interest', *Telos* (1977) No.34.
VANDERVELDE, Emile, *Collectivism and Industrial Evolution* (London: ILP, 1907).
VAZQUEZ, Adolfo Sanchez, *The Philosophy of Praxis* (London: Merlin, 1977).
VEBLEN, Thorstein, *The Theory of the Leisure Class: An Economic Study of Institutions* (London: Unwin, 1970).
VOLGYES, Ivan (Ed.), *Hungary in Revolution, 1918–19: Nine Essays* (Lincoln, Neb.: University of Nebraska Press, 1971).
WALKER, Jack L., 'A Critique of the Elitist Theory of Democracy', *The American Political Science Review* (1966) Vol.LX, 285–95.
WALTON, Paul & Andrew GAMBLE, *From Alienation to Surplus Value* (London: Sheed & Ward, 1972).
WALTON, Paul & Stuart HALL (Eds), *Situating Marx: Evaluations and Departures* (London: Human Context Books, n.d.).
WATERHOUSE, Roger, 'Heidegger: an Assessment', *Radical Philosophy* (1981) No.27, 22–8.
WATERS, Mary-Alice, *Rosa Luxemburg Speaks* (New York: Pathfinder, 1970).
WATNICK, Morris, 'Relativism and Class Consciousness: Georg Lukács', in Leopold Labedz (Ed.), *Revisionism* (London: George Allen & Unwin, 1962).
WATSON, David, *Why is There no Socialism in the United States?*, Winchester Research Papers in the Humanities (Winchester: King Alfred's Centre, 1981).
WATT, Richard M., *The Kings Depart: The Tragedy of Germany: Versailles and the German Revolution* (London: Literary Guild, 1968).
WEBER, Marianne, *Max Weber: A Biography* (New York: John Wiley, 1975).
WEBER, Max, *The Theory of Social and Economic Organization*, Part One of *Wirtschaft und Gesellschaft* (New York: Free Press, 1947).
WEBER, Max, *The Methodology of the Social Sciences*, eds Edward A. Shils & Henry A. Finch (New York: Free Press, 1949).
WEBER, Max, *Economy and Society: An Outline of Interpretive Sociology* (Berkeley: University of California Press, 1968).
WEBER, Max, *The Interpretation of Social Reality*, ed. J.E.T. Eldridge (London: Michael Joseph, 1971).
WEBER, Max, *From Max Weber: Essays in Sociology*, eds H.H. Gerth & C.W. Mills (London: Routledge & Kegan Paul, 1974).
WEIL, Simone, *Oppression and Liberty* (London: Routledge & Kegan Paul, 1958).
WEINSTEIN, James, *Ambiguous Legacy: The Left in American Politics* (New York: New Viewpoints, 1975).
WELDES, Jutta, 'Marxism and Methodological Individualism', *Theory and Society* (1989) Vol.18, No.3, 353–86.

WENGER, Morton G., 'Lukács, Class Consciousness, and Rationality', in Norman A. Fischer, Philip Goldstein, N. Georgopoulos & Louis Patsourasi (Eds), *Continuity and Change in Marxism* (New Jersey: Humanities Press, 1982).

WESSELL, Leonard P. Jr., *Karl Marx. Romantic Irony and the Proletariat: The Mythopoetic Origins of Marxism* (Baton Rouge: Louisiana State University Press, 1979).

WESTERGAARD, John & Henrietta RESLER, *Class in a Capitalist Society: A Study of Contemporary Britain* (London: Heinemann, 1975).

WIENER, Martin J., *English Culture and the Decline of the Industrial Spirit, 1850–1980* (Harmondsworth: Penguin, 1985).

WILLENER, Alfred, *The Action-Image of Society: On Cultural Politicization* (London: Tavistock, 1970).

WILLIAMS, Raymond, Culture and Society 1780–1950 (Harmondsworth: Penguin, 1963).

WILLIAMS, Raymond, *Marxism and Culture* (Oxford: Oxford University Press, 1977).

WINCH, Peter, *The Idea of a Social Science and its Relation to Philosophy* (London: Routledge & Kegan Paul, 1958).

WINDELBAND, Wilhelm, 'History and Natural Science', *History and Theory* (1980) Vol.XIX, 165–85.

WOLIN, Richard, 'Review of Agnes Heller (Ed.), *Lukács Revalued* (London: Basil Blackwell, 1983)', *Telos* (1984) No.60, 231–40.

WOLIN, Richard, 'Recent Revelations Concerning Martin Heidegger and National Socialism', *Theory, Culture & Society* (1990) No.7, 73–96.

WOLPE, Harold, 'Some Problems Concerning Revolutionary Consciousness', *Socialist Register 1970* (London: Merlin, 1970).

WOOD, Ellen Meiksins, *The Retreat From Class: A New 'True' Socialism* (London: Verso, 1986).

WRIGHT, Erik Olin, *Class, Crisis and the State* (London: New Left Books, 1978).

YAFFE, David, 'The Crisis of Profitability: A Critique of the Glyn-Sutcliffe Thesis', *New Left Review* (1973), No.80, 45–62.

YAFFE, David S., 'The Marxian Theory of Crisis, Capital and the State', *Economy and Society* (1973), Vol.II, No.2, 186–232.

YOUNG, James D., *Socialism and the English Working Class: A History of English Labour 1883–1939* (Hemel Hempstead: Harvester Wheatsheaf, 1989).

ZEITLEN, Irving M., *Ideology and the Development of Sociological Theory*, 2nd Edition (Eaglewood Cliffs, N.J.: Prentice Hall, 1981).

ZINOVIEV, Gregory, *Lenin: Speech to the Petrograd Soviet, September 6, 1918* (London: Socialist Labour League, 1966).

ZITTA, Victor, *Georg Lukács' Marxism. Alienation, Dialectics, Revolution: A Study in Utopia and Ideology* (The Hague: Martinus Nijhoff, 1964).

ZWEIG, Ferdynand, *The Worker in an Affluent Society: Family Life and Industry* (London: Heinemann Educational, 1961).

Index